P9-BIP-974

PRAISE FOR *The Historical David*

"All praise be—again—to those biblical studies scholars who can make ancient history matter and can shed light on long-held beliefs. In clear prose and with a documented command of what others have said before him, Baden offers a provocative reinterpretation of one of Western culture's heroes. . . . With a Jewish sensibility and a critical scholar's eye, Yale Divinity School Professor Baden sifts out the myth and political spin from the biblical evidence that shows that King David was a subjugating usurper who unseated the popular and able King Saul. . . . Baden opens up the text to the lay reader. He presents the plausible historical events leading to David's claiming of the throne, the nature of his reign, and, somewhat speculatively, the significance of Solomon's succession."

—*Publishers Weekly*

"This is an invigoratingly grown-up reading of the Bible, taking it seriously but not literally. Baden treats the biblical narratives of David as informative history based in reality, but thereby also sees them for the near-contemporary propaganda accounts that they are. David emerges no longer as the author of the Psalms or the slayer of Goliath, yet Baden's scholarly analysis leaves the usurper-King as one of the most crucial shapers of world history in the last three millennia."

—Diarmaid MacCulloch, professor of the History of
the Church at University of Oxford and author of
Christianity: The First Three Thousand Years

"Reading between and behind the lines of the biblical text and its silences, Baden gives an engaging reconstruction of who the true David may have been. This is a brilliant synthesis, with some unexpected and even daring twists of interpretation. A tour de force!"

—Michael Coogan, Harvard Divinity School lecturer,
director of publications for the Harvard Semitic
Museum, and editor of *The New Oxford Annotated Bible*

"This revisionist take on King David—as brilliant politician but despicable human being—combines the best of historical study and literary imagination. Baden's challenge to traditional understandings of Israel's king is always provocative, often compelling, and completely fascinating."

—Amy-Jill Levine, professor of New Testament and
Jewish Studies at Vanderbilt University and author of
The Misunderstood Jew

"In *The Historical David*, Joel Baden both accomplishes that reconstruction superbly and exemplifies how it should be done anywhere else within the biblical (and many other) traditions. He succeeds positively, powerfully, and persuasively in locating Israel's once and future king as an actual historical figure. The multiple layers of fact and fiction, history and theology are cleanly and clearly distinguished but without either modern apologetics or contemporary polemics."

—John Dominic Crossan, author of *The Historical Jesus*

"Joel Baden's lively account of David's reign is at once a defense of the historicity of the founding father of the Davidic dynasty and a deconstruction of the biblical narrative that shows how much of it is either fabricated or exaggerated. This is a provocative book that raises questions about the nature of biblical narrative and also about the historical continuity of the Davidic line."

—John J. Collins, Holmes Professor of Old Testament
at Yale University

"For readers open to debating this beloved biblical figure, *The Historical David* will make compelling reading."

—*Arkansas Democrat-Gazette*

THE HISTORICAL DAVID

THE HISTORICAL DAVID

THE REAL LIFE OF
AN INVENTED HERO

JOEL BADEN

HarperOne
An Imprint of HarperCollins*Publishers*

HarperOne

All biblical translations are the author's.

HarperCollins books may be purchased for educational, business, or sales promotional use. For information please e-mail the Special Markets Department at SPsales@harpercollins.com.

HarperCollins website: http://www.harpercollins.com

HarperCollins®, 🏭®, and HarperOne™ are trademarks of HarperCollins Publishers

FIRST HARPERCOLLINS PAPERBACK EDITION PUBLISHED IN 2014

Maps by Beehive Mapping

Library of Congress Cataloging-in-Publication Data
Baden, Joel S.
The historical David : the real life of an invented hero / Joel Baden. — First edition.
    pages cm
ISBN 978–0–06–218837–3
1. David, King of Israel. I. Title.
BS580.D3B2135 2013
222'.4092—dc23 2013011646

14 15 16 17 18   RRD(H)   10 9 8 7 6 5 4 3 2 1

For Gillian

CONTENTS

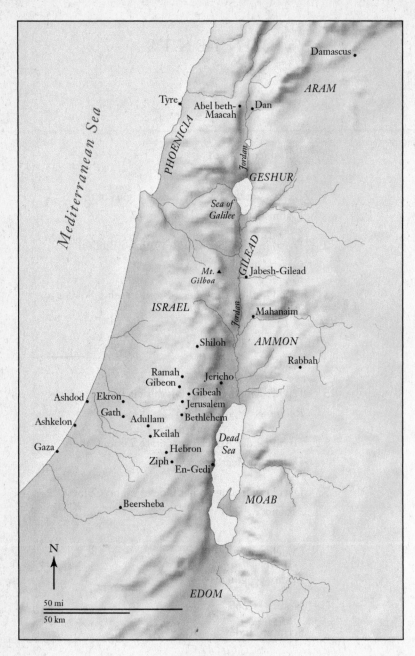

Damascus

ARAM

Tyre
Abel beth-
Maacah
Dan

PHOENICIA

Jordan

GESHUR

*Sea of
Galilee*

Mediterranean Sea

GILEAD

Mt. ▲
Gilboa
Jabesh-Gilead

Jordan

ISRAEL
Mahanaim

Shiloh
AMMON

Ramah
Gibeon
Jericho
Rabbah

Ashdod
Ekron
Gibeah

Gath
Jerusalem

Ashkelon
Adullam
Bethlehem

Keilah
*Dead
Sea*

Gaza
Hebron

Ziph
En-Gedi

Beersheba

N

MOAB

50 mi

50 km

EDOM

Major Sites in the David Story

INTRODUCTION

IN A SMALL VILLAGE IN Israel, some three thousand years ago, there lived a man and his wife who owned flocks of sheep and goats that grazed in the fields some distance from the village. One spring day, ten men appeared in the village. They were messengers from a larger gang of fugitives from society who roamed the countryside living as they could. They presented the man with a request: they had been protecting the man's flocks and shepherds out in the fields and no harm had come to the man's property, so now they would like the man to give them some money or food for their efforts. The man, who had never encountered this gang before, much less asked them to protect his property, refused to give them anything and turned them away. The next day, the leader of the gang showed up at the man's door with his full entourage, four hundred men armed to the teeth. Shortly thereafter, the man lay dead, and the gang leader had married the man's widow, thereby assuming legal ownership of the man's flocks, servants, house, and fields.

What do we make of this sequence of events? If this were a modern court case, the circumstantial evidence against the gang leader would look bad. It would be hard not to conclude that what we have here is a classic protection racket: the initial message from the gang would be seen as a thinly veiled threat, a threat embodied in the gang leader's appearance with his armed men and fulfilled, in the end, in the man's death. The device of marrying his widow would be understood as a "legal" means of justifying the acquisition of the man's property—essentially a cover-up. And the widow, taken by force—after all, her husband lay dead before her and she was surrounded by his killers—would be as much a victim as the dead man himself.

Though it may be the most plausible explanation given the information we have, this is only one possible way of explaining the events. How we understand what happened, what meaning we make of a plain series of events, depends greatly on who is telling them, and why. As is so often the case, particularly with events from the distant past, we do not have an objective reconstruction of the story. We have no court records, no eyewitness accounts. We have only a single version of these events, and that one is counterintuitive. It presents the gang leader as the hero and the dead man as the villain. For three thousand years, it is this version that has been taken unquestioningly as the truth. For this story comes from the Bible, and the gang leader was none other than David, the future king of Israel.

WHEN I TEACH THE life of David in my Introduction to the Old Testament class, even in the setting of a prominent divinity school most of the students are unfamiliar with David's early career as the leader of a band of misfits wandering the wilderness of Israel. Indeed, considering that David is one of the most famous characters from the Hebrew Bible, it is remarkable just how little of his life story is part of our shared cultural knowledge. This is undoubtedly in large part because most of us learn our Bible stories as children, in religious school, and most of the biblical stories about David, as we will see, are decidedly inappropriate for young ears. We know of David, but we can't say that we know him particularly deeply. The most famous image of him is Michelangelo's, carved in pure white stone. Compare this with Moses, who, thanks to Cecil B. DeMille's movie *The Ten Commandments* (and, for a younger generation, DreamWorks's *The Prince of Egypt*), is rendered in full color and motion: from his birth to the burning bush to the plagues to splitting the sea to the tablets of the Ten Commandments and the golden calf, all the way to his death.

Our knowledge of David exists not as a full-length film, but as short clips and still frames. Our first image is of him as a young man, bravely going forward to battle the Philistine giant Goliath, carrying nothing but a sling and a stone. We see Goliath towering over the Israelite army, in full armor, holding his great sword, taunting the Israelites to send someone out to fight him. We hear David recounting his tales of fighting off lions and bears to protect his family's flocks and then see him stepping out from the crowd to deliver to Goliath the immortal words: "You come against me with sword and spear and javelin, but I come against you in the name of the Lord of Hosts!" And we see the smooth stone striking Goliath in the forehead, the giant falling, the Philistines scattering in terror before their fallen hero.

From Goliath's death we fast-forward to David sitting on the throne of Israel, not merely as king, but as the composer of the immortal psalms. He has a lyre in his hand, the emblem of the great poet. Perhaps he is speaking those lines most familiar to us from the King James Bible: "A Psalm of David: The Lord is my shepherd, I shall not want." This is David at rest, the stately ruler of a peaceful realm, offering his praises to the God who granted him victory over Israel's enemies and who spared him from disaster.

These are the two moments that best represent David in the popular imagination. But there is far more to his story. The full narrative of his life takes up forty-two chapters in the Bible, spanning from 1 Samuel 16 to 1 Kings 2. The story of Goliath takes up only one chapter—and the writing of the psalms is in fact nowhere in the narrative at all. There is much more to tell of David.

The details of the biblical account of David's life, even those we are familiar with, are largely subsumed by the *idea* of David: an abstracted, romanticized, idealized figure, less a person of flesh and blood than a symbol of a nation's glorious past and promising future. We may know Moses better, but we love David more. When I was a child, I, like every other Hebrew school student, learned a simple, one-line song, accompanied by hand gestures and repeated at increasing tempo until we could no longer keep up. *David, melech yisrael, chai chai ve-kayam*—"David, king of Israel, lives and endures." The song has no story—there is nothing to be learned about David's life from these five words. What they represent, rather, and what was being instilled in us subconsciously, is David's status in tradition. We were surely too young to understand, but it is noteworthy that this song describes David not as a figure of the past, but as a part of the present: he "lives and endures." These words obviously cannot be used to describe a mere king from three thousand years ago. Nor, for that matter, would they be appropriate for any other character from the Hebrew Bible: we would never say that Moses lives and endures, or Abraham, or Jacob, or Isaiah. All of these figures also have legends attached to them, but David is uniquely timeless.

This timelessness is largely due to the third idea commonly associated with David, though it is one without any visual imagery: his role at the head of the lineage leading to the messiah. This idea begins already in the Hebrew Bible. At 2 Samuel 7:16 God promises David an everlasting kingship: "Your house and your kingdom shall be secure before me; your throne shall be established forever." As the prophets of Israel began to look ahead to a messianic future, it was only natural that they should imagine the future redemptive king as one from David's line. Thus Isaiah famously announces the birth of the "shoot from the stump of Jesse" who will rule in "peace without end upon David's throne and upon his kingdom" (Isa. 11:1; 9:6). Jeremiah speaks of the time when God "will raise up a righteous branch of David's line" (Jer. 23:5) and even more explicitly describes the time of Israel's restoration as one when "they shall serve the Lord their God and David their king, whom I will raise up for them" (Jer. 30:9). Ezekiel similarly foresees the return of David in the messianic era: "I will appoint over them a single shepherd to tend them—my servant David. . . . I the Lord will be their God, and my servant David shall be a ruler among them" (Ezek. 34:23–24).[1]

In early Jewish traditions from the first century BCE, the messiah was known as the "son of David," a title that continued to be used in the Talmud.[2] It is most famous, however, from the New Testament, where it is used fifteen times in the Gospels of Matthew, Mark, and Luke, including the very first words of the New Testament: "An account of the genealogy of Jesus the Messiah, the son of David" (Matt. 1:1). In the Gospel of John we read, "Has not the scripture said that the Messiah is descended from David?" (John 7:42). Jesus is said to be "descended from David according to the flesh" (Rom. 1:3), "a descendant of David" (2 Tim. 2:8), and "the root and descendant of David" (Rev. 22:16). In the book of Acts, a brief history of Israel is recounted, beginning with the Exodus (in the telling of which, notably, Moses is not mentioned) and culminating with David—because "of this man's posterity God has brought to Israel a savior, Jesus, as he promised" (Acts 13:23). In Christianity, Moses, as the preeminent law-giver, is downplayed, if not outright rejected; David is raised up.

The legend of David is deeply woven into the fabric of Western culture: one need think merely of the range and frequency of uses to which the "David and Goliath" comparison is put. This particular image, certainly the most dramatic from the story of David, resonates deeply with both contemporary Judaism and Christianity. The Israeli War of Independence in 1948 and the Six-Day War of 1967 were at the time, and have often been since, portrayed as a modern David and Goliath story, with Israel playing the role of David. In 1948, the small, largely ineffective (but noisy) mortars that Israel deployed against their Arab enemies were called Davidkas, "little Davids." Even now, when Israel's strength relative to that of its Arab neighbors is obvious, the size of the state and its vulnerable geographical position keep this metaphor alive and well. On the Christian side, one can easily find numerous websites that equate creationism with David and evolutionary theory—with all of the media, scientists, and universities that stand behind it—with Goliath. Not surprisingly, this rhetoric has entered political discourse as well: members of the conservative Tea Party have characterized themselves as David, fighting the Goliath of the liberal media.

It is human nature to idealize figures from the past, particularly those who are associated with origins. In the United States we may think of George Washington, whose legend, from the cherry tree to the crossing of the Delaware, is only loosely if at all connected with historical reality. Or we may recall the national uproar at the revelation of Thomas Jefferson's romantic exploits, a reaction caused by the sudden intrusion of reality in the previously unblemished image of one of our founding heroes. Idealizing foundational figures is a natural and perhaps unavoidable part of constructing identity. If we identify ourselves as Americans, then we look to our origins, and to the people responsible for the existence of America, as models for what we stand for. It becomes of the utmost importance that these figures from the past be not only exemplars, but exemplary: as their descendants, literally and nationally, we attribute to them the values and virtues we want to see in ourselves. How they really were, what they really did, becomes shrouded in the mists of time—set aside and then forgotten. What remains is the glory, in the stories we (mis-) remember and the stories we (re-)create.

If this idealization happens with the founders of a nation barely two hundred years old, how much more so with the founder of the messianic line that started three thousand years ago. And in the case of David, we have both: he is the founder of the nation of Israel and the ancestor—even, for some, the prototype—of the messiah. It is thus not surprising that those aspects of David's life that are known are those that attest to his glory: his youthful bravery, his lasting poetry, his imperial kingship. It is similarly unsurprising that the most famous description of David, stated first in the Hebrew Bible and repeated in the New Testament, is that he was "a man after God's own heart" (1 Sam. 13:14; Acts 13:22). The idealized cultural memory of David in Judeo-Christian tradition serves the important purpose of providing a model for the messiah and for ourselves, as peoples and as communities of faith. We leave the historical David to the past, and in his place we admire an eternal David constructed of our own hopes and aspirations.

THE CONSTRUCTION OF AN idealized David is not a recent phenomenon; it began already in the earliest writings about David. As an illustration, we may return to the story we began with, recalling the salient features: David, at this point in his life the leader of a band of fugitives from society living in the wilderness of Israel, sent some of his men to request food or money from a wealthy man in exchange for having "protected" his shepherds and flocks in the wilderness. When the man refused, David arrived at his house with his fully armed entourage; soon enough, the man was dead and David had married his widow, acquiring the man's property in the process. There are probably innumerable ways to fill the gaps in this sequence of events, but none, it is safe to say, could be as tilted in David's favor as the biblical version.

According to 1 Samuel 25, the man's name was Nabal—and his name already predisposes the reader against him, for in Hebrew *nabal* means "fool." What's more, he is described upon his introduction in the story as "a severe and evil man." His wife, on the other hand—Abigail—is called "clever and beautiful," thereby setting up the reader for what is to follow. When David's men speak to Nabal, they do so with the utmost politeness, with formal greetings and obsequious expressions. Nabal, however, responds coldly, even aggressively, accusing David of being no better than a runaway slave. David's claim of having protected Nabal's shepherds—though it is clear that Nabal never requested such protection—is justified by the unsolicited speech, delivered to Abigail, of an unnamed shepherd, who confirms that David had indeed protected Nabal's men—and who throws in an insult to Nabal in the process: "He is such a base fellow that none can speak to him." A remarkable exchange follows between Abigail and David, in which she also insults her husband—"pay no attention to that base fellow . . . his name means 'boor' and he is a boor"—and praises David to the skies, even going so far as to predict, like a prophetess, his eventual reign over Israel. She gives David and his men an elaborate gift, to make up for Nabal's stinginess, and effectively condemns her husband: "Let your enemies and those who seek evil against my lord fare like Nabal!" David responds by blessing her for her prudence and for keeping him from doing any harm to Nabal. Though he admits that he had intended to harm Nabal—how could he say otherwise, standing there with four hundred armed men?—he makes eminently clear that he will no longer attack. And thus it is a truly miraculous coincidence when, ten days later, God strikes down Nabal and he dies. The meaning of this divinely ordained death is proclaimed by none other than David himself: "The Lord has brought Nabal's evil down on his own head." In the very next moment, David sends men to propose marriage to Abigail, which she accepts without hesitation—after all, she has already foreseen David's rise to power, and she obviously had little regard for her late husband.

Without altering the basic sequence of events, the biblical version of what happened dramatically tilts the moral balance of the story. Nabal, the ostensible injured party—as the one who ends up dead—is positioned as the bad guy, as an evildoer, nasty, a fool, his character impugned even by his own wife. David, the ostensible aggressor, is rendered as the aggrieved party. Abigail can no longer be seen as a victim but becomes a willing participant and a willing newlywed, even a prophetess of David's glory. Nabal's death is the work of no human hands—least of all David's, as the story emphasizes more than once—but is in fact divine punishment.

How do we evaluate the claims of the biblical story? We begin by recognizing that the Bible is not objective history, nor was it ever intended to be. The idea, and much more so the practice, of "objective history" was unavailable to its authors. To state it baldly, the Bible is not history: it is the Bible. The biblical narrative breaks most of the fundamental rules of modern history writing. We find in the biblical story, presented as fact, aspects that no historian could know: private and unverifiable elements, including events that occurred behind closed doors; dialogues; and even internal monologues. We find characterizations of the various individuals in the story that are far from unbiased. And, perhaps most notably, we find the introduction of divine intervention as an explanation for the course of events. We can hardly blame the biblical author for failing to follow conventions of history writing that developed thousands of years after he wrote his narrative. At the same time, however, we cannot read the biblical text as if it were a piece of modern history writing. It may be describing the past, and in that sense it is historical in nature, but it describes the past using conventions more familiar to us from the genre of historical fiction. Moreover, these conventions serve a particular purpose: in our case, they glorify and idealize the Bible's main character and most prominent hero, David.

Thus the aspects of this narrative that are foreign to the modern genre of history writing—those that are more biblical than historical—all work toward the same ends: to denigrate Nabal and to raise up David. This can hardly be coincidence—especially when, as we will see, this pattern holds for the entirety of the David story in the two books of Samuel. Nor should it be surprising, since David is the unparalleled hero of the Hebrew Bible. He is the king against whom the Bible measures all subsequent kings and who stands unsurpassed by any who followed him. He is, as we have seen, the symbol of Israel's incipient messianic hopes. We should not be surprised that the biblical version of his life is weighted in his favor.

To realize that the biblical narrative is pro-David, however, is also to realize that it cannot be read at face value if we want to know the *real* history of David's life. But recovering the historical David is not, unfortunately, as simple as merely reading and remembering the often overlooked biblical account of his life, as if a deeper reverence for the scriptures would lead to historical truth. Quite the contrary: the Bible is a necessary source of information, but it is neither sufficient nor particularly trustworthy. For much of the past three thousand years, and for many people still today, such a statement is impossible to accept. For some, the biblical narrative is considered to be unimpeachably true, as the Bible bears the stamp of God. If it was written by God or with divine inspiration, there is no reason to doubt it—although, it may be noted, the books of Samuel and Kings with which we are concerned here make no claims for divine origin or inspiration, and indeed no one considered them to have such qualities for several hundred years after they were written. The unassailability of the biblical text is a faith commitment, not a historical fact. The attempt to recover historical fact means relinquishing, at least for this purpose, the faith commitments that preclude any challenge to the received tradition.

This means recognizing that the Bible is a product of human minds, and that, like all literature, it is subject to the biases and agendas, both conscious and unconscious, of its authors. The critical study of the Bible entails pressing against those biases, peeling back those agendas. Scholars of literature call this reading with a "hermeneutic of suspicion"—being aware that the conclusions to which a piece of writing leads us are those to which its author wants us to be led, and stepping back to ask how and why such efforts were made. We must first remove the nonhistorical pro-David elements from the story, to expose the basic events underneath. When we do this, it is harder to maintain the overwhelmingly positive picture of David we get from the Bible. In the case of the David and Nabal story, for instance, we are left with the stark sequence of events as presented at the beginning of this introduction—and, when we attempt to understand those events from an objective historical perspective, we are left with the strong possibility that David may in fact have been running a protection racket, may in fact have killed Nabal, and may in fact have covered up his acquisition of Nabal's property by marrying Abigail. Given this potentially damning depiction of David, it is no wonder that the biblical author went to such lengths to render the story in pro-David terms. To use a modern analogy, the biblical narrative may be considered the ancient equivalent of political spin: it is a retelling, even a reinterpretation, of events, the goal of which is to absolve David of any potential guilt and to show him in a positive light.

As spin, it has been remarkably effective, in no small part for the simple reason that it is from the Bible. The revelation of private thoughts, conversations, and events; the characterizations of the participants; the divine intervention—all of these, and with them the decidedly pro-David interpretation of the events, have been taken as representing the historical truth, or at the very least the moral truth. The Jewish historian Josephus, retelling the story in the first century CE, plays up Nabal's wickedness and David's innocence: "Nabal had died through his own wickedness and had given [David] revenge, while [David] himself still had clean hands . . . the wicked are pursued by God, who overlooks no act of man but repays the good in kind, while he inflicts swift punishment upon the wicked."[3] The ancient rabbis, perhaps realizing that the biblical account did not sufficiently justify Nabal's death, devised a number of rationales not found in the text, from greed to pride to idolatry.[4] Matthew Henry's commentary on this chapter, from the early eighteenth century, portrays David as exceedingly humble in his request and emphasizes his need: "David, it seems, was in such distress that he would be glad to be beholden to him [Nabal], and did in effect come a begging to his door. What little reason have we to value the wealth of this world when so great a churl as Nabal abounds and so great a saint as David suffers want!"[5]

Ironically, while postbiblical readers and commentators bought into the pro-David spin in Samuel, other biblical authors writing about David were made uncomfortable by it. The author of Chronicles, one of the latest books of the Hebrew Bible, seems to have recognized that even when interpreted in favor of David, the events described in Samuel are still rather unpleasant stories to be telling about Israel's glorious king. Thus in Chronicles we find no trace of the David and Nabal story—in fact, David's entire time in the wilderness, which occupies twelve chapters in Samuel, is reduced to the list of warriors who went to the wilderness to support David as king. It is noteworthy that these men are described as warriors—this is the Chronicler's revision of Samuel's description of David's band as "every man who was bitter of spirit." Any potentially negative aspect of David's life and actions to be found in Samuel, down to the smallest detail, is fully expunged in Chronicles. The David of Chronicles is unimpeachable—which seems to be precisely what the Chronicler had in mind when he rewrote the narrative of Samuel.

Our modern cultural memory of David, then, stands in a long line of increasing idealization and reconstruction. From the spin of Samuel to the cleansing of David's image in Chronicles to the messianic connection in the New Testament to the present, the historical David has been successively and successfully diminished, replaced by the legend we are now familiar with.

RECOGNITION THAT EVEN THE Bible presents an idealized David—and that the Bible is the only written source of information we have about David's life—has led some scholars in the past few decades to claim that David never existed at all. They argue that the biblical David is not the idealization of a real historical figure, but is rather an invention out of whole cloth, a projection into the past by later kings who wanted to legitimate their lineage and status and who created a legendary founding figure against whom to compare themselves. Yet this is akin to claiming that England's Henry V never existed if we had no source of information other than Shakespeare's idealized good king. To a certain extent, these scholars have bought the spin of the Bible just as fully as those who, like Matthew Henry, call David a saint.

It is, in fact, the very existence of the biblical spin that argues in favor of David's existence. There is no need to spin a story that has no basis in reality. If the fundamental aim of spin is to say "it may seem that the event happened one way, but it really happened another way," then there has to have been an actual event in the first place. And who, given the chance to create a legendary figure from the past to serve as an ancestor and model, would invent a story such as that of David and Nabal? When the stories in the two books of Samuel are understood as pro-David spin, the question of David's existence is rendered moot: he must have existed for the text to look like this. Moreover, the stories about David must have been written relatively soon after the events they describe, for they are grounded in the assumption that their audience knew something about those events.[6]

The task, then, is to find the middle ground between accepting the biblical narratives at face value and rejecting them altogether. This entails digging beneath the pro-David spin of the two books of Samuel—removing, as we did with the David and Nabal story, those elements of the narrative that we recognize as generically nonhistorical—in order to access the fundamental events of the past, and then trying to reconstruct the more likely story of what really happened.

In doing this, it is important to remember that the historical David was part of a very different place and time, the ancient Near East. The political conventions of the ancient Near East, and the cultural history of early Israel, provide a crucial lens through which we must view and evaluate David's actions as he seeks to attain and retain the throne. Similarly, understanding the literary conventions of the ancient Near East will reveal that the literary techniques used in the retelling and interpretation of David's life—the spin—were not uncommon, especially in stories about and by kings. David as a person and David as a literary figure participate equally in their ancient context and are illuminated by that context.

Such is the aim of this book: to bring the historical David to life by reaching back through the accumulated legend, beyond the pro-David agenda of the biblical text, into the ancient world in which David roamed. This process is revealing: the flesh-and-blood man is far more interesting than the mythical king. The legendary David is more a marble statue than a living personality, more a symbol than a man. The historical David, by contrast, is ambitious and clever, persuasive and threatening, not always in power but almost always in control. He is not someone we might want to emulate, but he is someone that we might recognize.

The process of uncovering this long-lost man also means revealing something about the biblical authors: why they wrote, what they wanted, and how they accomplished their goal of transforming David into the legendary figure we know today. They did their job remarkably well: the biblical depiction of David has held sway for thousands of years. These human authors are part of the story of David, almost as much as David himself. They are equally a part of David's world, and neither the king nor his hagiographers can be understood in isolation from each other.

WE ARE CULTURALLY INVESTED in a particular view of David as a central figure in the founding of both a nation and a religion. David the man is not easily dissociated from David the legend. And his legend has been of lasting importance to Jews and Christians alike. Those who consider themselves part of the nation of Israel, either literally or metaphorically, look to David as their founding figure. Both Judaism and Christianity recognize him as the origin of much practice and belief. The religious cult that he inaugurated in Jerusalem would become the temple, where Israel would worship almost uninterrupted for a thousand years and the sacrificial offerings of which would serve into the present as the basis for Jewish prayer and ritual. The psalms that David is said to have written have entered every Jewish and Christian liturgy and are held up throughout Judeo-Christian faith as models of prayer and piety. The messiah—the one who has already come in Christianity, and who is yet to come in Judaism—is believed to be a descendant of David, the original "man after God's own heart."

Past, present, and future are all tied back to David. Every culture values its founding myths, the stories of how it came to be. They provide definition; they explain why a culture exists and why it is different from other cultures. George Washington is venerated in the United States because he embodied the sort of steely resolve and steady leadership that this country aspires to demonstrate to the world. The legend of Washington and the cherry tree speaks to the value of honesty. We set aside aspects of Washington's life, such as the fact that he was an extraordinarily wealthy slave-owner, that do not comport with our vision of him. For Judeo-Christian tradition, David serves the same purpose. God singled David out despite his humble beginnings, just as he singled out Israel. David actively demonstrated his faith in God, both in action and in words, just as Jews and Christians seek to do. Because David is seen as the model, it is natural that his failings should be excised from his legend. They undermine the purpose of having the legend in the first place.

At the same time that founding figures are understood as models, they are also mirrors for the values of later generations. This can be seen already in the biblical texts about David: the two books of Kings, written at the close of the monarchic era (mid–sixth century BCE), elevate David to the perfect king; the two books of Chronicles, written when the temple dominated Israelite society (ca. 400 BCE), value David as a religious leader. And so it is in every generation. The rabbis of the Talmud discussed David's prayer practices because that was central to their worldview.[7] John Calvin in the sixteenth century focused on David as a model of piety.[8] When Israel became a state in 1948, it adopted as its flag the symbol known as the Star of David, an ancient Jewish emblem traditionally believed to have been emblazoned on David's shield when he went to war. The symbolism of recalling David's military glory in the moment of Israeli independence is hard to miss.

What we say and think about David, both as a model and as a mirror, is directly and deeply connected with what we say and think about ourselves as modern Jews and Christians. What would it mean if we discovered that the historical David was in fact quite different from what we imagine or desire? For almost three millennia we have had only increasingly good things to say about him. We have basked in the reflected glory of Israel's great king—his deeds, his words, his faith. To challenge David's legend is thus to open to debate what it means to be a descendant of David, be it nationally, ethnically, or religiously.

It is because the idealized David is important to us now that the historical David has any significance at all. To rediscover the historical David is to realize that behind the accumulated legend there was a living, breathing man, in a distant place and time, whose deeds, and the telling of them, were responsible for much of who we are today. It is this link across the millennia that makes the search for the historical David both risky and necessary. It is surely easier to rest content with the pleasant image of David preserved in tradition. But in doing this, we allow tradition to eclipse the past in which it is rooted. Some parts of the past—the Exodus from Egypt, for example—might never be recovered, and tradition is all we have. But when the history is there to be rediscovered, we ignore it at our peril. We are defined by the distance between what happened and how we tell the story. It is therefore necessary to know what happened, what didn't happen, and how to tell the two apart.

CHAPTER I

David's Youth

THE MYTHICAL ORIGINS OF THE PSALMIST AND GIANT-SLAYER

VERY OFTEN IN THE BIBLE a character's birth story anticipates and identifies his or her significance. Isaac is the miraculous child of Abraham and Sarah's old age, the very embodiment of God's promise to make Abraham into a great nation. Jacob emerges from the womb clutching Esau's heel, foreshadowing his life of trickery and usurpation. The infant Moses is saved from death by being hidden in a basket among the reeds of the Nile, just as years later he would save the Israelites from destruction at the Sea of Reeds. Samson's birth is announced to his mother by an angel, because Samson, the angel reveals, will be the one to defeat the Philistines. Samuel, the great prophet and judge, is born in accordance with Hannah's faithful prayer. And, of course, Jesus is marked even from before his birth as conceived by the Holy Spirit and destined to redeem Israel from its sins.

Given the litany of biblical heroes who are provided with birth narratives, it is somewhat surprising that of David's birth—indeed of his entire childhood—we know absolutely nothing. The Bible gives us only the barest facts: David's hometown is Bethlehem. The name of his father is Jesse. He has seven older brothers, only the first three of whom are named.[1] The family profession is shepherding. In short, David is a nobody. He is from a minor village in the (then) unimportant region of Judah, the youngest son of a man with no claim to wealth or fame, a mere shepherd. His conception and birth go unnoticed by any divine being, and even by the Bible itself.

At the same time, everyone loves an underdog, and David fits the bill perfectly. If someone with a background like David's could eventually become the great king of Israel, then, it would seem, there is hope for all of us. The Bible relates two stories of how the teenage David rose from his humble origins to prominence in Saul's kingdom: as Saul's lyre-player and as the slayer of Goliath.[2] These stories, from 1 Samuel 16 and 17, respectively, are the most famous episodes from David's life, though they resonate in different ways.

The first image of David to appear in the Bible is as a musician: he is the youth brought to Saul's court to play the lyre and ease the king's troubled mind with his sweet music. This is also the story with the longest afterlife, as David's youthful skill with the lyre is intimately connected in the popular imagination with his lifelong status as the author of the psalms. David is the quintessential lyricist, and he is perhaps just as famous for the songs he wrote as for anything else he may have done. After his death, David's authorship of the psalms quickly became the defining act of his life.

David's connection to the psalms was recognized and valued already in very ancient times. At the end of his life he recites a song to the Lord, recorded in 2 Samuel 22, and this song is none other than what we know as Psalm 18. According to Chronicles, David was the first to institute the regular singing of songs to the Lord in the temple (1 Chron. 16:7). Most notably, a full 73 of the 150 psalms in the Hebrew Bible have David's name in their superscriptions. Even before the turn of the common era the psalms had become so thoroughly associated with David that they could be referred to simply by his name: in the Dead Sea Scrolls we find references to "the book of Moses and the books of the prophets and David."[3] The same is true of the New Testament: only in Acts 1:20 is a quotation from Psalms introduced as such: "For it is written in the book of Psalms . . ." Most often, the words of the Psalter are introduced with reference to David: "For David himself says in the book of Psalms" (Luke 20:42), or, far more frequently, simply "David said . . . ," or "David declared. . . ."[4] David has become synonymous with the book of Psalms, just like Moses with the laws of the Torah and Solomon with the wisdom of Proverbs and Ecclesiastes. The rabbis of the Talmud stated this outright: "David wrote the book of the Psalms."[5]

The equating of a biblical character with a distinct biblical corpus does more than simply attribute authorship; it defines the fundamental character trait of that figure. Moses, by being identified with the Torah, becomes the archetypal law-giver (for better or worse, depending on one's religious background). Solomon, for all his many deeds as king of Israel, is most widely known for his wisdom, as exemplified in the books associated with his name. And for David, the connection with the book of Psalms positions him as the ultimate model of faith and worship. The psalms, after all, have been recognized from antiquity to the present as the most personal expressions of humanity's relationship with God. They exhibit the full range of emotions, from anguish to rejoicing, from fear to security. As John Calvin said, "I have been accustomed to call this book, I think not inappropriately, 'An Anatomy of all the Parts of the Soul'; for there is not an emotion of which any one can be conscious that is not here represented as in a mirror."[6] For thousands of years the words of the psalms have been at hand for expressing one's deepest feelings, just as they were for Jesus: "My God, my God, why have you forsaken me?"; "Into your hands I commend my spirit"—the last words spoken on the cross (Mark 15:34; Luke 23:46), found first in the Psalter (Pss. 22:1; 31:6). Members of many contemporary religious groups, from Christians to Hasidic Jews, read the psalms daily as a devotional act. They have been enshrined in liturgy in every branch of Christianity and Judaism, stretching back even to the biblical period.

David, as the author of the psalms, is the genius who gave poetic expression to Judeo-Christian belief. Whatever deeds he may have done, his innermost nature is exhibited through his songs of praise, thanksgiving, and lament. The Psalter stands as clear testimony to his faithfulness and devotion to the Lord. Through all the ups and downs of his life, David maintained in his psalms a clear and unbending commitment to God as the source of success and salvation. God says that David is "a man after my own heart" (1 Sam. 13:14; Acts 13:22); the truth of this statement seems to be manifested most concretely in the psalms. When the youthful David takes up the lyre in 1 Samuel 16 and soothes Saul's troubled spirit, we understand this to be not just the first of his acts, but the foremost of them. David's music defines him: in the narrative he is worthy of the king's attention, and in tradition he is worthy of God's—and our—affection.

The second episode of David's youth, the slaying of the Philistine giant Goliath, is quite different. The David who plays the lyre is a young man at peace; the David who faces Goliath is a young man very much at war. David the musician is sedentary amid the chaos of Saul's court; David the warrior is, by contrast, full of motion amid the static face-off between the two armies. The Israelites and the Philistines are dug in on either side of a ravine, with Goliath stepping out day after day to challenge any Israelite to face him in single combat. No one moves. David journeys from his home, arrives into this repeating set piece, speaks with Saul, rejects the heavy armor that prevents him from moving freely, and runs forward to encounter Goliath. He is courage and nobility embodied. Though only a youth, he proves himself to be the biggest man on the battlefield.

This nobility finds expression in the most famous and beloved image of David, Michelangelo's glorious sculpture. It is ironic that this story of David's bold movements is most effectively captured by a motionless figure. For as evocative as the image of the stone sinking into Goliath's forehead may be, the picture that stays with us is that of David taking his stand, slingshot in hand, with not a shred of fear in his eyes. We may not ever have to face down a giant in one-on-one combat, but everyone knows the feeling of confronting that which is terrifying, and David's self-possession in the face of grave danger stands as a lasting example for all. This is undoubtedly why, despite the fact that David was at war nearly his entire life, it is this first battle that lasts in the imagination—for this is virtually the only time that David is not in a position where he holds some degree of power. Only here does he stand alone, against the odds.

Perhaps even more significantly, David's stance is not one of pure bravery, but rather of the bravery that comes from a deeply held trust in God's power. His speech to Goliath ranks as one of the great declarations of faith in the face of adversity, worthy of any Sophoclean or Shakespearean hero: "You come against me with sword and spear and javelin, but I come against you in the name of the Lord of Hosts, the God of the ranks of Israel" (1 Sam. 17:45). It is a thrilling statement that reshapes the entire story, changing it from one of combat to one of belief. And it further opens the story to readers in any desperate situation: anyone can emulate David's stance.

If David playing the lyre is an image of faith expressed in words, David defeating Goliath is an image of faith expressed in action. Taken together, they present a complete picture of the authentic man of God, one as emotionally insightful as he is physically courageous, all parts of his character testifying to his devotion. David stands as a model for all who pray and act in God's name. This is where the defining stories of a character's youth are more valuable than birth narratives. The story of a character's birth imbues that figure with a sense of predestination for greatness, with an otherworldly quality that adds to the character's glow. At the same time, however, birth stories are distancing for the reader, for there is no possibility of emulating them; by the time one reads the story, after all, it is too late to imitate it. But when characters emerge from an unremarkable background and define themselves by their own actions, the reader has a visceral reaction: here is something I could do, too, someone I could aspire to be. It is not a coincidence that many of our modern heroes are defined not by their births, but by some relatively youthful experience, whether legendary or true—George Washington admitting to chopping down the cherry tree, or John F. Kennedy saving his crew at sea during the Second World War. The character traits we associate with our heroes are frequently sought, and found, in the defining stories of their youth. (Notably, especially for our purposes, this remains the case even when our heroes conduct themselves later in life in less than heroic ways—we downplay Kennedy's marital infidelities in favor of his martial exploits.)

David with the lyre and David facing the giant—these are the very first stories that we read about David in the Bible. They are also the first stories about him that we learn as children—not because they are first in the text, nor because they are about a young man, but because they instill the fundamental values of faith. For many, these are in fact the *only* stories we know about David. And why would we need any others? Everything anyone could want in a hero, in a king, in an ancestor of the messiah, is present here. The David we meet in the first two chapters of his story is the David of our cultural memory, the David we hold on to in popular imagination.

And yet: despite their cultural resonance, despite the values they encapsulate, despite the complete picture of the faithful hero they paint, when we try to read these two stories as a narrative history of David's youth, something is fundamentally askew. To put it bluntly, both stories cannot be true as they are told in the Bible.

David's Dueling Origins

THE NARRATIVE IN 1 Samuel 16 of David playing the lyre for Saul is, on its own terms, relatively straightforward. We are first introduced to David when the prophet Samuel goes to anoint one of Jesse's sons secretly as king. We meet Jesse and David's brothers, each of whom is rejected in turn. Finally, David is found, having been brought in from shepherding the flock; Samuel duly anoints him, and David is seized by the divine spirit from that day forward. Meanwhile, Saul's spirit is troubled, and his courtiers suggest finding someone who might play the lyre to make Saul feel better. One of the young men immediately thinks of David: "I have seen a son of Jesse the Bethlehemite who is skilled in music, a man of valor, a warrior, sensible in speech, a handsome man, and the Lord is with him" (16:18). Saul promptly sends for David, who comes as asked. Saul finds David pleasing and appoints the lad as one of his arms-bearers, sending word to Jesse that he intends to keep David with him. And so, we are told, whenever Saul felt the evil spirit descend upon him, David played his lyre and the spirit would depart from Saul.

This is all well and good, until we begin to read the story of David and Goliath in 1 Samuel 17. Suddenly, it is as if the previous story had never happened. We are again introduced to the family of David, in terms that make it clear that they are being introduced for the first time: "David was the son of a certain Ephrathite of Bethlehem in Judah whose name was Jesse" (17:12). A certain Ephrathite whose name was Jesse? This is the way that the Bible regularly introduces new characters.[7] But Jesse is hardly a new character; why should he be introduced again? We are told "he had eight sons" (17:12)—but again, we already knew this. Furthermore, "the names of his three sons who had gone to the battle were Eliab the first-born, the next Abinadab, and the third Shammah; and David was the youngest" (17:13–14). Not only did we already know that David was the youngest, we already knew the names and the birth order of his three eldest brothers. In fact, we know them relatively well, since it was precisely these three whom Samuel rejected in the previous story. It would be one thing if the second story gave us the names of the other four sons, but it doesn't; there is not a bit of new information here. What's more, both stories use the eldest brothers in the same way: as a foil for David. In the first story, they are explicitly rejected by Samuel; in the second, they are among those who stand by while Goliath challenges the Israelites to fight.

Then there is the question of where David is when the second story begins. We learned in the previous chapter that Saul had taken him into his service as arms-bearer. Since Saul was now out on the battlefield, surely David should be with him, bearing his arms. But no—he is back home with Jesse, and he goes to the battlefield only to bring food to his brothers; he is even supposed to go right back home with news of how his brothers are faring (17:17–18). Admittedly, the second story seems to recognize this confusion about how David spends his time, and so we are told that "David would go back and forth from attending on Saul to shepherd his father's flock at Bethlehem" (17:15). But even this explanation is scarcely acceptable. Are we to imagine that during peacetime David was in constant attendance on Saul as arms-bearer, but during a time of war he was there only occasionally? Furthermore, the narrative does not really match with this back-and-forth movement between Saul and Jesse: when David goes to the battlefield, it is not to attend on Saul at all, but only to check on his brothers. And it is clear that this is in fact David's first time going to the battle, since when he sees Goliath and hears the giant's challenge, he seems to have no idea that this has been going on for forty days already. All of which is to say that the verse stating that David went regularly between Jesse and Saul is not only illogical, but it stands as fairly clear evidence that the discrepancies between the two stories were felt even by the biblical authors, who made a half-hearted and transparent attempt to reconcile them.[8]

But from there the problems only grow. When David goes to Saul and declares his intention to fight Goliath, Saul's response is, in light of the previous story, rather surprising: "You are only a boy, and he has been a warrior from his youth!" (17:33). This can hardly be the same David who was introduced to Saul in the previous chapter as "a man of valor, a warrior" (16:18). David then describes himself entirely in terms of his career as a shepherd—"Your servant has been tending his father's sheep"—although surely he should have said that he had been Saul's arms-bearer.[9]

The disconnect between the two stories comes to a head at the end of 1 Samuel 17: "When Saul saw David going out to confront the Philistine, he said to Abner, the army commander, 'Whose son is that boy, Abner?'" (17:55). This question is, by any reckoning, inconceivable. Saul took David into his service in the previous chapter. David was especially pleasing to Saul. Saul appointed him his personal arms-bearer. David regularly played the lyre to soothe Saul's spirit. Saul even communicated directly with Jesse. How could he now not know who David is? Only when we reach this unfathomable question do we realize that nowhere in the second story has Saul addressed David by name, nor has David offered it. It seems that, to Saul, David is just a youth who has volunteered to fight, and only when he is successful does it occur to the king to discover who the lad might be. But he should have known, and known well.

The conclusion of the Goliath story is to be found in the first verses of the next chapter, 1 Samuel 18, where we read that "Saul took him [into his service] that day and would not allow him to return to his father's house" (18:2). And with this the parallel nature of the two stories is fully revealed. Both begin with no foreknowledge of who David is, such that we have to be introduced to him, and to his family: his father, his three eldest brothers, and his four unnamed brothers. Both describe how David comes to Saul's attention: through his skill at playing the lyre, and through his bravery on the battlefield. Both have Saul being pleased with David: because he soothes Saul's spirit, and because he is victorious against Goliath. And both conclude with the explicit notice that Saul took David into his permanent service, thereby severing David from his home in Bethlehem.

In short, what we have in these two chapters are two stories of David's rise to prominence in Saul's court—two stories that are identical in function and parallel in structure, but thoroughly incompatible as sequential episodes in a historical narrative. The parallel and independent existence of the two accounts is, remarkably, proved by the evidence of the Greek translation of the Hebrew Bible from the third century BCE, the Septuagint. For in the Greek text of 1 Samuel 17, huge chunks of the Goliath story we know from the Hebrew Bible are missing—and those chunks are precisely the ones that contain almost all of the contradictions with 1 Samuel 16 noted above.[10] The Hebrew version preserves a fully separate account of David's defeat of Goliath, one that likely circulated independently—hence its reintroduction of the main characters, its distinctive description of David, its ignorance of David's established relationship with Saul, and structural parallels with 1 Samuel 16. Only at a much later point was this independent story of David's victory over Goliath combined with the alternative story found in the Septuagint, thereby creating the literary mess that is the canonical text of 1 Samuel 16–17.[11] We therefore have two independent and truly irreconcilable stories about how David emerged from obscurity to become a presence in the royal court of Saul.

It is easy enough to see why both would be valuable to the biblical authors. As we have already seen, both stories present David in a flattering light as a young man faithful to both his king and his God. But both cannot be historically true, for they contradict each other at almost every turn. These contradictions illustrate one of the main difficulties with reading the Bible as history: the Bible preserves disparate and frequently irreconcilable traditions, even about a single figure. These traditions may have great value from a theological perspective—and after all, the Bible is nothing if not a theological work—but they cannot provide us with firm grounds for historical reconstruction. In a situation like that presented by these two chapters, we are forced to make a decision as to which tradition seems more likely to have any historical value, a decision that we can make only on the basis of a close analysis of each tradition independently.

Unfortunately, when we look closely at these two famous biblical traditions about David—as the musically gifted author of the psalms and as the uniquely courageous slayer of Goliath—we find that not only can both not be historically true, but in fact neither is historically true.

The Author of the Psalms?

SO MUCH OF OUR standard image of David depends on the words of the psalms. These words of faith and devotion that David is said to have composed in his times of crisis and triumph color the traditional characterization of him and allow us to relate to him on an emotional and a spiritual level. It is therefore more than mere historical detail that is at stake here—David's connection with the psalms is integral to his status in Judeo-Christian culture.

Any discussion of the authorship of the psalms must logically begin with the book of Psalms itself. There we find, as noted above, that 73 of the 150 psalms in the Hebrew Bible have David's name in their superscriptions, in the Hebrew phrase *le-David*. Tradition takes this phrase to mean "by David," and if such an understanding is correct, there would seem to be some evidence for Davidic authorship. The problem, though, is what to do with the many psalms that use the same Hebrew construction but with a different name in place of David's: "the sons of Korah" (Pss. 42; 44–49; 84–85; 87–88), "Asaph" (Pss. 50; 73–83), and "Ethan" (Ps. 89). The superscriptions to two psalms mention not David, but Solomon (Pss. 72; 127). One says "Moses" (Ps. 90). And there is even one without a proper name, simply "a poor man" (Ps. 102). If *le-David* means "by David," then all of these alternatives should mean the same thing: "by the sons of Korah," "by Asaph," etc. In which case, one cannot say that David wrote the psalms—at most, one could say that David wrote seventy-three of the psalms, and that other people wrote the rest.

Further complications ensue in those psalms that mention more than one figure in this sort of superscript: "the sons of Korah" and "Heman" in Psalm 88; "Jeduthun" and "David" in Psalm 39. Again, if the Hebrew phrase really does intend to ascribe authorship, then evidently we have here jointly composed psalms. Finally, we may consider the very common superscription mentioning "the conductor," evidently referring to the person who would perform or lead the performance of the psalm in question. The very same Hebrew construction with *le-* is used in these cases also, so if we are to be consistent, we should translate this too as "by the conductor," which is somewhat awkward. But here the problem is especially acute, because only two Psalms mention "the conductor" alone (Pss. 66–67); everywhere else, the phrase appears in conjunction with another such phrase: for example, "By the conductor. By David" (Ps. 11); "By the conductor, with instruments. A psalm by Asaph" (Ps. 76); "By the conductor. By the sons of Korah" (Ps. 85); and so on.

This is all to say that if we take the superscription *le-David* as attributing authorship, then we are faced with a large number of psalms that are either attributed to someone else or jointly attributed, including the very many Davidic psalms that also mention "the conductor"—thirty-nine of the seventy-three, in fact, or more than half.[12] This is problematic enough for the claim of Davidic authorship. The more substantial difficulty is that the Hebrew preposition *le-* has a fairly wide range of meanings, but "by" is not among them.

Nowhere outside of the book of Psalms does *le-* signify authorship. It means, rather, "to," "for," "regarding," or "belonging to." These meanings open an entirely new array of possibilities for understanding the superscriptions to the psalms. At this point, however, it is necessary to look briefly at the way that Chronicles presents David's relationship with these songs. Chronicles repeatedly claims that David was the first to institute the regular praising of God through song in the sanctuary in Jerusalem.[13] As David was, by all accounts, the one who initiated the formal worship of Yahweh in Jerusalem, this is perfectly sensible as a historical premise. Nowhere in the Chronicles account, however, does it say that David actually wrote any of the songs. Rather, his innovation was to assign certain Levites, the priests who ministered in the sanctuary, to be in charge of the singing. The premise of Chronicles here seems to be that these songs were already in existence and that David simply organized their formal recitation as part of the cultic ceremonies.

More striking are the names of the Levites whom David picked to lead the singing, names that ought to be familiar to us: "Heman son of Joel and, of his kinsmen, Asaph son of Berechiah; and, of the sons of Merari their kinsmen, Ethan son of Kushaiah" (1 Chron. 15:17); "Heman and Jeduthun had with them trumpets and cymbals" (16:42). Heman, Asaph, Ethan, Jeduthun—these are precisely the names we find in the superscriptions in the book of Psalms. As for the sons of Korah, they are mentioned later, during the reign of Jehoshaphat, but with the same function: "Levites, from among the sons of Kohath and of the sons of Korah, got up to extol the Lord God of Israel at the top of their voices" (2 Chron. 20:19). These figures are not presented as authors of psalms; they are, rather, professional singers and likely represent guilds of cultic singers that bore their names. The superscriptions that mention them should not mean "by Asaph," for example, but rather something like "of Asaph," in the sense of "to be performed by" or even "according to the style of" if we imagine that each guild had its own particular manner of singing. This rendering conforms well also to "the conductor": "to be performed by the conductor" is far more sensible than "composed by the conductor." It also explains the frequent addition of "with instruments": these superscriptions are instructions, detailing who is to perform the psalm and how.

Can this understanding apply also to the superscriptions that say *le-David*? It is certainly possible. The phrase might signify that there was a particular style of performance that was attached to David's name—maybe with a lyre?—or that there was a guild, perhaps part of the royal court, that took David's name to signify the guild's origins. Some scholars have suggested that these superscriptions signify psalms that were meant to be performed by the king himself during the cultic ceremonies, just as we know that in neighboring cultures the king regularly offered certain sacrifices as part of the ritual proceedings.[14]

Alternatively, we might understand the phrase *le-David* to mean "regarding David" or even "about David"—that is, the psalms bearing this heading were viewed as particularly appropriate to certain experiences in David's life. As we noted earlier, the psalms capture virtually the full range of human emotions—and no character in the Hebrew Bible had nearly as many ups and downs as David. Since these cultic songs were already associated with David in Chronicles, and since David was a talented musician according to 1 Samuel 16, the association of particular psalms with David's life is almost obvious. Thus in the Psalter we find headings that are remarkably specific—not just "about David," but, for example, "A psalm about David when he fled from his son Absalom" (Ps. 3:1). There is, however, nothing in Psalm 3 that explicitly mentions either David or Absalom, or anything else related to that biblical narrative; it is simply a song of lament, asking God to save the speaker from his enemies—one among many such laments in the book of Psalms. Such a song fits perfectly with that episode from David's life, however, and it is easy enough to see how someone might intend the reference to David to illustrate the type of situation in which one might recite this particular psalm.[15]

If these sorts of superscriptions seem rather haphazard—after all, many psalms could say "about David" but don't—this impression is justified. The very randomness of the Davidic headings is highlighted by the Septuagint. Its version of Psalms has not seventy-three but eighty-five psalms with David's name in the superscription. We can hardly imagine that the Septuagint was trying to ascribe Davidic authorship to these extra twelve psalms; if that were the case, we would expect that all of the psalms without any superscription would have been treated in the same manner. The Septuagint seems not to have equated the entirety of the book of Psalms with David; rather, it continued the recognizable trend of associating particular psalms with their famous promulgator. The process of linking psalms with David's name, it seems, was ongoing, stretched over centuries.[16]

The superscriptions to the psalms, so often taken as proof of Davidic authorship, therefore show themselves to have been rather unfixed in ancient times. They are not the only element of the book of Psalms that is unfixed in this way, however. There is evidence that the entire book is made up of smaller collections of psalms, each of which once had its own independent existence. Note the concluding line of Psalm 72, not even halfway through the book: "End of the prayers of David son of Jesse." The use of the plural, "prayers," in this verse shows that it is intended to conclude not merely the psalm to which it is attached, but an entire group of psalms. The problem is that this is not at all the end of the Davidic psalms; indeed, they appear again beginning with Psalm 86. The existence of independent collections within the Psalter may help to explain why one psalm seems to be repeated: Psalms 14 and 53 are virtually identical. The same psalm, it seems, was taken up into more than one collection. This may suggest yet another rendering of *le-David:* the phrase may identify those psalms that were, at some point, included in a collection that was understood to have been compiled—but not necessarily composed—by David.

Even more remarkable is the evidence from outside the Hebrew Bible. The Septuagint not only has some of the psalms in a different order, but actually includes a psalm that is not found in the Hebrew, Psalm 151—a psalm that even has a good Davidic superscription: "About David, when he fought Goliath in single combat." The Dead Sea Scrolls also present the psalms in a radically different order and include not one but seven psalms unknown to the Hebrew Bible. In short, the evidence strongly suggests that the Psalter was not a closed collection of authentically Davidic compositions, but was rather an open assembly of cultic poetry that was constantly being reshaped and supplemented, right down to the beginning of the common era.

The final piece of evidence that explodes the notion of Davidic authorship is the presence in the psalms of anachronisms: references to things and events after David's death. Thus we find mention of the temple (Pss. 27:4; 42:5; 48:10; 65:5; 66:13; 116:19; 117:26), which was built by Solomon after David had died; the destruction by the Babylonians of the temple and the cities of Judah (74:7–8; 79:6–7), which occurred in 586 BCE, nearly four hundred years after David; and hopes for the subsequent rebuilding of the walls of Jerusalem (51:20) and the cities of Judah (69:36). Most famously, there is Psalm 137, which also recalls the Babylonian exile: "By the waters of Babylon, there we sat and wept when we remembered Zion. . . . Remember, O Lord, against the Edomites the day of Jerusalem's fall" (137:1, 7). The recognition that David did not write the psalms emerged relatively early in biblical scholarship and was the source of some embarrassment, considering how well entrenched the idea was in tradition. As one commentator—a Christian bishop, no less—said in 1798, "the misapplication of the Psalms to the literal David has done more mischief than the misapplication of any other part of the Scriptures, among those who profess the Christian religion."[17]

With all of this evidence, we may well wonder how it is that tradition came to claim that David was in fact the author of the psalms, such that this is usually the first, and sometimes the only, thing that is known of him today. It is possible to trace at least the outlines of how this belief developed, beginning where we began: with the story of David playing the lyre for Saul, which established David as a musician. The narrative of David's life in Samuel and Kings, however, makes no mention of David writing the psalms. Even in 2 Samuel 22, where David sings what we know also as Psalm 18, the text does not actually say that David composed the song himself; it says only that "David recited to Yahweh the words of this song" (22:1). As far as the narrative is concerned, David may just as well have taken up a preexisting song of thanksgiving, one that he found, correctly, to be appropriate to his situation.

It is, in fact, even more likely the case that the biblical author, or a later hand, inserted this psalm into the narrative of David's life. It is the introduction to the song that gives this away: "David recited to Yahweh the words of this song, on the day that Yahweh had saved him from the hands of all his enemies and from the hand of Saul" (22:1). As an original part of the David narrative, this deliberate contextualizing of the song seems unnecessary. We know precisely when in David's life these words were spoken—why do we need it stated so explicitly? Notably, the very same introductory line is found in the book of Psalms, where it makes far better sense, as it matches with all of the similar superscriptions there. Thus it appears likely, if not provable, that 2 Samuel 22 was lifted entirely from Psalm 18, complete with its superscription, and inserted into the David narrative at the appropriate moment. The earliest records of David's life mention only the youthful lyre-playing, and nothing of the psalms.

In the later books of Chronicles, dated by most scholars to around 400 BCE, the psalms do seem to appear in connection with David, though not explicitly by name. In Chronicles, as noted above, we are told that David assigned certain Levites to be in charge of the cultic music—a notion that is not found in Samuel. As a whole, Chronicles is particularly invested in the cult and in arguing for David's role in instituting virtually every part of it except for the physical structure of the temple (which was left for Solomon). This is an innovation of the Chronicler; in Samuel, David is credited only with bringing the ark of the covenant to Jerusalem. We may understand why the Chronicler goes to such lengths to link David with as much of the temple and cult in Jerusalem as possible: in the fourth century BCE, when Chronicles was written, Israel no longer had a king. The recently rebuilt temple was the sole cultural and political center of society. By associating the temple with David, the beloved first king of the united Israel, Chronicles positions the temple as the functional continuation of the Davidic dynasty, even as the actual line of David has ceased to rule. In the absence of a king, the temple carries on the tradition of David. It is therefore easy to recognize the political utility of the Chronicler's portrayal of David as instituting the cult and all its trappings, including the cultic music, that is, the psalms. This at least suggests, if it does not demonstrate conclusively, that even this depiction may be without any historical basis. At the same time, whether it is true or not is less important for our current purposes than the fact that it was claimed at all. The claim of Chronicles, that David instituted the cultic music of the psalms, entered tradition and contributed to the link between the two. After Chronicles, the songs of the cult, the psalms, become David's songs—not by authorship, but by patronage.

When, two or three centuries later, the Dead Sea Scrolls refer to the psalms by David's name alone, this sort of patronage may well be what is intended: David is not necessarily the author of the psalms, but his name is synonymous with them. The step from there to authorship is a small one: David became viewed as the author of the psalms just as Moses became viewed as the author of the Torah, though in neither case does the Bible actually make these claims. Indeed, there is a consistent and quite ancient trend toward associating essentially anonymous texts with famous figures from the past, especially those already linked somehow with a particular corpus. If one wanted to lend authority to a work, for instance, it was typical to do so by putting it into the words of a founding figure: Moses, as in the case of Jubilees, a Jewish text from the second century BCE that introduces itself as having been dictated to Moses on Mount Sinai; or Ezra, as in the late first-century CE composition known as 4 Ezra, written in the first person in Ezra's voice.

This process can be witnessed also within the Bible: an anonymous prophet of the sixth century BCE who gave eloquent voice to the hopes of the exilic Jewish community attached his work to, and thereby borrowed the authority of, the writings of the famous eighth-century BCE prophet Isaiah.[18] It is likely, then, that as the association of David with cultic poetry increased over time, more and more such poetic material was attributed to him—and, as we have seen, there is even evidence that this was the case, in the expanded attributions of psalms to David in the Septuagint. What we see, then, is a shift from the psalms having been authorized by David to the psalms having the authority of David, from text perceived as associated with David to text perceived as authored by David.

It is not my intention to suggest that the shift from David as lyre-player to David as author of the psalms was actually accomplished by these aforementioned texts; texts are, more often than not, reflections of the changing traditions in the societies from which they emerge, rather than instigators of change themselves. Thus it is most likely that the view of David's authorship of the psalms developed gradually over time, from the simple playing of the lyre for Saul to the full-blown composition of the entire Psalter. What is important, however, is that the notion of Davidic authorship of the psalms is not rooted in any historical fact—not even in the ostensibly historical narratives of the Hebrew Bible itself. It belongs, rather, to the growth of traditions, about the psalms and about the figure of David. When the traditions are unraveled and the evidence examined, it becomes apparent that David did not write the psalms.

With this realization the traditional image of David is irrevocably altered. The lyre has dropped from his hands; these magnificent songs, full of joy and suffering, hope and faith, have vanished from his throat and pen. The psalms have lost none of their power, nor, for the most part, their great antiquity; but they can no longer represent David. Without them, the David we have inherited as a culture becomes something of an empty vessel: the words that we have for so long associated with his inner life, that have for generations provided us with a direct link to his heart and mind, serve that purpose no more. This newly created vacancy in the standard portrait of David provides us with an opportunity, however—a chance to understand the man anew, without any preconceptions imposed by the accumulated weight of tradition.

We also may now take a step back and ask whether there is any truth to the story that lies at the root of the notion that David wrote the psalms, that is, the narrative of his coming to Saul's attention in 1 Samuel 16. There are two distinct elements to this story, each of which plays out independently in the rest of the David narrative. The first is that David soothed Saul's spirit with his lyre-playing; the second is that he entered Saul's military service as his arms-bearer. It seems probable that the second of these has some historical veracity. As the rest of the story demonstrates, and as we will see, David's rise to greatness in Israel was largely the result of his military prowess. At some point, therefore, David almost certainly joined Saul's army.

As for David's playing of the lyre, it is important to recognize the circumstances under which this is said to occur. According to the biblical narrative, the only reason David needs to play the lyre for Saul is because the authors deem Saul to be, in essence, mentally unfit to rule: "the spirit of Yahweh had departed from Saul, and an evil spirit from Yahweh overwhelmed him" (1 Sam. 16:14). In the next chapter, we will have the opportunity to critically examine the biblical depiction of Saul's mental state. Suffice it to say for the moment that the popular notion of Saul's insanity is dubious at best. And if Saul's "evil spirit" is an invention of the biblical authors, so too is David's lyre-playing, for the two are always linked.

What we can say at this point is that the evil spirit said to descend on Saul is carefully counterposed in the Bible with the claim that "the spirit of Yahweh gripped David" from the day that Samuel went to Bethlehem to secretly anoint him as king (1 Sam. 16:13). The narrative intentionally constructs Saul as David's foil, and David as predestined to replace Saul as king. And it does so by means of a historically unverifiable indicator: the invisible, indescribable "spirit of Yahweh."

From a faith perspective, such a thing cannot be challenged; from a historical perspective, it cannot be substantiated or corroborated. The "spirit of Yahweh" is a theological explanation for the historical circumstance of Saul's eventual downfall and David's rise in his place. It is also an explanation unique to the narrative of Samuel, as it is absent from the history of David's life presented in Chronicles. It is a literary construction, not a historical record.

Equally unverifiable is the story of Samuel anointing David in Bethlehem in 1 Samuel 16:1–13. A central part of this narrative is its secrecy: only Samuel, Jesse, and David's brothers witness the anointing. What's more, this anointing is never again mentioned in the David narrative. Not only does no one outside of David's immediate family see it happen, but no one is ever told that it happened. No historical event can be extracted from this episode; it exists only for the reader's benefit, as a means of legitimating David as the future king even before he has proved himself worthy of kingship.

Just as the "spirit of Yahweh" serves to elevate David at Saul's expense, so too the story of David's anointing is intentionally counterposed with the selection of Saul as king in 1 Samuel 10. In that story, Samuel gathers all of Israel and, using lots, narrows the search down to the tribe of Benjamin, to the Matrite clan, and finally to Saul; Saul, however, is not present but is with the baggage. When he is finally brought forward, he is the tallest man there, and both Samuel and the people acclaim him as king (10:17–24). The similarities between this and the story of David's anointing are evident. Both feature Samuel; in both, possible candidates are winnowed until the true king is identified; and in both, the future king is elsewhere and must be retrieved to receive the kingship. The selection of David replicates the selection of Saul, though with one important difference. Saul is acclaimed as king because of his impressive stature: "When he stood among the people, he rose a head taller than all the people. Samuel said to all the people, 'Do you see the one whom Yahweh has chosen? There is none like him among all the people'" (10:23–24).

When it comes time to anoint David, however, the very characteristic that signified Saul's kingship is explicitly rejected, and rejected by Yahweh himself. For when David's eldest brother Eliab stands before Samuel, Yahweh says: "Do not take note of his appearance or his stature, for I have rejected him. For not as man sees does Yahweh see; man sees only what is visible, but Yahweh sees into the heart" (1 Sam. 16:7). Although Eliab is under discussion here, it is hard not to hear in this a clear rejection of Saul as well. As one biblical scholar has put it, "Eliab is something of a 'new Saul,' so that in his rejection Saul is denounced in effigy."[19] Again, Saul is a literary foil for David; Saul was selected on illegitimate grounds, but David was chosen for all the right reasons.

It is immensely difficult to extract any historical information from the beginning of the David story. We are faced with a combination of unverifiable elements, such as the "spirit of Yahweh" and the secret anointing ceremony, and manifestly polemical passages, in which David is positioned as the positive counterpoint to Saul. So it is not just the traditional attribution of the psalms to David that is in doubt. As we try to get beneath the biblical story, at every stage we find a narrative that has been constructed with the goal of glorifying David, not with the aim of presenting a historical account of what really happened. At the most we can say that David probably entered the military under Saul. And this is the essential result of the David and Goliath story as well.

Slayer of Goliath?

WHEN WE TURN TO the story of David slaying Goliath, we confront a different sort of problem. It is not that the biblical story itself is in any way empirically unbelievable. Admittedly, the height given for Goliath, "six cubits and a span tall" (1 Sam. 17:4), works out to a fairly incredible nine and a half feet—though the Septuagint here says four cubits rather than six, a more likely measurement (around six and a half feet, still unusually tall for that time and place), thus suggesting that the Hebrew version has been altered to make the giant even more mythically imposing. But there is nothing impossible about David facing and defeating Goliath the way the text says—remarkable, even unlikely perhaps, but not impossible.[20]

What makes the biblical story of David's defeat of Goliath impossible to accept as historical fact is that elsewhere in the Bible an entirely different person is said to have killed Goliath. In 2 Samuel 21:19 we read: "Again there was a battle with the Philistines at Gob; and Elhanan son of Yaare-Oregim the Bethlehemite killed Goliath the Gittite; the shaft of his spear was like a weaver's bar." This can hardly be a different Goliath: both are Philistines, both are from the Philistine city of Gath, and, most remarkably, both have the same impressive spear: the words "the shaft of his spear was like a weaver's bar" are found verbatim in both 2 Samuel 21:19 and 1 Samuel 17:7. How is it possible that two different people could have slain the same giant at two different times and places? This is not a problem of modern readership, as if we are simply too far removed from the conventions of ancient literature to understand these texts. The ancient author of Chronicles saw precisely this same problem. His rendering of the note about Elhanan reveals a transparent, even desperate, attempt to overcome it. In 1 Chronicles 20:5 we learn that "Elhanan son of Jair killed Lahmi, the brother of Goliath the Gittite; the shaft of his spear was like a weaver's bar." Elhanan has been stripped of his victory over Goliath, which is replaced with a victory over, of all people, Goliath's brother—though note that the description of the giant's spear remains the same. The earliest readers of Samuel, biblical authors themselves, grappled with the fact that two different people are said to have killed the same Philistine.

Surely one of the two accounts is a duplicate of the other. The question then becomes: which story is the original and which the duplicate? It hardly seems likely that anyone would think to take a story originally about David and retell it with a different protagonist—especially a protagonist who is otherwise a nonentity in the Hebrew Bible.[21] It is equally unlikely that anyone would take the very full narrative of David's victory and reduce it to a single verse. This notice about Elhanan's defeat of Goliath is very similar to other such brief notices about the valor of David's warriors. It is stuck unremarkably in the midst of one such little collection, in 2 Samuel 22:15–22, in which we hear about the exploits of some of David's men as they fought a series of Philistine giants; Abishai son of Zeruiah, Sibbecai the Hushathite, and Jonathan son of Shimei are all said to have won battles of single combat against Philistines who had huge weapons (a heavy spear and a new suit of armor) or physical abnormalities (twelve fingers and twelve toes). The story of Elhanan defeating Goliath is simply part of this list—that is, it is an organic part of the material in which it is found, and it is not given any special prominence there.

Other stories about David's warriors are preserved in the biblical text as well: Adino the Eznite, who killed eight hundred men single-handedly (2 Sam. 23:8); Eleazar son of Dodo, who alone fought off an entire Philistine army (23:9–10); Shammah son of Age, who did the same (23:11–12); Abishai son of Zeruiah, who defeated three hundred men by himself (23:18); and Benaiah son of Jehoiada, who killed a lion—just as David claims to have done in the Goliath story—and a giant Egyptian (23:20–21).

These brief accounts are obviously legendary, mythical triumphs that attached themselves to heroes. They are the sorts of stories we find in Homer about the heroes of the Trojan War. Although clearly invented, these warrior legends have their own internal logic. They explain why David's handpicked soldiers were chosen, and why their names are worthy of preservation for posterity. Elhanan has no reason to exist in the Bible except as a result of his heroic defeat of the Philistine giant Goliath. And so it is increasingly difficult to believe that he would have been invented merely for the purposes of giving him glory that was rightfully and originally due to David, the ultimate biblical hero.

It is, however, entirely plausible that David's legend could have been embellished by appropriating the glory of a relative nobody. This sort of transferal from the unknown to the known is a well-attested feature of heroic tales. The legends of Robin Hood are borrowed from a wide range of real-life, but otherwise virtually unknown, outlaws. Some traditions about King Arthur have their basis in actual events, but these events have been linked only secondarily with the mythical king. Stories accrete to famous figures, just as quotations accrete to famous speakers (proverbs to Confucius, or folksy humor to Mark Twain). When one wants to say more about a character than one knows to be true, there is an infinite amount of material to choose from. A story can be invented out of whole cloth, or it can be borrowed from the life of someone otherwise unknown.

In fact, it seems as if the story of David and Goliath was borrowed not only from the exploits of Elhanan, but also from those of Elhanan's brother Eleazar—who is also, naturally enough, from Bethlehem, also one of David's warriors, and also unmentioned anywhere else in the narrative. While Elhanan's story specifically mentions the figure of Goliath, he of the mighty spear, Eleazar's story is the origin for the narrative framework of the battle: the Philistines challenge the Israelites to fight, and all the Israelites but Eleazar fall back, afraid, while Eleazar wins a great victory. Not only is this the same situation we find in the David story, but the location of the battle is even the same: Epes-dammim (1 Chron. 11:13; 1 Sam. 17:1). With two stories paralleling the David narrative, it becomes even more unlikely that the David story is original; we would have to believe that someone took the glory away from David, split it in two, and gave it to relative nobodies. It is far easier to see David as the borrower.[22]

And who better to borrow from than two soldiers from Bethlehem, David's own hometown? Minor legends about minor characters have been taken up and dramatically expanded, complete with mythical descriptions of Goliath's size and grand declarations of faith by the young David. (Somewhat ironically, the legends explaining why Elhanan and Eleazar deserved to be part of David's military retinue are reused to explain how David acquired his position in Saul's army.) As we have seen, this greatly expanded narrative of the Goliath story serves its purpose well, presenting us with a David who is faithful and fearless, unique among his peers, and eminently worthy of the kingship that will soon be his. The original legends of Elhanan and Eleazar were but two among many such tales; the embellished story makes David out to be a man like no other. At its heart, however, it is not truly David's story. The Goliath of 1 Samuel 17 is a secondhand creation, and the entire narrative is a literary exercise in Davidic glorification.

WHEN WE FIRST ENCOUNTER David, in 1 Samuel 16–17, we find a young man destined to be king, anointed by God's true prophet, the antithesis of all that is wrong with Saul. He is not only destined, but, more important, he is worthy—gripped by the spirit of Yahweh, a musician who will one day give lyrical voice to the faith of his people, a warrior for God among timid men. The most famous images of David, the most important ideals associated with him, are laid out right at the start of his story. And this is precisely what the biblical authors intended. Everything that David does from this point forward, and everything that we think about him, is colored by these first stories and the theological weight that they bear.

As we have seen, however, these stories of David's youth have no basis in reality. The only minimal facts that we might be able to extract are David's origins—his hometown and his father's name—and the fact that he entered Saul's military service. Everything else is invented for the purpose of glorifying David, even in advance of his kingship. The David of popular imagination, the insightful author of the psalms and the valiant warrior for God, is a construction of the biblical authors and the traditions that subsequently grew about this greatest of all Israelites.

David did not write the psalms. David did not kill Goliath. The defining features of David in the modern imagination are merely that: imaginary. They are what the biblical authors, and we too, want David to be, not what he was. These, then, are the questions we have to reckon with: if David did not do what we imagine him to have done, what did he really do? If David was not who we think he was, then who was he?

CHAPTER 2

David in Saul's Service

REVEALING A BIBLICAL COVER-UP

WHEN WE TRY TO RECONSTRUCT the life of the historical David, we are at a significant disadvantage. Everything we know about David comes exclusively from the Bible. Yet we have already seen that the biblical authors are not above inventing episodes for the sake of portraying him in a particularly positive light. The fundamental question the historian must ask is whether any material in the Bible can be judged to be historically accurate; or, to put it another way, why shouldn't we assume that it is all invention? What clues are there to suggest that David really existed, and even may have done some of the things described in the Bible?

As it turns out, the first two chapters of the David story are rather unlike the rest of the narrative of his life. After those chapters, there are no more mythical battle scenes and only a very few explicitly theological passages (which are easy enough to spot) like the secret anointing in 1 Samuel 16. The majority of the story is an ostensibly chronological recounting of the significant events in David's life, with special concentration on his relationships with others: with Saul, with Jonathan, with the inhabitants of Judah, with the Philistines, with Saul's descendants, with his opponents, and with his children. In virtually every part of the text, however, the program is identical to that of the first two chapters: to demonstrate that David is righteous, innocent of any wrongdoing, and fit to be the king who inaugurates a glorious dynasty—despite the fact that he, born to a shepherd in Bethlehem, had no obvious right to the throne. In this, the David narrative belongs to a well-established ancient literary genre: the apology.

We are remarkably fortunate to have an example of this genre from the centuries just before the Bible began to be written. In the thirteenth century BCE, a Hittite king named Hattušili promulgated an account of how he came to rule.[1] Hattušili was the younger brother of the reigning Hittite monarch, a position of significant power but one that did not lead to the throne. Hattušili's brother had a son, and so the kingship would by rights pass to Hattušili's nephew, thereby skipping Hattušili. Hattušili explains in this text how he had been in charge of the Hittite armies under the reign of his elder brother, and how he enjoyed success after success in battle, with the divine assistance of his patron goddess. Evidently his nephew, upon gaining the throne, saw Hattušili's military victories, and the favor the goddess bestowed on him, and became envious, or perhaps nervous. The new king took away many of the properties that Hattušili had previously been granted, and soon enough, according to Hattušili, "He sought my destruction." Hattušili, however, claims to have shown great restraint: "Out of regard for the love of my brother I did not react at all." When he did eventually take over the kingship, by capturing his nephew in battle, he did so not just of his own accord, but with the blessing of the deity, who "had already early foretold kingship for me," and of the populace at large: "All of Hatti supported me."

What we have here is a man who had no right to the kingship; who was a great military leader, aided by divine providence; whose successes aroused the envy of the king; who was unjustifiably pursued by the king; who proclaims his innocence; who is beloved by his deity and by the people of his land; and who, despite his station, becomes king. To anyone who knows the story of David, this should sound very familiar. What Hattušili says for himself is almost exactly what the biblical authors say on David's behalf, as we will see in detail. This Hittite text has been called "The Apology of Hattušili." Many scholars have seen fit to describe the narrative of David's life as "The Apology of David,"[2] for, similarity of details aside, it serves the same literary purpose: to demonstrate the greatness of the protagonist and even his God-given right to the throne despite what we would expect to happen in the normal course of events.

When we recognize that the David story is an apology, even though it remains a literary creation rather than what we might consider a historical one, new avenues of historical inquiry open for us. For it is the nature of an apology that it must apologize for something. That is, an apology is always written as a response: either to custom or to tradition or, most often, to a counternarrative that challenges the text's version of things. If we understand the apology as the ancient version of political spin, this notion will be obvious: in today's media-driven world, spin is always and only produced as a means of explaining something differently from what one might think, or from what others have said. This has significant ramifications for historical reconstruction, for with both spin and apology, there is no need to explain something that never happened. The point of an apology is that something *did* in fact happen, and that something requires explanation.

Understanding the David story as an apology therefore allows us to take three major steps. First, and broadly, we can reject the notion that David never existed. There would be no need to apologize for a fictional character. If David were invented, we are safe in assuming that many of the stories we read about him would never have been told. We would have an entire narrative that looked like the first two chapters of his life. If the Bible apologizes for David, then he must have existed. This literary conclusion is borne out in dramatic fashion by the recent discovery of a late ninth-century BCE inscription in Aramaic that refers to Judah as the "House of David."[3] It is one thing to surmise that ancient Israel invented its glorious founder. It is quite another to think that a foreign people would also invent David.

Second, recognizing the text as an apology allows us to date it to a period roughly contemporary with the times it describes. An apology needs to explain events that its audience knows happened—and an audience centuries removed would have no way of accessing the real facts. This is why the stories of David in Samuel are apologetic, whereas those in Chronicles, written some six centuries later, are not. Chronicles can tell the story however it wants and so leaves out everything that is potentially embarrassing for David, but Samuel doesn't have that freedom. It must therefore be from a period relatively close to David's own time.

Third, on the methodological front, once we know that we are reading an apology, we know what to look for and how to proceed. The historian's task when reading an apology is to identify those features of the text that belong to the level of the apology—that cast David in a flattering light, that justify his actions (frequently in unlikely ways), and that denigrate his opponents.[4] When those aspects are stripped away, we may see what it is that is being apologized for—what it is that David may have done, or was thought to have done, that the Bible is eager to cast in a positive light. There is little in the biblical text that we can rely on. Removal of the apologetic elements entails the removal of many narrative details, especially dialogue. So the task of reconstruction must be based only in part on the biblical account and in larger part on what we know of the ancient world in which David lived. What do we know of the political structures, the social norms, the international relations, even the geography? All these will play a part in filling out the picture, helping to explain who David was, what he did, and why.

Saul's Kingdom

THE FIRST SIGNIFICANT PERIOD in David's life for which we can propose any historical basis is the time he spent in Saul's service. From 1 Samuel 16–17 we learn that David joined the military under

Saul. The subsequent chapters, 1 Samuel 18–20, venture to tell us what transpired between that moment and David's being forced to flee from Saul and go into exile in the wilderness. To understand David's position in Saul's kingdom and the relationship between Saul and David that is the main focus of these chapters, we have to understand just what kind of kingdom Saul ruled over, and what sort of king he was.

First, we must recognize what territory Saul could lay claim to. We use the term "Israel" to denote the entire nation, but in the time of Saul and David, "Israel" meant specifically the northern tribes and did not include the region of Judah to the south. Saul himself was from Benjamin, which along with Ephraim and Manasseh constituted the central region of Israel, both geographically and politically. Farther to the north, through the tribal territories of Issachar, Zebulun, Naphtali, Asher, and Dan, settlements were sparser; to the east, across the Jordan, there were some Israelite tribes, Gad and Reuben, and some semi-independent regions such as Gilead. Saul's power was concentrated in the heartland of the Israelite hill country, and his influence to the north and east was probably less clear.[5]

Saul's reign in Israel was something of a grand experiment. Israel had never before had a king. Indeed, before Saul there had never been an entity called Israel. The northern tribes were independent clan units, each lacking any sort of formal centralized leadership. Only in the face of an external attack would a tribe produce a leader, known in the Bible as a judge, who would organize and lead the tribe to battle. When the threat passed, the judge's work was done and things would go back to the way they had been before, until the next threat emerged and the cycle began again. Given the ad hoc nature of the position, judges did not pass their status on to the next generation.[6] Eventually, the realization dawned that this was an ineffective way for the tribes to defend themselves. As Israel's neighbors grew in power, the emergence of a particularly gifted leader in every generation could hardly be counted on. What was required was consistency—and that is precisely what a dynastic monarchy provides.[7]

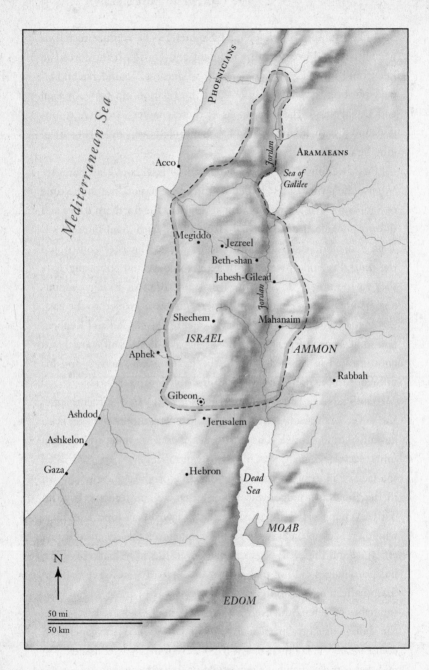

Saul's Kingdom

Saul's kingship, therefore, was a novelty in Israel on two fronts. First, the position was no longer ad hoc—Saul would be king in times of war *and* in times of peace. Second, the position was hereditary; after Saul, it was understood that, as with kingship everywhere, the crown would be passed on to his offspring, and to theirs in turn. Despite these two innovations, however, Saul's kingdom was not drastically different from what came before it.[8] There was no significant royal or national infrastructure. Saul had no palace, nor a proper capital: he ruled from beneath a tree in his hometown (1 Sam. 22:6). The tribes continued to operate as they always had, without any intrusion from the crown. They would have had no interest in giving up their long-established self-sufficient ways, but they realized the need for regular mutual cooperation in battle. Israel under Saul was more a permanent military alliance than a proper political state, and Saul was more commander in chief than king: the Bible ascribes to Saul no role on the national stage other than as leader of the army.[9] Indeed, his only recorded acts before David's arrival on the scene are set in a military context, just as was the case with the judges who preceded him.[10]

Even Saul's military, however, was not particularly advanced compared with those of his predecessors. In the days before the monarchy, each tribe would muster its own troops under its own commander, to defend itself either against a foreign enemy or, at times, against another Israelite tribe. On rare occasions an external threat would be severe enough that multiple tribes would combine their forces, with the understanding that one of the tribal officers would take the lead. This is the situation described in the ancient poem of Judges 5, in which a number of Israel's tribes rally behind the prophetess Deborah and the general Barak, from the tribe of Naphtali. There is no indication that Saul changed this basic system. Before he waged the first battle of his kingship, he sent messengers to each of the tribes calling for their participation. Saul had no standing army, at least not on the national level. The tribalist nature of the army, central to the days before the monarchy, persisted during Saul's reign. His military commanders were not the highest officers from each tribe, as might make sense if the armed forces were truly national. Instead, Saul kept it in the family: his son Jonathan was a military captain, and his cousin Abner was the army commander. Kin relations were the basis for social organization before Saul, and they remained so after he became king.[11] The real change from the judges to Saul with regard to kingship was simply Saul's enduring presence and the tribes' understanding that, when their king called, they would send men to fight for him. The kingship was thus a position of trust: the people had agreed to put their fate in Saul's hands when it came to matters of the military, and they were willing to grant him a royal dynasty as long as he was able to protect them.

The Israelite decision that the independent tribal system of defense was no longer feasible, and that a king was needed, was probably not so sudden as it is presented in the Bible. It was rather a gradual process, largely conditioned, as scholars have long realized, by the steady rise of a significant threat on Israel's borders, one that showed no signs of going away any time soon.

David's Military Exploits

IN THE TWELFTH CENTURY BCE, about two centuries before David, a wave of mysterious immigrants arrived in Egypt and the Levant. Because they were ethnically diverse and came largely by ship, the Egyptian pharaoh Merneptah called them the "Sea Peoples," and so they are still called today.[12] The origins of the Sea Peoples are not known with any certainty, but some of the names by which their subgroups are identified in the Egyptian inscriptions strongly suggest that they came from the Aegean: the Ekwesh (= Greek Achaeans), the Denyen (= Greek Danaans), the Sherden (= Sardinians), and the Shekelesh (= Sicilians). The Sea Peoples tried to invade Egypt during the reign of Ramesses III but were roundly defeated. Many then turned to the northeast, to find less well-defended territories to settle. They seem to have succeeded; scholars think that the Sea Peoples may have been responsible for the collapse of the once mighty Hittite empire in Anatolia (modern Turkey). But the most famous of the Sea Peoples were those who traveled the least distance from Egypt, who displaced the local inhabitants along the coast of Canaan. These were the Peleshet—the Philistines.

The Philistine invasion of coastal Canaan was swift. The archaeological record shows that almost immediately the Philistines conquered and resettled five major Canaanite cities, known as the Philistine Pentapolis: Gaza, Gath, Eqron, Ashdod, and Ashkelon. Within a generation, they had spread farther.[13] It was at just this time that the earliest proto-Israelite communities were being settled in the hill country to the east. It is likely, in fact, that the arrival of the Philistines increased the early Israelite process of settlement, as coastal inhabitants were pushed eastward by the expanding Philistine culture. This displacement is probably reflected in the biblical stories about the tribe of Dan, which was forced from its ancestral homeland on the coast to a new inland territory far to the north (Judg. 18).[14]

The disparity between the two territories, and the two peoples, could hardly be greater. The coastal plain occupied by the Philistines had fertile soil and historically large cities, enriched by both agricultural abundance and the ancient trade routes between Egypt to the south and Mesopotamia to the north: the Fertile Crescent. The central highlands region where the proto-Israelite communities emerged was, by contrast, difficult to work, requiring specialized techniques to allow for even the most basic of agriculture. It was on no significant route—who would trek through the hills when the coast offered a straight and flat path? The Philistines came from the relatively advanced Aegean culture and brought with them military organization and equipment, notably chariots, unmatched by anything the Israelites had. This is why, according to the biblical story of the Israelites' conquest of Canaan, Joshua was unable to take control of the Philistine territory: "They were not able to dispossess the inhabitants of the plain, for they had iron chariots" (Judg. 1:19).

The relative situations of the two peoples made them natural adversaries. The powerful Philistines would have seen the emerging Israelite population as a roadblock to their continued expansion into Canaan and a potential threat to their regional dominance. The Israelites would have regarded the Philistines as foreign invaders who had taken control of the best land available. Given the disparity in power, it is not surprising that the Philistines should have been the aggressors. Yet the geography that minimized Israel's capacity for agricultural wealth also provided them with a natural defense system. As a prominent archaeologist has noted, "had the Philistines accomplished their military goal, it would have been the first time in recorded history that a lowland polity had succeeded in bringing the highlands under its control."[15] The chariots that gave the Philistines such an advantage in the open field of battle were useless in the wooded hills. As a result, the relationship between the Philistines and the Israelites was one of regular conflict but was largely a stalemate, with neither side able to impose its will on the other.

The Bible traces this rivalry. The first major conflict with the Philistines occurs in the story of Samson from the book of Judges. Samson's birth is marked by the prophecy that he will oppose the Philistines: "He shall be the first to deliver Israel from the hand of the Philistines" (Judg. 13:5). His entire life is dedicated to defeating the Philistines, culminating with his final act of pulling down the Philistine temple: "Those whom he killed as he died outnumbered those whom he killed when he lived" (16:30). The wars with the Philistines continue in the life of Samuel, the great prophet and judge, as recounted in 1 Samuel 4–7, during which the Philistines actually capture the ark of the covenant for seven months.

Saul, too, fights against the Philistines throughout his kingship: "There was constant war against the Philistines all the days of Saul" (1 Sam. 14:52). And it is in this context that the Bible narrates the rise of David, in the battle against Goliath, the champion of the Philistines. The biblical authors go to great lengths to make David out to be even better at fighting the Philistines than Saul had been. This process begins in the Goliath story: Saul, like the other Israelites, is afraid to face the giant, but David steps forward into the breach. It continues in the accounts of David's repeated victories over the Philistines and the reports of the love of the troops and the populace at large for their young hero. According to the text, even Saul recognizes David's military prowess, appointing him as the head of the entire army: "David went out and was successful whenever Saul sent him, and Saul put him in command of all the fighting men; this pleased all the people and Saul's courtiers as well" (18:5). We are repeatedly told that David was always victorious in his battles: "David was successful in all his undertakings" (18:14); "The Philistine chiefs marched out to battle; and every time they marched out, David was more successful than all the other officers of Saul" (18:30); "David went out and fought the Philistines; he inflicted a great defeat upon them and they fled before him" (19:8). David is, in short, depicted as the perfect general.

His successes are not lost on the army or the general populace of Israel, who laud him for his leadership: "The women sang as they made merry, saying, 'Saul has slain his thousands, David his tens of thousands!'" (18:7); "All Israel and Judah loved David, for he marched before them" (18:16); "His reputation soared" (18:30). Given that David seems to be constantly laying waste to Israel's great enemy, the Philistines, the popular response seems well deserved. More than mere appreciation is being expressed here, however. The people's love for David, as the Bible presents it, is both comparative and political. It is not just that he is a great military leader; he is a greater military leader than even Saul. This is no small matter. Saul's kingship was marked by his triumphs in battle: "After Saul had secured his kingship over Israel, he fought against all his enemies on every side: against the Moabites, Ammonites, Edomites, the kings of Zobah, and the Philistines; and wherever he turned he worsted them. He was triumphant, defeating the Amalekites and saving Israel from the hands of those who plundered it" (14:47–48). Saul's reputation was built on his military prowess. Yet in a matter of mere moments, at least narratively, David exceeded Saul by a factor of ten.

On the military front, therefore, David is presented as a superstar.

He is not only exceptionally successful in every battle, he is increasingly famous and beloved, and in ways that emphasize his superiority to Saul. When we read the accounts of David's military career, brief though they may be, we are witnessing the opening scenes of a swift rise toward the ultimate position of leadership in Israel. David, at least in military terms, has all the makings of a king.

From a literary perspective, this makes perfect sense. David's military successes, and his superiority to Saul, justify David's eventual supplanting of Saul on the throne. Yet there are elements of the biblical account that should give reason for pause. Foremost among these is the lack of specificity throughout: no places are named, no dates are given, and no enemies are named aside from the broad term "the Philistines." This lack of information makes it impossible to judge the accuracy of these reports. Furthermore, the fact that every notice of a victory by David is followed directly by an attempt by Saul to have him killed—a topic we will return to presently—suggests that these notices serve an important literary function, highlighting David's valiant service and Saul's incommensurately jealous response.

This does not mean, of course, that David did not actually fight in any battles. Since he does appear to have garnered some popular approval—an element that may be exaggerated but seems probable to some degree, as we will see—he must have done something. What is doubtful is that his victories were of any major significance. David wins battle after battle against Israel's great enemy, yet he never seems to make any progress in the broader war. From the people's response to David's military successes, one would think that Israel was gaining the upper hand, even perhaps winning. Yet after each battle, the status quo seems not to change. Indeed, the Philistines continued to be a persistent threat to Israel long after David: the Bible tells us that during the reign of Hezekiah, almost three hundred years later, Israel was still trying to conquer Philistine territory (2 Kings 18:8). For the first few hundred years of its existence, Israel was in a state of perpetual war against its Philistine neighbors, a war in which neither side was able to make any substantial headway.

Given this situation, we may ask: for what, precisely, was David so lauded? What sorts of victories did he enjoy?

At the very least, we can say that these were not major conquests of Philistine territory. For one thing, the reports of David's victories lack any details: not a single town or city or territory is named. We are told only that David was successful. Had he captured a Philistine town, even a minor one, it surely would be mentioned, and perhaps even reflected in the archaeological record. Moreover, the relationship between the Philistines and the Israelites during this period was very one-sided. The nascent state of Israel may have had some vague expansionist ambitions, but it was the Philistines, well established along the coastland for two centuries, who had all the power. Success, from the Israelite side, meant repulsing Philistine advances, not conquering any Philistine territory proper. Even this sort of defensive success was considered remarkable, and even divinely aided, given the relative strength of the two forces: "The Philistines were subdued and did not enter the territory of Israel again; and the hand of the Lord was against the Philistines" (1 Sam. 7:13). Momentary truces were marked by the restoration of captured Israelite territory, and not the reverse: "The towns that the Philistines had taken from Israel were restored to Israel. . . . Israel recovered all its territory from the hands of the Philistines" (7:14).

If David's victories were not offensive conflicts, then perhaps they were defensive. This is what is portrayed in the Goliath story: after David has slain Goliath, the Israelite victory consists of driving the Philistines back to their proper territory—at which point the Israelites do not continue the pursuit into Philistia, but turn back home. Simply maintaining border security is victory enough for them. So too it may be with all of David's victories: they may be no more than defensive battles. Yet even in this we notice again the absence of any named towns or territories in which David's battles took place. Major biblical battles, even fictional ones as in the case of Goliath, are virtually always located somewhere. What does it mean that David's famous victories are essentially placeless?

At the beginning of the first millennium BCE, neither Israel nor Philistia was a politically defined state as we understand the word today. There were no cartographers to draw lines indicating where one territory began and another ended. Such clear demarcations would come only with the subjugation of Canaan by foreign empires—Assyria, Babylon, Persia, Greece, and Rome—that divided the land into administrative districts for taxation purposes. The inhabitants of Canaan lived in city-states, with surrounding villages and agricultural lands that fell under their spheres of influence. The Philistines, for their part, had no centralized government but rather five kings for the five cities of the Pentapolis, which were united by ethnicity and language. Israel, though it did have a king in Saul, was similarly a group of towns brought together by common religion, language, and foreign enemies. The geography of Canaan was such that the major inhabited sites were often quite some distance from each other, separated by hills or by stretches of wilderness. There were no clear borders between Israelite and Philistine territory; there was merely open space. This geopolitical situation meant that small scouting and raiding parties moved constantly back and forth between Israel and Philistia—much as today regular skirmishes occur in the spaces between nations, such as between Pakistan and India. These sorts of minor encounters happened in uninhabited and unnamed locations. And they happened regularly, unlike the relatively rare major pitched battles between the Israelites and Philistines that we read about in the Bible.[16]

In short, these sorts of small skirmishes fit perfectly not only with the historical situation, but with the biblical description of David as having been constantly successful—"in all his undertakings," "every time the Philistines marched out." David fought at the head of Saul's troops for what would appear to be only a short time. It would be surprising if numerous major battles had occurred during those few months or perhaps years, but we would expect there to have been a constant series of border skirmishes. This would also account for what we already observed, namely, that after each one of David's victories, the status quo seems to have been unchanged. Major battles, even Israelite defensive victories, would have affected the relative status of the two parties, but minor encounters in the middle of the wilderness would not.

We may also note that this description of David's military role suggests that he was not, in fact, the head of all of Israel's armed forces. In the ancient Near East, it was typically the king's duty to lead the army into battle. In the Bible this notion is so taken for granted that it is even used to mark time: "At the turn of the year, the season when kings go out to battle . . ." (2 Sam. 11:1). But should the king be unable to go, that job would fall to the next in line for the throne. This was more than a matter of training; it had practical political benefits. Leadership in battle was a way a prince gained the respect and affiliation of the army and thus secured the backing of the military before he took the reins of leadership.[17] And this seems, quite naturally, to have been the role of Saul's son Jonathan before David arrived on the scene. The first time we hear of Jonathan in the Bible is in a military context. Saul chooses three thousand men to fight a battle. He takes two thousand of these men for himself and puts the remaining thousand under Jonathan (1 Sam. 13:2). Jonathan seems to have been a relatively good officer, winning in battle (13:3), taking on a dangerous solo mission (14:6–15), and gaining the admiration of his men (14:45).[18]

Given this situation, it seems unlikely that Saul should elevate David to a higher military position than his son Jonathan or his cousin Abner. Doing so flies in the face of both tradition and common sense. Indeed, as we have seen, David's job seems to have been warding off minor incursions into Israelite territory—the role of a military officer, no doubt, but not necessarily of the highest officer in the land. There is some ambiguity in the biblical text as to what position David held. It says in one place that Saul put David in charge of all the soldiers (1 Sam. 18:5), but it says in another that he appointed David as "chief of a thousand" (18:13). "A thousand," it should be noted, is not a precise numerical designation but rather a technical term for a military unit.[19] Thus, according to at least one biblical passage, David was just one officer among many. This seems a more historically likely scenario.

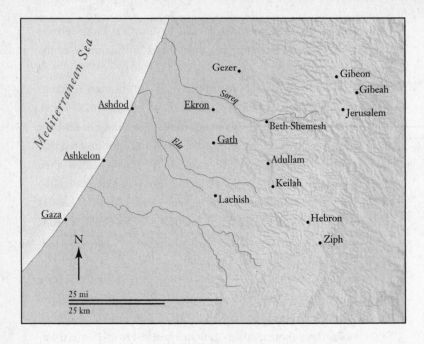

Philistia and Judah

Key: Philistine cities (underlined); Israelite towns (not underlined)

We may better define David's role by considering his homeland: the territory of Judah. As we have already noted, Judah was not officially part of Saul's kingdom, yet it was a crucial part of Israel's defense against the Philistines. The Philistine Pentapolis was on the southern coastal plain, and so it was Judah that directly bordered on Philistine territory. Since the Philistines would almost always have to cross Judah to reach the territory controlled by Saul, it was a buffer region for the north. When the Philistines tried to capture Samson in Judges 15, they "came up and encamped in Judah" (15:9). When they sent the captured ark back to Israel (1 Sam. 6), it went through Beth-Shemesh to Kiryath-jearim, both towns on the northern border of Judah. And the battle against Goliath took place in Judah: "The

Philistines assembled their forces for battle and gathered at Socoh of Judah" (17:1).

Saul's need to protect Judah, and Judah's need for Saul's military help, necessitated a mutually beneficial arrangement. As noted above, such arrangements were standard practice in early Israel. Even before the monarchy, the individual tribes would unite in ad hoc military collectives to fight off external enemies. Although the tribes would fight under a single general, each would send its own military leadership. This, it may be suggested, is a good parallel to what happened under Saul. Though Saul as king would be the commander in chief, Judah, still an independent territory, may well have had its own military officer: David. Presumably, David rose to this position by proving himself capable or intelligent enough to hold it.[20] It is not unlikely that Saul would have been the one to appoint him; Judah, though descriptive of a region, was not yet a self-standing political unit. David would have been responsible for warding off the constant minor incursions of Philistines into his territory. As part of the larger Israelite defense strategy, he would have reported to Saul and been considered an arm of Saul's royal forces.

The best historical description of David's military career under Saul, then, is that of an officer—not a general—who had some minor successes in battle. David probably was responsible for defending the porous Judahite frontier region against minor incursions by Philistine raiding parties. For a small nation in constant fear of the mighty Philistine city-states to the west, even the defensive successes of repelling small bands of Philistines along the border might well have been seen as worthy of praise. Judah was the front line, and David was the one holding it, protecting Israel at large from the Philistine threat. At least, it is easy enough to see how David's role could be presented that way to the populace.

It is very much part of the biblical authors' program to exaggerate David's successes. As we saw in the previous chapter, they are even willing to take the semimythical victories of lesser-known warriors and attribute them to David. It should not surprise us, then, that these authors may take minor victories and ascribe great significance to them, for in this way David's military exploits can be held up against those of Saul. David is shown to be worthy of the kingship in the terms most important to the fledgling Israelite state.

In today's world, exaggerating or embellishing one's accomplishments is frowned upon—and it is fraught with peril, as we see in almost every election season. In the ancient world, however, such exaggeration was standard literary practice. Scholars have noted that something very similar occurs in the royal annals of the Assyrian king Tiglath-Pileser I, who reigned about a century before David. Tiglath-Pileser boldly proclaims that he conquered "the land of Kathmuhu in its entirety," which would seem more impressive were it not that he evidently had to go back the next year and conquer it all over again—just as David seems to have had to repeatedly "defeat" the Philistines. Conquest is in the eye of the conqueror. In the case of Tiglath-Pileser, he counted as conquered everything from those territories he fully annexed to those he merely looted before withdrawing his troops. As one biblical scholar has put it, "in Assyrian royal inscriptions . . . the torching of a grain field is the conquest of a whole territory behind it."[21]

We don't have royal annals from ancient Israel, though they may well have existed. What we have instead, serving the same self-congratulatory function, are the biblical narratives. What Tiglath-Pileser does in his annals is what the biblical authors do in 1 Samuel: they credit David with great laudable victories for military encounters that failed to register on the larger political stage. This is not the case only with David, of course. We may note again the description of Saul's own military successes: "he fought against all his enemies on every side: against the Moabites, Ammonites, Edomites, the kings of Zobah, and the Philistines; and wherever he turned he worsted them" (1 Sam. 14:47). Saul conquered none of these peoples; all of them would be Israel's neighbors and occasional adversaries for centuries. At best, he maintained his incipient kingdom in the face of potential threats from the surrounding nations (though in fact we have no evidence of any of these wars from outside the Bible). From the Israelite perspective, that's impressive enough to warrant high praise.[22]

The reports of David's military victories may have some truth behind them, but they have been colored by the desire of the biblical authors to denigrate Saul and elevate David. As noted above, the primary purpose of this presentation of David is clear enough: David, the biblical hero, must have been a magnificent warrior. Moreover, he must have excelled in precisely the area where Saul himself was so prominent, in battles against the Philistine archenemy. At every turn, David must exceed Saul. David was undoubtedly an excellent military leader, as his later exploits will demonstrate. But we can say next to nothing about his actions in Saul's service, because the victories ascribed to him in the Bible are free of detail and are exaggerated. At most, we may give David credit for successfully repelling minor Philistine advances in Judah.

The Biblical Portrayal of Saul

THE BIBLICAL DEPICTION OF David as a mighty warrior for Saul dovetails with another part of the biblical authors' agenda: the portrayal of Saul as unfit to rule. Speaking about David, Jonathan says to Saul, "His actions have been very much to your advantage" (1 Sam. 19:4)—and yet, according to the narrative, Saul seems to care about nothing so much as killing David. He is driven to extremes of rage and envy by David's successes and the popular admiration for the young officer: "When Saul saw that he was successful, he dreaded him, but all Israel and Judah loved David, for he marched before them" (18:15–16). We can, however, conclude that the biblical account of David's popularity is, if not entirely invented, at least exaggerated. The manner in which David is praised is part of the Bible's rhetorical goal of downplaying Saul in favor of David. When the Israelite women famously proclaim that "Saul has slain his thousands, David his tens of thousands!" (18:7), the hyperbole is obvious. The entire

Philistine population at its height numbered around thirty thousand; David could hardly have killed more than half of all the Philistines in one battle, or even in all of his battles combined.[23] Even Saul's "thousands" is undoubtedly false. But these are not supposed to be actual body counts. The numbers used here are, just as today, simply representative of "a lot"—which is defined by the speaker. "A lot" for Israel in a battle against the Philistines could be, from our perspective, a very small number indeed. Elsewhere in the Bible these same numbers are used similarly: "Our flocks number thousands, even tens of thousands, in our fields" (Ps. 144:13); "Would the Lord be pleased with thousands of rams, with tens of thousands of streams of oil?" (Mic. 6:7). These numbers are self-conscious exaggerations.

As for the comparison between Saul and David, here it seems that the biblical authors are having some fun at Saul's expense. Biblical poetry regularly uses increasing numbers in parallel clauses, which often are to be read not as a comparison, but as a distributive equation: "Saul has slain his thousands, David his tens of thousands" can be understood as "Saul and David have killed their thousands and ten thousands."[24] This would, in fact, be a logical reading of the verse in 1 Samuel 18, since we are told that "the women of all the towns of Israel came out singing and dancing to greet King Saul" (18:6)—Saul is the returning hero, and David his chief warrior. The women may very well have meant to praise both Saul and David as having defeated a great number of the Philistine enemy. If so, the authors make Saul out to be not only unjustifiably jealous, but even unfamiliar with the standards of his native language when he responds in anger that "to David they have given tens of thousands, but to me they have given thousands" (18:8). The women's chant thus serves two purposes: to elevate David by the numerical exaggeration, and to make Saul out to be a fool by his response to it—the two essential goals of this section of the narrative.

In his jealousy, Saul is said to try just about every way possible to get rid of David. He throws a spear at David while David is playing the lyre for him—twice. He sends him to the front lines of battle in hopes of having him die at the hands of the Philistines. He offers him his daughter Michal in marriage, for the grotesque bride-price of a hundred Philistine foreskins, a price he is sure David will die trying to pay. He sends his men to David's house to kill him in his sleep.

In scene after scene, Saul tries everything he can think of, direct and indirect, with his own hands and by various proxies, to kill David. Nothing works. Nor, of course, should we expect it to, since we know that David succeeds Saul as king. What these episodes reveal, then, is Saul's growing fear—a fear that is driven by his uncertain hold on his own royal position and by David's increasing popularity. It is important, however, to recognize that the biblical account depicts Saul's fears as unreasonable—not just intellectually, insofar as David seems to be devoted to Saul's service without giving any thought to his own advancement, but literally: Saul is portrayed as mentally unstable. The biblical authors link Saul's jealousy over David's military successes with the "evil spirit of God" that afflicts the king: after every one of David's victories, Saul tries to kill him. The Bible makes clear that Saul is losing control not only of his kingdom, but of his mind. The reader of these episodes instinctively sides with David and is made to feel that Saul is losing any legitimate claim to power. At the same time that David is proving himself fit to be king, Saul is gradually proving himself unfit to rule.

Almost every aspect of the biblical presentation is unrealistic. As we saw in the last chapter, David's lyre-playing and the "evil spirit" that afflicts Saul are closely linked to the secret anointing of David and are historically unverifiable. Moreover, the entire setting of these episodes, with David by Saul's side at court, seems unlikely. If David was really an officer in Judah, responsible for defending the front lines against Philistine raids, then he was probably not a regular fixture in the royal court to the north. Like the other tribal military officers, David was not part of the central army apparatus led by Saul, Jonathan, and Abner, the familial inner circle. His place was in Judah, and if he ever went to Saul's capital, it would be only on rare formal occasions—perhaps Saul, like other Near Eastern monarchs, required his officers to appear before him once a year to reaffirm their loyalty.[25] But it is improbable that David lived permanently at Saul's court as the text suggests. Thus the spear-throwing episodes may be safely discounted.

So too the notion of Saul sending David to the front lines in the hopes that he will fall in battle. The narrative makes clear that David was always victorious—it would seem that sending him to war would only increase his stature, rather than result in his death. Furthermore, David's death in battle would be entirely contrary to Saul's own good. Saul's reputation is built on his ability to protect Israel from the Philistines—a Philistine victory over David would be disastrous for Saul's claim to the throne. Saul's placing of David at the head of the troops is a literary move, again intended to demonstrate David's invincibility in battle, and Saul's own reticence to fight.

The offer to David of Saul's daughter Michal in marriage is historically highly unlikely.[26] The reward, in Saul's mind, is the likelihood that David will die in attempting to meet the bride-price. But the risk far outweighs any reward: should David succeed, as indeed he does twofold, then the man that Saul is trying to eliminate would become a member of the royal family, and potentially in line for Saul's throne. Furthermore, any children born to Michal and David would have Saul's royal blood in their veins and would be potential heirs themselves. We should probably credit Saul with being smart enough not to set in motion such a sequence of events. In addition, when David is forced to flee, Michal does not go with him, which would be inexplicable if they were in fact married (and if she was as supportive of David against her father as the text makes her out to be).

But this marriage does serve a number of significant literary purposes for the biblical authors. The first and most obvious is that David is presented as having a justifiable claim to the throne: he is Saul's son-in-law. Thus when David eventually becomes king in Israel, it appears to be at least nominally a regular succession, rather than a usurpation by someone outside the royal line. In addition, marriage to the king's daughter positions David as something like royalty himself. It was common custom in the ancient Near East for kings to marry their children to royal descendants of other nations. A full millennium before David, Mesopotamian kings were marrying their sons to foreign princesses to cement political ties; nearly three millennia later, royal houses in Europe did the same.[27] Even Solomon is said to have married the daughter of the Egyptian Pharaoh (1 Kings 3:1). Thus the marriage to Michal makes David out to be Judahite royalty, and it serves as an implicit treaty between Saul and David. Ironically, in the biblical presentation, the unification of the northern and southern kingdoms, though accomplished by David, was set in motion by Saul himself. Finally, David did end up marrying Michal— but only after he became king in Judah. The problem is that Michal had long been married to someone else, and David took her by force, as we will see. For the biblical apologists, this was unacceptable—the preferred narrative would be that David was her rightful husband and that Saul had taken Michal from him. And that is precisely what the Bible says (1 Sam. 25:44). Thus the marriage to Michal at this early stage of David's life is both a bit of literary foreshadowing of David's kingship and a defense of his character. But in no case is it historically accurate.[28]

This conclusion also renders doubtful the story of Saul trying to have David killed in his sleep. That story depends on Michal's protection of David from Saul's men. If David and Michal were not really married, then the entire scenario falls apart. The story is also mostly comic, as it involves a classic teenager's ruse: Michal puts an idol into the bed, with some goat's hair on its head, and pulls the covers over it while David escapes out the window.[29]

All of these episodes are literary constructions, intended to demonstrate Saul's unreasonable jealousy of David and thereby to mark the king as mentally compromised. (Indeed, if these stories were true, then we would have to judge David as the more unreasonable of the two: who would willingly return again and again to the service of a homicidal maniac?) The authors' agenda is most clear in the final attempt on David's life. After escaping from Michal's bed, David is said to have fled to the prophet Samuel, in Ramah. And there, something very strange happens. Saul sends his men to capture David, but when they arrive, they are seized with the spirit of God and begin to prophesy ecstatically. Saul sends another group, and then a third, but the same thing keeps happening. Finally, Saul goes himself, and he is also seized with the spirit of God: "He too stripped off his clothes and he too spoke in ecstasy before Samuel; and he lay naked all that day and all night" (1 Sam. 19:24). The king of Israel, naked and mumbling nonsense: as Shakespeare knew when he created Lear, there can hardly be a more damning picture of a once powerful man. He is an embarrassment. His dislike of David results in his complete abasement.[30]

This latter episode is particularly striking, as it is by far the most humiliating depiction of Saul; but it is manifestly a literary construction, not a historical account. It conforms to the standard biblical pattern of "the rule of three"—Saul sends his men to find and kill David three times before he himself goes, just as Noah sends the dove out from the ark three times, three divine beings appear to Abraham, Israel travels three days into the wilderness during the Exodus, Balaam strikes his donkey three times, the spies visit Jericho for three days . . . the list could go on and on. What's more, the story culminates in an apparent etiology for what must have been a well-known, if now somewhat obscure, saying: "Is Saul too among the prophets?" (1 Sam. 19:24). In the context of this episode, the saying carries a distinctly pejorative tone, mocking the royal figure writhing naked on the ground. But this is in fact the second time this saying has been introduced in the Bible. The first time occurs when Samuel has just privately anointed Saul as king, and the ecstatic prophecy serves as a divine sign acclaiming the anointing. Samuel tells Saul: "The spirit of the Lord will rush upon you . . . you will be changed into another man. And once these signs have happened to you, do as you see fit, for God is with you" (1 Sam. 10:6–7). When indeed Saul is possessed by the spirit and begins prophesying, the people with him marvel at the sight and say, "Is Saul too among the prophets?" (10:11–12). Far from a negative saying, in its first context the remark about Saul's prophesying is positive, indicating God's favor. The second occurrence, in the context of the David story, is an intentional reversal of the earlier acclamation of Saul as king. It plays on the popular saying and subverts it. This is a literary device, not a historical record. It tells us only that the Bible wants to go to some lengths to portray Saul's irrationality as graphically as possible.

The biblical depiction of Saul has been remarkably persuasive, not only for those who take the text at face value, but for critical scholars as well. In the past century scholars tended to try to diagnose Saul's illness in modern terms, with the most common suggestion being bipolar disorder.[31] After all, he seems to vacillate wildly between affection and hatred for David, between periods of docility and of nearly hyperactive pursuit. But this attempt to diagnose Saul is doomed to failure. First, it imposes modern clinical categories on a text and culture to which they are utterly foreign. To say that Saul was bipolar does nothing to explain how his behavior would have been viewed by a culture that knew nothing of modern science. As one commentator correctly observed, "Saul's suffering is described theologically, not psychopathetically or psychologically."[32] Second, and most important, it assumes that the biblical account is describing Saul accurately. And this is very much in doubt.

From a historical perspective, for Saul to qualify as unfit to rule it is not enough that we are told that he was so; his actions must testify to it. What does Saul do that marks him as unbalanced? As noted above, his irrational behavior is always linked with his attempts to kill David. From the pro-David perspective of the Bible, this is indeed madness. But let us understand events from Saul's point of view. Saul was the first king of a small and fragile nation. His kingship was maintained by sheer force of will and the promise of continued military success. He had every right to be concerned about the succession of his line—as he was the first king, there was no established dynastic protocol.

Saul could not have known it, but the people over whom he reigned, the northern kingdom of Israel, would prove themselves largely incapable of maintaining a stable dynastic succession. Over the nearly three hundred years of the kingdom's history, the longest dynasty lasted only five generations (compare this with the southern kingdom, where the royal succession was unbroken for the more than four hundred years of its existence). The principle of dynastic succession, though common throughout the ancient Near East, still would have required an initial example, preferably two, to set it firmly in place. Even the Bible has Saul recognize this, as he says to Jonathan, "Neither you nor your kingship will be secure" (1 Sam. 20:31). Genealogical succession to the throne was not just a matter of genetic loyalty; it was a way of ensuring that one's name would be properly remembered and praised (as the example of David's legacy demonstrates). Kings who are succeeded by outsiders are denigrated; those who are succeeded by their offspring have the royal line named after them and gain fame even in the eyes of non-Israelites. Thus we have an Aramean inscription that mentions "the House of David" and an Assyrian obelisk that refers to "the House of Omri," the founder of one of the northern kingdom's short-lived dynasties.[33] In a largely preliterate world, this sort of fame was the highest honor to which one could aspire—and thus the possibility of a failed dynastic succession would have been of the highest concern to Saul.

Saul had been acclaimed as king largely because of his ability to fight off Israel's enemies. Someone else arising who seemed to garner popular approval for the very same reason could spell potential trouble. Throughout the ancient world, as indeed is still the case today, usurpers came most commonly from the military, from the ranks of the officers who could command the allegiance of the army even more effectively than could the king himself. We have already seen the example of Hattušili, who was a successful Hittite general before he seized the throne. Later in Israel's own history, the northern king Elah would be killed and usurped by his commander Zimri (1 Kings 16:9), who would himself then be the victim of a military coup by Omri, the head of the army (1 Kings 16:16). Saul's fears were more than theoretical.

Being king in the ancient world meant constantly watching one's back. The royal succession of every ancient Near Eastern nation was riddled with coups and usurpations. David may have been of use to Saul, but he was at the same time a very real threat, if solely because of his position in the military. If the troops really were pleased with having David as their commander, the boost in morale would hardly make up for the increased risk of a coup from Saul's point of view. If the populace at large really did have affection for David, even if not at Saul's expense but merely alongside the king, it would be unacceptable. Power was not so secure in the ancient world, especially in the nascent Israelite state, as to allow for any divided affections.

The entire program of depicting Saul as unfit to rule is a literary construction. The denigration of one's predecessors was a standard feature of ancient royal rhetoric. In the biblical account, it has an obvious literary purpose: to rhetorically depose Saul so as to make room for David to ascend the throne. It is noteworthy, perhaps, that Saul's reign did not come to an end because anyone in ancient Israel realized that he was unbalanced or unfit—he died in battle, just where any good king ought to have been, and indeed a classically glorious way for a military leader to die. There is no evidence even from the Bible's own account that anyone thought Saul was irrational. Indeed, the most important rationale for judging Saul to be sane—even if he had tried to kill David repeatedly—is that, as it turns out, Saul was absolutely right. David would indeed succeed him as king. Saul's dynasty would never come to be. Far from being unreasonable, Saul was prescient. His fears were justified. Even as the Bible describes him as mentally unstable, the history it records proves the opposite.

David and Jonathan

ASIDE FROM SAUL, THE other person in Israel who had the most to fear from David's success and popularity was Saul's eldest son and heir, Jonathan. As already noted, Jonathan had been a successful and popular military leader before David arrived, thus positioning himself as ready to ascend to the throne after Saul. In fact, Jonathan may have had even more at stake than Saul: Jonathan's succession would be the most important indication that the newly inaugurated kingship in Israel was a lasting proposition. Any challenge to Saul's reign was equally a challenge to Jonathan.

And yet the Bible does not present Jonathan as someone who fears or is threatened by David. On the contrary, he is said to have loved David. He defends David to Saul, he protects David from Saul, he even conspires with David against Saul. And throughout it all, in the biblical account, Jonathan effectively abdicates his natural right to the throne in favor of David. In their first scene together, Jonathan and David make a covenant, and, though it is unclear exactly what the contents of the covenant are, the ceremony by which they cement it has great importance: "Jonathan stripped off the robe he was wearing and gave it to David, together with his outer garment, his sword, his bow, and his belt" (1 Sam. 18:4). Though this may seem a rather strange thing to do, remember that Jonathan is not just any youngster—he is the king's son, the crown prince, the presumptive heir to the throne. His clothing and equipment would not be that of the common man or soldier. He would be wearing royal garb, equipped with royal arms. Giving these to David is highly symbolic. It is simultaneously an act of abdication and of anointment. David, not Jonathan, is dressed as the next in line to be king.[34]

When Jonathan agrees to find out Saul's intentions regarding David, he again debases himself before David, though this time verbally. He says that if Saul is in fact trying to kill David, "May the Lord be with you as he used to be with my father. . . . Thus has Jonathan covenanted with the House of David; and may the Lord requite the enemies of David!" (20:13–16). This speech is remarkable not for Jonathan's unwavering support for David, but for the basic assumptions implicit in it. "May the Lord be with you as he used to be with my father"—in this Jonathan is effectively transferring the kingship from Saul to David, rather than to himself. "Thus has Jonathan covenanted with the House of David"—here Jonathan uses royal terminology, "the House of David," even before David has become king, much less founded a dynasty that could be described as his "house." "May the Lord requite the enemies of David"—again Jonathan puts David in the position of king, surrounded by enemies vying to remove him from the throne. Just as he did when he gave David his royal clothes, here too Jonathan rhetorically abandons the throne to his beloved friend. And we, as readers, have little choice but to begin seeing David as the presumptive heir to the throne.

To justify David's unlikely kingship, the biblical narrative must establish three things. The first is that David is worthy of kingship, a claim substantiated by both the invention of stories (such as the secret anointing of David and the defeat of Goliath) and the exaggeration of David's actions (as in the description of his military exploits). The second is that Saul is unworthy, as demonstrated by his irrational behavior and the notion that God has abandoned him. The third, and least obvious, is that Jonathan, the presumptive heir to Saul's throne, approves of being replaced by David in the royal succession. It is not enough simply to make Saul look bad and David look good. All the comparisons in the world between the two would not override the expectation that Saul should be succeeded by his son according to the custom of dynastic kingship. So the biblical narrators need to persuade us that David and not Jonathan is the natural choice to follow Saul as king.

The biblical account portrays Jonathan as symbolically and rhetorically abdicating his royal inheritance in favor of David: first by giving David his royal clothes and arms, and then by speaking in terms that put David in the position of authority, complete with a dynastic house. From the moment he enters the story, Jonathan is subordinated to David. He is gullible, while David perceives the situation keenly. He ferries messages between David and Saul. He has no discernible role other than as David's defender. As Jonathan continues to praise David in the highest terms and to express his devotion, he is diminished practically to the point of nonexistence when compared with the brave and noble David.

But the historical reality of these elements is very much open to doubt—precisely because they all contribute to the goal of rhetorically removing Jonathan from the line of succession. The bestowal of the royal clothes on David is very similar to other biblical stories in which the gift of clothing symbolizes the passing on of status—such as the moment when Elisha dons the mantle of his predecessor Elijah and thereby acquires his prophetic powers (2 Kings 2:13–15), or when Aaron's priestly garments are passed on to his son Eleazar (Num. 20:28). The private speeches in which Jonathan defends David's innocence and treats him as the presumptive king are unverifiable, but they are so fully in keeping with the message that the biblical narrative is trying to convey that we must doubt their historical accuracy.

The Bible replaces Jonathan with David. There is no claim, however, that Jonathan is incompetent, as is the case with Saul. The biblical authors have no need to question his fitness to rule, for Jonathan will never have the chance to ascend the throne—he is killed, by happy coincidence, side by side with his father (a coincidence to which we will return). What is required is the demonstration that Jonathan willingly accepts David's replacement of him—and this is accomplished by portraying Jonathan as being in love with David.

Many scholars have raised the possibility that David and Jonathan had a homosexual relationship.[35] Certainly the Bible comes close to saying so. Over and over we are told that Jonathan loved David. And while frequently the word "love" in the Bible and the rest of the ancient Near East has a nonromantic meaning of "covenant loyalty"— this is probably what it means when it says that Saul loved David, for example—the use of the word in the case of Jonathan seems to go beyond that.[36] Jonathan does not just "love" David: "Jonathan's soul became bound up with the soul of David" (1 Sam. 18:1). Jonathan "delighted greatly in David" (19:1)—the same Hebrew word used in Genesis to describe Shechem's desire for Jacob's daughter Dinah (Gen. 34:19). When Jonathan dies, David laments for him in these words: "More wonderful was your love for me than the love of women" (2 Sam. 1:26).[37] The comparison to the love of women can hardly have a political connotation; this is as close to an expression of romantic attachment between two men as we find in the Bible.

There is nothing historically objectionable about the idea that David and Jonathan were lovers. We need not suppose that David was gay, in our modern understanding. It is clear enough that were we to apply such contemporary labels, we would be more justified in calling him bisexual, considering his multiple marriages and explicitly sexual attraction to Bathsheba. But any such terms—homosexual, bisexual—are inappropriate when describing people in the ancient world. Sexuality as we understand it today is a social construct, a category imposed on people to define them within a larger cultural system.[38] No such categories or constructs existed in the ancient world. There was no notion of a person being "gay" or "straight." People engaged in heterosexual or homosexual acts in various degrees.[39] Much of the time these were, by the standards of their contemporary societies, entirely unobjectionable—consider the famous example of Alexander the Great. Even the Hebrew Bible, despite what many people think, has virtually nothing to say on the matter—only two verses in Leviticus, from the hand of a priestly author with a particular agenda who did not speak for the entirety of ancient Israelite culture. If David and Jonathan were lovers, there is no indication that anyone at the time would have batted an eye over it, much less been morally outraged—certainly the Bible seems to be unbothered by its own hints in that direction.

At the same time, the Bible does not intend explicitly to condone a homosexual relationship between David and Jonathan, as some have suggested.[40] The point is that if such a relationship existed, the biblical authors present it as mere fact. The physical expression of Jonathan's love for David is not important. What is important, from the biblical point of view, is the political ramifications of that love, the benefits that accrued to David as a result of Jonathan's affection. Sex is power, in the ancient world as today, and David is depicted as using Jonathan's love for him to his advantage.

That said, the relationship between the two men appears to be a literary construct from beginning to end. It justifies David's future rule by rhetorically removing the natural heir apparent. Jonathan would have had every expectation of being king some day—the first Israelite to succeed his father to the throne. Perhaps even more than Saul himself, Jonathan had reason to be protective of the kingship and wary of David's popularity. There are no comparative examples of princes willingly relinquishing the throne in favor of someone outside the royal family. Jonathan's love for David, and the elaborate relationship they enter into, is historically unrealistic.

Jonathan is a cipher for the reader. His view of David mirrors and makes explicit the view that the reader comes to—or is intended to come to. Everything that Jonathan sees in David—his innocence, his devotion to Saul, his goodness—is the opposite of what Saul sees. It is, however, exactly how *we* are supposed to understand David. Jonathan says to Saul: "Let not the king wrong his servant David, for he has not wronged you; indeed, all his actions have been very much to your advantage. . . . Why should you be guilty of shedding the blood of an innocent man by killing David without cause?" (1 Sam. 19:4–5). Jonathan puts into words what the reader is meant to be thinking: David is blameless, fighting tirelessly for Saul's army, and Saul's pursuit of David is unjustified. The rhetorical power of having this view expressed by Saul's own son cannot be overstated: the one person besides Saul who should be most wary of David's growing fame puts David's innocence, and evident lack of ambition, front and center. If Jonathan, of all people, believes in David's goodness, then who is Saul—or the reader—to think otherwise?

Jonathan is not the only one portrayed as loving David. In these first few chapters of David's life, he is explicitly said to be loved also by Saul (1 Sam. 16:21), by the people of Israel and Judah (18:16), and by Michal (18:20). What is clear enough from the biblical story is that every time someone loves David, it results in a distinct advantage for David. Saul's love leads to David's being taken into the royal court. The people's love is necessary for David to be accepted as king, when the time comes.[41] Michal's love provides an opportunity for David to become part of the royal family proper, and it saves his life. And Jonathan's love protects David from Saul's jealousy and allows David to escape more than once. All this affection is literarily useful: David succeeds not by his own machinations, but by the free choice of others. David does nothing in the biblical account that could be deserving of condemnation. Saul appoints him head of the army, and David fills that role bravely and without any self-aggrandizement. It can hardly be David's fault that the troops and the people grow fond of him; he is simply doing his job. When Saul tries to kill David with his spear—twice—David is doing nothing threatening, merely playing his lyre. When Saul offers his daughter in marriage, David's response is self-effacing: "Who am I and who are my kin, my father's family in Israel, that I should become the king's son-in-law?" (18:18); "Do you think that becoming the son-in-law of the king is a trifling matter, when I am but a poor and trifling man?" (18:23). Jonathan and Michal love David of their own free will, like the rest of Israel; David did not coerce them into helping him. He is, from start to finish, utterly innocent of his own success.

This is both manifestly apologetic—it is strongly reminiscent of "The Apology of Hattušili"—and entirely unlikely. To put it bluntly: one does not become king against one's will, especially when one is not of the royal family. David became king, so David must have *wanted* to become king. One does not simply stumble onto the throne. Virtually the entire narrative of David's time in Saul's service has been revealed to be fictional: his military exploits, his popularity, Saul's attempts to kill him, Jonathan's and Michal's love for him. The authors go to great lengths to prove again and again that David neither desired the kingship nor did anything to motivate Saul's hatred and his eventual expulsion into the wilderness. All of which suggests that David actually did want the kingship and did do something, did force Saul's hand—for, eventually, Saul really did cause David to flee. The biblical authors have created an entire counterreality in their depiction of the period before David entered the wilderness. Our question must be, what is the reality that they are trying to cover up? What was it that brought Saul to the breaking point with David?

The Breaking Point

THE BIBLE PROVIDES LITTLE explanation for how David finally came to push Saul over the edge. This is, of course, because the biblical authors try at every turn to downplay David's role in his own rise to power, a rise that they want to attribute to the working out of the divine plan. Indeed, in the biblical account, there is no edge for Saul to go over—he has sought David's life from the very beginning, and so David's flight is merely the result of a long-simmering hatred. Since all of the stories exemplifying Saul's hatred can be historically discounted, however, we are required to posit a moment when Saul realized that David was not simply a potential threat, but a very real one.

We can safely say that David was ambitious. Much of this may have been attributable to his position: being a military officer may have fueled his aspirations for the kingship. Saul became king because he fought off Israel's enemies—David was doing the same. David also may have looked to the history of Israel's political leadership and, reasonably enough, considered Saul to be no more than a glorified judge, destined to pass from the scene without leaving a permanent mark or a hereditary successor. As one biblical scholar has noted, "traditional societies . . . often do not move directly from a segmentary tribal organization to a hereditary, permanent, centralized monarchy."[42] It was not necessarily self-evident to all that Saul would have a dynasty, as it would be the first of its kind in Israel.[43] And this may have been the perspective especially from David's home, the independent territory of Judah, which had not participated in the selection or anointing of Saul as king. David may have seen Saul more as a model than as a monarch.

How did David's ambition manifest itself? What did he do to deserve Saul's wrath? Indeed, what could he have done? Regicide (the murder of a monarch) was an impossibility—not for lack of opportunity, but because it wouldn't result in David's gaining the throne. Saul seems to have been liked well enough by his people; as much as they may have appreciated David, there was no groundswell of support for deposing the king. But the biblical story does suggest that David made an attempt to change that, to gain allegiance for himself at Saul's expense. Saul, in a moment of fury at his inability to capture David, screams at his courtiers: "Will the son of Jesse give fields and vineyards to all of you? And will he make all of you captains of thousands or captains of hundreds? Is that why all of you have conspired against me?" (1 Sam. 22:7–8). Saul's accusation is a damning one: that David has attempted to buy off Saul's closest supporters. In truth, this is less overt bribery on David's part than an attempt to present himself as a royal figure. David is playing the role of patron, a role that normally belonged to the king. In the stage between tribal societies and full-fledged kingship—the stage that Saul and, to a large extent, David occupied in Israel—the leader may be defined as one who "redistributes goods (such as spoils of war and agricultural produce) that have come to him, and those who benefit from the redistribution wish to maintain the power of the chief so that they may continue to benefit."[44] David already had the military credentials to rule, at least in his own eyes; what he required was the allegiance of the powerful members of society. If he could provide them with grants of land and high position, they might transfer their support from Saul to himself.

If we can trust Saul's statement as having some historical basis, we can suggest that David made overtures to members of Saul's court, perhaps testing the waters.[45] This would have infuriated Saul. Yet there is evidence that David's fall from favor came as the result of an even more spectacular attempt to take the crown away from Saul.

It appears at first glance as if David fled to the wilderness alone—even Michal, his wife according to the narrative, does not go with him. In the wilderness, he takes a new wife, Abigail (Nabal's wife, whom we met earlier; see also chapter 3). But after the notice of David's marriage to Abigail, the biblical text says something curious: "David had married Ahinoam of Jezreel, so the two of them were his wives" (1 Sam. 25:43). This is unexpected news to say the least—we never heard of David's marriage to anyone named Ahinoam, yet here she appears almost as an afterthought. And she will continue to appear throughout the story, always first in the mentions of David's wives, and as the mother of his eldest son. She is thus more than an afterthought—but who is she, and when did David marry her? And why do the biblical authors bury the notice of their marriage here?

In the entire Bible, only one other woman is named Ahinoam. Remarkably enough, she lived at the same time as David. David even would have known her—for Ahinoam is the name of one of Saul's wives, the mother of Jonathan and his two brothers (1 Sam. 14:50). Scholars have suggested that the two Ahinoams, Saul's wife and David's wife, are one and the same.[46] The coincidence of names is telling on its own, but there is another indication that the two Ahinoams are one. Saul is said to have had two other sons born after Jonathan and his brothers. These younger sons, however, were born not to Ahinoam, but to Rizpah, Saul's concubine (2 Sam. 21:8). In other words, after David is said to have married Ahinoam, she disappears from Saul's household, replaced by Rizpah. It seems, then, that David took Saul's wife for his own. But how could this have happened?

In ancient Israel, the wives and concubines of a king were markers of royal status. They were also indicators of the king's power. If someone was able to sleep with a member of the king's harem and get away with it, it meant the king had lost the ability to control even that which was closest to him. To sleep with a royal wife or concubine was to declare a coup—not metaphorically, but literally. It was to announce to the world one's desire for the crown and one's belief that the current king was incapable of holding it.[47] There is no other logical scenario in which Ahinoam would have come to be David's wife before he entered the wilderness. Saul would hardly have parted with her willingly—this is far less likely than the already improbable idea that he gave his daughter Michal in marriage to David. If Ahinoam became David's wife, David must have taken her in an act of rebellion.

This, above all else, must have been the precipitating event for Saul's attempt on David's life. There is no doubt that Saul would have wanted David dead for it: it is unthinkable that he would have willingly let David survive to seek the crown another day. That David would even attempt such a rebellion implies that he must have enjoyed some popular support—not to the degree that the Bible suggests, but enough that he felt he might succeed in his venture. The fact that David was forced to flee, however, also means that his coup failed. He made the grand traditional gesture of usurpation, but it turned out that Saul had the power to fight back. David miscalculated his position. In one failed act, David went from popular military officer to exile, on the run for his life. This scenario explains other aspects of the story as well. Whether Ahinoam was a willing participant in David's coup or not—it is impossible to know—once David had slept with her, she hardly could be welcomed back into Saul's household. In biblical terms, she would have been seen as "defiled" (Deut. 24:4). Thus even without any formal ceremony, by sleeping with Ahinoam David effectively made her his wife, and she was forced to flee along with him—since the traditional punishment for adultery was death (Deut. 22:22). David's coup attempt also explains why Saul went to such great lengths to hunt him down in the wilderness after he had fled. David was not just some ordinary criminal. He had tried to seize the crown from Saul's head. He could not be allowed to live.

From the perspective of the biblical authors, this story simply could not be told. Their objective was to portray David's kingship as an act of the divine will. If these chapters have no record—or even a hint—of David as ambitious, then surely the authors could not re-count that he attempted a direct coup by sleeping with Saul's wife. The entire narrative of David's time in Saul's service—from Saul's crazed attempts on David's life to the marriage to Michal to Jona-than's love for David—is effectively in the service of covering up this one unspeakable fact. The Bible could hardly ignore the common knowledge that Ahinoam did become David's wife. But it could defer the mention of the marriage until later in the narrative—in fact, until the very point when it became absolutely necessary, when David took Abigail as his second wife. Abigail couldn't be cast as the first, for Ahinoam was the mother of David's eldest son. So at the moment that David marries Abigail, then, and only then, are we told that he had been married before. And the authors took the further step of not mentioning that this was the same Ahinoam previously identified as Saul's wife, though they could do little about the identical names. Ironically, however, it is the biblical authors themselves who provide us with one of the most substantial hints that David had indeed taken Saul's wife for his own. In 2 Samuel 12, the prophet Nathan castigates David for his behavior with Bathsheba and lets this slip in the name of God: "I gave you your master's house and your master's wives" (12:8). The house is obviously the kingship, but the mention of the wives is inexplicable—unless it is referring to Ahinoam. No cover-up is per-fect. The most significant act of David's time in Saul's service is also the one the Bible seeks to hide. David attempted an outright coup.[48] And he failed—for now.

A CLOSE READING OF this period of David's life gives us a picture quite different from that presented in the Bible. No great victorious general, David was in fact an officer in the relatively backwater terri-tory of Judah, with the important but hardly glorious task of warding off Philistine raiding parties. Far from being innocent, David seems to have been keenly aware of his situation and how to manipulate those around him to serve his own ends. Saul, for his part, was not unstable or unfit to rule but was rather entirely justified in his pursuit of David. David was no idle threat.

Even while a young officer, David managed to combine ambition, a sharp knowledge of how to elevate his status, and a willingness to do whatever it took to reach his goals. As it turned out, he reached too far and was forced to flee. In the wilderness, however, without the constraints of custom or allegiance, these personality traits came to full expression.

CHAPTER 3

David in the Wilderness

FROM ISRAELITE SOLDIER TO
PHILISTINE VASSAL

THE WILDERNESS OF JUDAH IS a forbidding place. In the northern and central regions, the landscape undulates with small hills. Rainfall is plentiful enough for the hills to be well covered with evergreen trees, though in biblical times these trees were an impediment to habitation. Settlements in this area were possible only by deforestation, yet removing the trees also meant destroying the natural network that held the water in the ground. Habitation therefore required the use of specialized agricultural techniques such as terracing along the hillsides, which prevented the rainwater from simply cascading down to the valley below, washing away the soil with it. Between the hills the valleys were, and still are, largely void of any significant greenery aside from grasses and the occasional shrub.

To the east, toward the Dead Sea, even minimal vegetation effectively ceases. The landscape is true desert, with more substantial rocky outcroppings and deeper rifts between them. The rocky ground and sometimes impenetrable passes between the cliffs make traversing this landscape by foot difficult. What little rain does fall in this region is immediately directed into channels that rage torrentially but only momentarily, drying up quickly into a trickle at best and more frequently merely into a dry bed. Only the occasional oasis provides any support for habitation.

Toward the south, the hills gradually give way to the Negev desert. Here the rainfall is significantly less than in the central wilderness, and agriculture and even pasturage are nearly impossible. The land is flat and broad, the temperatures high. In ancient times, habitation in this region was sporadic, with most settlements originating as military outposts or trading depots. Between the settlements was, and is, empty space.[1]

This is the landscape to which David fled to escape Saul's wrath. Here, in the wilderness, David would manage not only to survive, but to accumulate substantial power. He entered the wilderness alone, but he emerged from it a king.

David at Nob

ACCORDING TO THE BIBLE, David's first stop was at Nob, a small town east of Jerusalem, on the edge of the desert leading down to the Dead Sea. There, we read in 1 Samuel 21, he was given bread by the local priest, Ahimelech, as well as the sword of Goliath—though we are not told how the sword ended up wrapped in cloth and stored in a minor sanctuary. As it turned out, one of Saul's officials, Doeg the Edomite, was at the sanctuary in Nob that same day. When Saul heard that David was there and had even been given provisions, he sent for Ahimelech and all the priests of Nob. The crazed king ordered his men to kill the priests for treason, but his servants refused. Doeg, however, was more than willing—he killed all eighty-five priests, and for good measure went to Nob and finished off the rest of the town: "He put Nob, the city of the priests, to the sword: men and women, children and infants, oxen, asses, and sheep" (1 Sam. 22:19). As is almost always the case in such stories, however, one priest managed to escape and fled to David. His name was Abiathar, and David promised to protect him.

This story serves a number of literary purposes. It gives David a measure of cultic approval, as he is helped by a priest. It emphasizes that God is on David's side, for Ahimelech gives David the bread only after having inquired of God whether to do so, to which God must have responded approvingly. It brings us back to David's innocent youth through the reference to Goliath's sword—David, we are to understand, is beginning again. It demonstrates the depth of Saul's unhinged anger: the destruction of Nob is an explicit bastardization of the Israelite law of *herem*, or "the ban." Israel, according to Deuteronomy and demonstrated throughout the book of Joshua, was to utterly destroy Canaanite settlements during the conquest. The description of Joshua's destruction of Jericho should look familiar: "They exterminated everything in the city with the sword: man and woman, young and old, ox and sheep and ass" (Josh. 6:21). This is precisely what Saul does to Nob—but this is long after the period of the conquest, and Nob is not a Canaanite town. In his rage, Saul has twisted Israel's laws and customs.[2]

The story of David in Nob participates in the same literary program that we are now well accustomed to in the David story: the elevation of David and denigration of Saul. It has no historical value. When these elements are stripped away, however, virtually nothing is left of the narrative. David leaves Nob essentially unchanged: the bread digested, the sword a myth—and never spoken of again in any case. Only Abiathar's presence continues through the rest of the narrative, and it hardly requires this elaborate story as justification. In short, the entire episode at Nob is a literary construction. There is no reason to think that David was ever there.

David and His Band

THROUGHOUT HISTORY, THE WILDERNESS of Judah has been a refuge for those seeking to avoid the eyes of those in power. In the second century BCE, members of the Essene sect moved there to practice their unorthodox religious beliefs in peace, founding the community at Qumran, where the Dead Sea Scrolls were found in caves in the nearby cliffs. The Maccabees fled to the wilderness at the beginning of their war against the Seleucid empire. During the Great Revolt against Rome in the first century CE, the Jewish rebels made their final stand from the forbidding mountain of Masada. A hundred years later, during the Bar Kochba revolt, some of Bar Kochba's men fled to caves in the Dead Sea area.

David knew precisely where he was going: "David escaped to the stronghold of Adullam" (1 Sam. 22:1), a small site in the hills about sixteen miles southwest of Jerusalem.[3] And he knew precisely what sort of people he would find there: "Everyone who was in straits and everyone who was in debt and everyone who was bitter of spirit joined him, and he became their leader" (22:2). The Bible makes no attempt to sugarcoat the fact that David surrounds himself with a band of misfits and outlaws. Given his whereabouts, he had little other choice. No one would willingly live in the middle of nowhere if there were any other alternative.

Israelite society was a kinship culture. People were expected to live with their close relations in a mutually protective group. Multiple generations lived under a single roof, or in adjoining houses. Marriages were endogamous, that is, people tended to marry within the extended family. Even when someone married outside the kin group, the two families would invent a common ancestry, a process known as fictive kinship, to maintain the kinship basis for relationships. Each kin group possessed its own land, and it was a priority to keep the land within the family at all costs. Communities were close, literally and figuratively, with each member responsible for the others.[4] Only under dire circumstances would someone be forced out of that community: for committing a crime, for going deeply into debt, for bringing shame on the family—or for rebelling against the king.

Unlike the story of David at Nob, the gathering at Adullam therefore rings true (though the number of David's band, four hundred, seems more symbolic than realistic). David would have needed others to help him survive in the wilderness, and the others would have recognized David as one of their own, on the run from the authorities—but also with a history of authority himself, making him a natural leader. David once commanded a royal military unit; now he commanded a private militia.

Just south of Adullam sat the town of Keilah. According to the Bible, Keilah was one day raided by a band of Philistines, and David took his men to protect it. It seems not to have been a particularly spectacular battle; all that is said is that "he drove off their cattle and inflicted a severe defeat on them" (1 Sam. 23:5). This is like the other reports of David's victories over the Philistines: devoid of detail, except for the rather unimpressive achievement of having scared off some livestock. But David is given his due glory: "Thus David saved the inhabitants of Keilah" (23:5).[5] Despite his efforts on their behalf, the people of Keilah do not appear to have been enthralled with David's arrival. When Saul hears that David is there, and prepares to pursue him, David learns by divination that the inhabitants of Keilah will turn him and his men over to Saul, so David is forced to move along.

It is not unlikely that the Philistines might really have attacked Keilah. As we have already seen, Judah, especially those towns to the west, nearer the Philistine heartland, was probably subject to regular incursions. (Keilah is not so far from Socoh, where the battle against Goliath is set.) What seems improbable is that David and his men would venture into battle against an established military force like the Philistines. Whatever arms they may have had, they undoubtedly would have been outmatched. The only plausible rationale for engaging in battle at Keilah would be to win the trust and admiration of the inhabitants. But this is precisely what they failed to do. What, then, was David doing at Keilah?

David's men were not fit for any sort of regular military engagement. Life in the wilderness did not lend itself to organized preparations for battle. Like most small militias, what David and his men had to their advantage was speed and mobility. Relatively few in number, relatively lightly armed, they had the capacity to move from place to place with ease. Facing the Philistines head-on was out of the question, but going to Keilah directly after the Philistines had finished plundering it would be no problem. Such an arrival would make sense on two fronts. First, David could, with some imagination, position himself as the one who drove the Philistines away. Keilah was a fortified town—"a town with gates and bars" (1 Sam. 23:7)—and the Philistines seem not to have actually entered it: they were only "plundering the threshing floors" (23:1). Threshing was an activity done in an open space, where the wind could blow away the chaff as it was tossed into the air. For a fortified city, this almost certainly meant that the threshing area was outside the city walls.[6] The arrival of the Philistine raiding party would have driven inside the city walls for protection those in the fields and at the threshing floor, leaving the Philistines free to plunder the agricultural produce left behind. As the people of Keilah watched, the Philistines finished the job and left of their own accord, at which point David and his men could have appeared and claimed responsibility for scaring off the enemy—driving away their cattle, securing provisions for which may have been the Philistines' primary goal.[7]

Second, David may have seen in the freshly attacked Keilah an opportunity. The town was vulnerable, as the Philistines had demonstrated. David and his men could provide a measure of security in case of future raids—in exchange for some security of their own. It seems that David did in fact enter the town with his men, for otherwise Keilah would not have had the chance to give him up to Saul. But it is hard to imagine the circumstances under which a settled community would willingly let a band of ne'er-do-wells into its walls. Such a group would be outside the usual kinship bonds and therefore accountable to no one in the town. They would have to be fed from the town's supplies—supplies that, given the landscape, hardly could have been abundant. They would have to be housed somewhere—either with resident families or in public spaces, neither of which would be desirable. This, of course, is just what David and his men needed:

food and shelter, the very basics that were hard to come by in the wilderness. If after an attack by the Philistines this second armed band showed up at the gates of Keilah, perhaps a polite but forceful request for entrance would have been difficult to decline.

But it is unlikely that the inhabitants would have seen David as a hero. Indeed, the moment that a greater power threatened to arrive on the scene, the people of Keilah were more than ready to turn David in—not only because his men were sapping their resources, but perhaps out of fear that sheltering him would lead to retribution against the town by Saul. Sheltering a rebel was a crime not taken lightly. In Judges 9 we read of a rebellion against the local ruler Abimelech. The leader of the rebels takes refuge in the city of Shechem, where the people are in league with him. Abimelech's response is to destroy the city: "he razed the city and sowed it with salt" (9:45). Whether this story is true or not, it reflects a common understanding of how rebellious towns are to be treated (and one that will recur later in the David story). The inhabitants of Keilah wanted none of this. It was in their best interest to make clear that they were not aligned with David. And David, it is clear, was not in any position to take on Saul's forces. His only choice was to leave.[8]

The western part of the wilderness having proved inhospitable, David and his men traveled southeast, toward the Dead Sea, into the wilderness of Ziph, named for its most prominent town. This place, however, was even less welcoming than Keilah had been. Saul did not even need to threaten to come down; the Ziphites themselves went to Saul to offer David up. Perhaps they had heard of David's behavior at Keilah, or perhaps they were better equipped to fend off his requests. In any case, David seems to have found no town to take him in but was rather moving around the wilderness of Ziph in search of hiding places. When the Ziphites returned from meeting with Saul, David had already shifted from the hill of Hachilah, where he had previously been, to the area of Maon, a bit to the south. The biblical account makes the arrival of Saul a very close thing for David, with Saul and his men on one side of a hill and David and his men on the other, each trying to outmaneuver the other—one trying to capture, one trying to escape (1 Sam. 23:26). David escaped only when Saul was called away to defend a new Philistine attack.

This last dramatic detail seems to be fictional, as it exists mostly for the purpose of providing an etiology for a place in the wilderness called "the Rock of Separation." But true or not, it highlights once again the respective powers and advantages of the two adversaries. David is trying not to confront Saul, but to escape him. Saul is stronger than David, yet David is mobile and moves quickly from place to place to avoid capture. Even when Saul is close, David has the ability to slip away. Hiding in the wilderness, constantly moving, he and his men resemble guerilla fighters, such as have operated in this way from time immemorial. Even today, with the most advanced technology, it is difficult to track down and capture small, highly mobile groups, as examples from Uganda to Sri Lanka to Afghanistan repeatedly prove. It is no surprise that David expected to be safe in the wilderness.

And yet Saul seems regularly to find him—which points to another salient feature of these episodes. Whatever affection the people once may have had for David, it evidently evaporated rather quickly, such that they are perfectly willing to turn him in. This may appear to be fickle behavior. After all, the people loved David when he was fighting off the Philistines. But this is precisely the point: David is no longer fighting off the Philistines. We tend to think of the conflict between David and Saul as one of good against bad, of the righteous against the oppressive. But David and Saul did not live in an abstracted black and white universe. They were participants in an established culture and political system. The tradition of leadership in Israel, as we have seen, was one of "what have you done for me lately?" Leaders were temporary employees, holding their positions only for as long as their constituents needed protection. When the job ended, the position ended. If the person was unable to do the job, someone else would have to step up. Popular affection was pinned not to a person, but to a persona. By trying to usurp the throne, and as a result being forced to flee from Saul to the wilderness, David relinquished his position as officer in the war against the Philistines. He now fought not for Israel, but for himself. As one biographer of David put it, "David's band survived in the wilderness by terrorizing the local population."[9] He was no longer of use to the Israelites—if anything, he was now a burden. For a people scattered in small towns and villages throughout the hills of Judah and Israel, what benefit would there be in supporting David any longer? His coup having failed, he could not provide the only service that was of value to them—protection from the Philistines. The one who could do that, as before, was Saul, and so it was Saul who commanded the people's allegiance. Indeed, throughout the story, up to the moment of Saul's death, there is no evidence that anyone in Israel or Judah has any objection to his rule. Nor should they, since he seems to have done his job perfectly well.

Should David have felt betrayed by the Judahites? He himself was from Judah, after all—why did his compatriots feel nothing special for him? The answer is that Judah was, biblical narratives notwithstanding, not yet a cohesive tribe; scholars believe that it was among the last tribes in Israel to coalesce.[10] Judah is strikingly absent from the earliest record of Israelite tribes, that of Judges 5. None of Israel's early leaders in the book of Judges are said to be Judahites. In fact, the one who comes from that region, Othniel, is identified as a Kenizzite (Josh. 15:17)—an ethnic group, potentially native to Canaan, that was eventually incorporated into Judah—but he is not yet considered a Judahite. The territory of Judah was far larger and less densely populated than that of the northern tribes. As noted above, much of it was uninhabitable wilderness, with occasional settlements dotting the landscape. In such a place communication was difficult and centralized organization much more so. Judah was a region, not a polity. Each town was its own self-enclosed community. Even after the Philistine threat made regional self-defense desirable, it was Israel, the northern kingdom, that provided it. Judah had no need to organize into a unified tribe. David, therefore, was not properly a Judahite—he was a Bethlehemite, from the region of Judah. The inhabitants of Keilah and Ziph had no responsibility for him. Nor does David ever seem to think that they should—he does not appeal to common ancestry in hopes of finding a safe haven. He goes to Judah because it is a wilderness, not because it is his homeland.

David's Innocence

THE BIBLE PRESENTS A pair of stories about David coming upon Saul unawares. The first, in 1 Samuel 24, takes place at En-Gedi, the oasis at the edge of the Dead Sea. There, Saul enters a cave to relieve himself, not knowing that David and his men are hiding in that very cave. David's men encourage David to attack Saul, but he refuses. Instead, he sneaks up and cuts off a corner of Saul's cloak—somehow accomplishing this without Saul noticing. As Saul starts to leave, David steps forward and shows him the swatch of cloth, thereby demonstrating that, though he had the opportunity, he did not lay a hand on the king. Saul admits that he has been in the wrong, even proclaims that David will be king and have a dynasty, and requests that David not wipe out Saul's family after he has achieved the throne. David agrees, and they part ways.

The second story, in 1 Samuel 26, happens in the wilderness of Ziph. There, Saul falls asleep, and David sneaks up beside him. Again, David's men encourage him to kill the king, but David refuses, saying that when Saul's time comes, his death will be by God's hand or in battle. Instead, he grabs the spear and water jug lying beside Saul and takes them some distance away. He calls to Saul from the top of a nearby hill and shows him the spear and water jug, thereby demonstrating, as in the incident in the cave, that he did not lay a hand on the king even though he had the opportunity. Again, Saul admits that he has been in the wrong and even proclaims that David will prevail. Then they part ways.

Even in their barest outlines, the two stories are virtually identical; there is no need to detail the many nearly verbatim verses. It is highly improbable that both stories are true. But, as with the stories in

1 Samuel 16–17 examined in chapter 1, in fact neither of these stories is anything more than a literary invention. Two major themes are at play in these passages. One is Saul's admission of guilt and acceptance that David will one day be king. Only according to the pro-David biblical account does Saul have anything to be guilty of. As we have seen, it is the biblical authors' aim to make Saul's pursuit of David unjustified both by repeatedly proclaiming David's innocence and by making Saul out to be mentally unstable. More confusing, however, is Saul's declaration that David will indeed be king. Even in the biblical narrative, why would Saul say such a thing? The only explicit reference to David's future kingship comes in the private anointing ceremony in 1 Samuel 16, of which Saul cannot have had any knowledge. In fact, part of the Bible's agenda is to make clear that David was definitively not seeking the kingship at all. What we have here, then, are two episodes composed with the larger literary scope of the David story in mind, with the knowledge both of the private ceremony in 1 Samuel 16 and of David's eventual ascent to the throne. Outside the literary world of the Bible—and even to a certain extent within it—Saul would never have said such a thing.

The second major theme, and perhaps the more interesting, is David's demonstration of his lack of desire to kill Saul. On the surface, this seems to be merely a response to Saul's aggression: David shows that he is not trying to attack Saul—again this affirms his explicit lack of desire for the kingship—so why is Saul trying to attack him? The more important statement, however, is not only that David did not kill Saul, but that David *would never* kill Saul: "Yahweh forbid that I should do such a thing to my lord, Yahweh's anointed—extending my hand against him—for he is Yahweh's anointed" (1 Sam. 24:7). "Who can lay hands on Yahweh's anointed and be innocent? . . . As Yahweh lives, Yahweh himself will strike him down, or his day will come and he will die, or he will go down to battle and perish. But Yahweh forbid that I should extend my hand against Yahweh's anointed!" (26:9–11). What David says in these lines is that he is bound by his own faith in God never to attack Saul.

Like Saul's acceptance of David's kingship, however, this too is confusing from a narrative standpoint: why should David have to deny so forcefully a desire to kill Saul? In the story to this point, David has never shown any aggression toward him. Rather, it has been quite the reverse: Saul has been constantly seeking David's life. All David has ever expressed is a desire to be allowed to live. The text's strong defense of David is at odds with the story, but it is absolutely comprehensible when understood as an apology. Saul would, after all, eventually die—in battle, just as David (coincidentally) predicts. David would become king after Saul, though he had no right to the throne. He had also already tried once to seize the kingship. Anyone in Israel may well have wondered whether David had a hand in Saul's death, given the way things turned out. These stories address that issue directly: not only did David not have a hand in Saul's death, but when he had the perfect chance to bring it about—twice—he didn't take it. As we will see, this particular apologetic defense of David will recur later. For now, we can simply note that it raises the question: if the Bible goes to such lengths to argue that David wasn't involved in Saul's death, should we consider the possibility that he might have been?

David and Nabal

SANDWICHED BETWEEN THE TWO episodes of David sparing Saul's life is the story of David and Nabal (1 Sam. 25).[11] We have already discussed this episode in the introduction, but it is worth considering again, now that we have a better sense of David's time in the wilderness. In this story, as a reminder, David sends ten of his men to the Calebite Nabal, a wealthy owner of flocks, indicating that since Nabal's shepherds had come to no harm under David's protection, Nabal might be inclined to give David some supplies. Nabal refuses, so David and all of his men arrive at Nabal's door fully armed. Abigail, Nabal's wife, greets David with some food and drink and denigrates her husband while proclaiming David's future kingship. David agrees not to harm Nabal—and yet, miraculously, God strikes Nabal down a few days later. David immediately sends his men to take Abigail as his wife, to which she readily agrees.

David's motivations in sending his men to Nabal should be obvious. For some time they have been in the wilderness, a hard place in which to survive, and have been forced to move constantly, away from Saul and away from the various local communities that want nothing to do with them. Perhaps, as seems to be the case with Ziph, their reputation has preceded them. Rather than gaining strength, they seem to be losing it. And as David and his men grow more desperate, they have to seek out sustenance in more direct ways. Thus a thinly veiled threat, clothed though it may be in polite language, might be a way of gaining access to a supply of goods, one that could sustain them for a long while.

Nabal knows precisely with whom he is dealing. David, after all, was once a reasonably well-known military leader, and his flight from Saul hardly could have gone unnoticed. David assumes that Nabal knows him, saying, "Greet him in my name" (1 Sam. 25:5). Though Nabal's response makes it seem at first as if he has never heard of David, a closer look reveals that this is not the case. "There are many slaves today who run away from their masters" (25:10), Nabal says. This is a cutting remark, aimed squarely at the relationship between Saul and David. David, Nabal implies, is no better than a slave to Saul, and his flight is equivalent to running away from a master. Nabal not only knows who David is, he knows which side deserves his allegiance. Here again we see two key features of David's wilderness experience: that he is known, and that he is unloved. As for David's men, they "come from I don't know where" (25:11)—the ultimate insult in ancient Israelite society. Almost everyone in the Bible is identified by his or her homeland, as kinship affiliation was the basis of personal identity. To be without a place and family of birth was to be virtually nonexistent. This is what it means to enter the wilderness—and we may note that once David enters the wilderness, he is never again referred to as being from Bethlehem. Like his men, he has effectively renounced his past affiliations. Even his father, Jesse, is mentioned again only as part of David's name. He disappears from the narrative. Nabal knows who David is, but he knows him as a man who has given up all that identifies him as Israelite, as part of a community, and has chosen to make his way in the wilderness.

To run a protection racket, one must be willing to do the dirty work if the victim refuses to pay up. David, never afraid to make the necessary effort, is certainly willing in this case, arriving with his men fully armed, even admitting his intentions to kill Nabal. Did Abigail really come out to greet David with provisions? It's not beyond the realm of possibility that she recognized what was about to happen and tried to forestall it. If this is the case, however, she seems to have miscalculated. By showing David that Nabal had plenty to spare, Abigail may have sealed her husband's fate. It is possible that she delayed it—after all, Nabal doesn't die right away, but a few days later. But once David's men had gone through what she gave them, they would have known that there was more where that came from. We may speculate that Abigail's gift tided David over for a moment but also ensured that he would return. And this time, there could be no further negotiations.

In Israel, when a woman's husband died, the husband's family was responsible for providing a new husband for her from within the clan, so that the family's landholdings would not pass to an outsider—a concept known as levirate marriage. This arrangement also ensured the security of the widow, for without protection from her husband's clan, she would be vulnerable. If a widow could not find a husband, she was to return to her father's house, for the same reasons.[12] Deuteronomy repeatedly aligns the widow with orphans and resident aliens, the two other classes of people who would not have kinship protection.[13] Abigail was particularly vulnerable, as she seems to have had no son and was therefore the sole inheritor of her husband's property. It would have been unthinkable for her to go off willingly into the wilderness with David and abandon her familial security and kinship obligations. It is therefore far more likely that David married her by force—on the strength of the armed men standing around Abigail and her newly killed husband.

But what advantage was it to David to marry Abigail? We can discount the possibility that he was in love with her—they had just met, after all, and under rather fraught circumstances. This being David, we have to imagine that he saw something substantial to be gained. And yet he had already taken Nabal's property, the prize he was ostensibly after. Abigail could neither prevent David from seizing her husband's possessions nor provide him with any additional goods. Something more must have been at stake.

The key to understanding David's motivation in marrying Abigail is to be found in the status of her husband. Nabal is described as extravagantly rich—he is said to own three thousand sheep and a thousand goats. For the purpose of comparison, when Solomon is said to receive tribute from his entire kingdom, it amounts to three thousand sheep per month (1 Kings 5:3). That's coming from all corners of Solomon's territory—Nabal is a single individual. In other words, Nabal is not merely wealthy—he is royally wealthy. In the independent territory of Judah, where there was no king yet, the only individuals who could possibly command such a fortune would be the chiefs of the various clans. It therefore seems likely that Nabal was not any old Calebite but was in fact the chief of the Calebite clan.[14] As noted above, when a widow remarried, her former husband's property—as well as, in theory, her husband's position—passed to her new husband. In marrying Abigail, David gained something far more valuable than tangible property. He gained the title of chief of the Calebites.

And yet David does not remain in Calebite territory to take advantage of his new position; he and his new wife, along with Ahinoam and David's men, leave immediately. It is safe to say that, despite holding the nominal title of clan chief, David did not have the power to enforce his newly acquired status. If he was not allowed to stay even for a few days in the small towns of Keilah and Ziph, it is unlikely that the entire tribe of Caleb would have permitted him to occupy the tribal leadership. David had, after all, killed their chief and broken the established custom of levirate marriage, thereby depriving the tribe of its rightful land. He was not prepared to impose his will on the Calebites, but he took what he needed and had prepared himself well for the future. Should the time ever come when David had enough power to return, he would bring with him Abigail, the living proof of his right to rule.

As the physical embodiment of David's newly acquired title, Abigail was the real prize. This raises the suspicion that the protection racket was not the endgame, but rather a preparatory move. What David needed was Nabal dead and Abigail to be his wife. It seems likely, then, that David knew very well that Nabal would never accept his terms. Nor should Nabal have been expected to; if he was the chief of the Calebites, he would have felt little threat from a band of hooligans, especially one that had been rejected at every previous stop. David must have known it would come to this.

We may intellectually comprehend David's actions toward Nabal and Abigail as part of his plan to gain power for the future. But we cannot simply pass over the death of Nabal. There is no moralizing to be done here. This was murder, plain and simple. David wanted Nabal's property, and more important his title, and to get it he killed the man in cold blood. Not even the most ardent admirer of David could justify his actions here—which is why the biblical authors take the only way out and attribute the death to the unknowable and unimpeachable God. Nabal's murder is disturbing also because, though it is not the only death for which David is responsible, it is the first. Up to this point, David has perhaps acted badly—in his attempted coup, in his unwelcome stay at Keilah—but he has not seriously harmed anyone, except perhaps himself. With the killing of Nabal, David has crossed a moral threshold. He can no longer be seen as put upon, as oppressed, as righteous. He is revealed as a thoroughly amoral individualist, concerned only for his own well-being. These properties serve him well in his attempts to gain and keep the throne, as we will see, but they are hardly the character traits one associates with the famous

King David. From this point forward, we cannot be surprised by anything David does: if he could kill Nabal, he could well do something just as bad, or worse. And that is precisely what he does next.

David and the Philistines

THE WILDERNESS, INHOSPITABLE TO all, was even more so for David. He had to contend not only with the landscape, but with the inhabitants, who were more than ready to give him up, and Saul, who mounted regular campaigns to track him down.[15] For these reasons alone, leaving the territory of Judah must have seemed a sensible decision. But there was also nothing David could accomplish in the wilderness. One could not find one's fortune there—at best, one might find temporary shelter, as in Keilah, or a momentary bounty, as with Nabal. But these were fleeting successes, and once the welcome was worn out and the supplies used up, David was back where he started. There were not enough outlaws in the wilderness for him to bring together and mount an effective challenge to Saul, or even to defend against one of Saul's search parties. Life in the wilderness was about survival, and David wanted to do more than just survive. He had to move elsewhere.

But his choices were limited. The desert to the east, the Dead Sea region, was and remains one of the least habitable places on the planet. To the south was the Negev, which was almost as bad, and to the north was Saul's territory. This left only the west—the heartland of the Philistines. And that is where David went.

Treason is a strong word. David had long since given up his position in Saul's army, and with it any affiliation with Saul's kingdom. He had been repeatedly rejected by the people of Judah. At this point, David was almost as much an enemy to Israel and Judah as the Philistines themselves. By seeking shelter among the Philistines, David was less a traitor and more a defector. And, like most defectors, he was welcomed with open arms. Surely, had a prominent Philistine gone to

Saul and offered his services, Saul would have been quick to accept. So, too, Achish, the king of Gath, accepted the sudden influx of both bodies and arms that David and his men provided.

Gath was a logical choice for David. The city was the closest of the Philistine Pentapolis to Judah (which is undoubtedly why it is featured most prominently in the Bible), so it was the easiest to get to and, should any trouble arise, the easiest to get away from.[16] And unlike some of the more far-flung parts of Philistine territory, Gath was beyond Saul's ability to capture, meaning that David knew himself to be safe there. Sure enough, "When Saul was told that David had fled to Gath, he did not continue to pursue him" (1 Sam. 27:4). Gath also controlled a large territory, especially to the south. This gave both David and Achish an opportunity. Rather than stay in Gath, where he and his men would be a drain on the royal resources and where they would have little to do, David asked Achish to grant him control of a small town near the Negev called Ziklag. This suited both parties. David could act as a vassal for Achish, as a garrison to the south, solidifying Philistine control over the area. He would finally have a secure base, and even some official power—albeit Philistine power—to wield from it.

We have already seen what the typical Philistine practice was regarding the treatment of Judah. Between the relatively rare major attacks, for which both armies would mass in an open field, the Philistines launched a regular stream of small raids against small towns and fields. And this was to be David's new career: raiding Judah. He was the perfect man for the job. He and his men had experience in raiding from their time in the wilderness, and they were familiar with the territory. And clearly Achish had no doubts that David would take up his new position without compunction, another reminder that no one—not Saul, not the Judahites, and not the Philistines—seems to have thought that David was allied with Judah or Israel. David's strong independent streak was more than a character trait; it was an ethnic and political stance. To call him an Israelite at this point would be purely nostalgic. David was his own man.

Still, it is understandably hard to imagine that David actually led raids against towns in Judah. This is the man who would one day become king of Judah, and of all Israel. Surely he could not have acted as Judah's enemy. At least, this is what the biblical authors want us to believe. According to the Bible, David raided "the Geshurites, the Gizrites, and the Amalekites" (1 Sam. 27:8)—inhabitants of the southern wasteland leading down to Egypt. But he would tell Achish that he had raided regions of Judah. To ensure that the truth would not come out, David is said to have left "no man or woman alive; he would take flocks, herds, asses, camels, and clothing" (27:9). Thus, no survivors of these non-Judahite settlements would remain to reveal where David had actually been.

This biblical scenario is thoroughly improbable. Although few people lived in the region to the south of the Philistine territory, it was by no means entirely deserted. The main trade routes between Egypt and Canaan moved through this area. An absence of dense settlements does not mean an absence of people. And trade routes carried more than just goods—they carried information. It seems unlikely that David could have raided this region, repeatedly, and wiped entire settlements off the map without word reaching the Philistines. The deception recounted in the Bible is only partially for the benefit of Achish. It is mostly for the audience—it is they who will be unable to find a Geshurite or Gizrite or Amalekite to contradict David's story. Not because David left none alive, but because he never attacked them. Unlikely as it may seem, David was probably raiding Judahite communities, just as he told Achish.

It should be remembered that Judah was not a unified tribe. Raiding one town would not have affected others. There was no collective defense, especially in the more sparsely settled south where David was located. And why should David not have raided Judah? It is only from a later perspective, after David has become king, that such actions become unthinkable. At this point, David was a Judahite, an Israelite, in name only. In practice—as an itinerant outlaw, a raider, a mercenary for hire—David was a *habiru*.

David the Habiru

NEARLY A THOUSAND YEARS before David, in the nineteenth century BCE, Sumerian texts describe a group of mercenaries, ethnically unaffiliated, who could be hired by local city-states. Other Sumerian texts from the eighteenth through fifteenth centuries fill out the picture somewhat: these people spoke a variety of languages, wandered the countryside, and yet had some semblance of internal military organization, such that it was necessary, on occasion, to treat them as a cohesive group—one text even records a treaty made with them. The Sumerian term used to identify this loose collective is SA.GAZ, which means "bandit" or "murderer." The Sumerian word is translated into the Semitic languages as *habiru*.[17]

On the other end of the Fertile Crescent, in Egypt, the *habiru* appear as well. In the fifteenth century BCE, an Egyptian general requested of Pharaoh Thutmose III that he be allowed to bring his horses inside the city walls of Joppa, out of fear that they might be stolen by the *habiru*. Around a century later, Pharaoh Seti I sent his troops in search of the *habiru* who had attacked one of his towns. The *habiru* appear to have been present also on the northern coast of Syria, in the city-state of Ugarit. Farther north, in Anatolia, the Hittites used the *habiru* as mercenaries as early as the sixteenth century BCE.

From another Anatolian state, known as Mitanni, we find even more remarkable data from a sixteenth-century inscription. A Mitanni prince named Idrimi was forced to flee his native land and traveled to Canaan, where he joined forces with and eventually became the leader of the *habiru*. Idrimi and his *habiru* attacked the city-state of Alalakh, in modern Turkey, and he became king there—and, fortunately for us, he inscribed his tale for posterity.[18] The archaeological excavations of Alalakh have uncovered a remarkable number of written records, including lists of these *habiru* that reveal they came from disparate backgrounds—they had been thieves, slaves, priests, and soldiers.[19]

And in Canaan proper, the *habiru* were a constant bother. One of the most important archaeological discoveries of the past two centuries was a cache of letters in the Egyptian city of Amarna.[20] For a brief period in the fourteenth century BCE, Amarna was the capital of Egypt, and so all diplomatic correspondence was sent and stored there. The letters discovered at Amarna come from city-states in Canaan and Syria, which at the time were vassals of Egypt. As is often the case with such correspondence, many of the letters from the vassals to the Egyptian overlords consist of complaints about various local problems, in hopes that the pharaoh might lend some assistance. A number of these letters specifically mention the *habiru*, who are accused of attacking the king of Byblos and even capturing a large portion of his territory. They are reported to have killed a number of local rulers south of Jerusalem and seized their territories. In these cases, the *habiru* seem to be acting independently. But often they were used as mercenaries in battles for regional dominance among the various city-states. One local king named Lab'ayu used *habiru* troops to seize control of neighboring territories, settling the *habiru* in conquered towns as an extension of his rule. Lab'ayu's sons continued the practice after him, paying *habiru* soldiers to wage war against the city-state of Megiddo. The king of the city-state of Jerusalem complains that his adversaries, among them the king of Gath, have given territory to the *habiru*, including the town of Keilah.

These mentions from across the Near East make it possible for us to draw a fairly good picture of the *habiru*. They were not an ethnic group—indeed, they seem to have come from a wide variety of ethnic backgrounds. Instead, the term *habiru* is descriptive of a social class more than anything else: they were people who were forced out of normal social structures for whatever reasons and who were compelled to make their livings however they could, wherever possible. They acted as bandits operating independently and as mercenaries available for hire to either side of a conflict. The parallels with David, both generally and, in some cases, with almost uncanny specificity, are obvious.[21] David—forced out of Israelite society, raiding and murdering across the wilderness of Judah, and eventually becoming a mercenary for the Philistines—participated recognizably in a centuries-old pattern.

If the word *habiru* has a familiar sound to it, there may be a reason. Scholars have long surmised that it is from the term *habiru* that we get the word "Hebrew."[22] The most common explanation for this etymology, which would not put the Hebrews in a particularly flattering light, is that some proportion of the early Israelite population that settled the small villages of the central highlands of Canaan were of *habiru* background, perhaps escaping the social structures of the major city-states. The emerging Israelites may have been seen as *habiru*, not because of their banditry or mercenary activities, but because they existed outside of the mainstream centralized societies. It is perhaps for this reason, as many have noted, that in the Bible it is often foreigners who describe the Israelites as Hebrews, rather than Israelites using the term themselves. One such example is found in our story: when the officers of the Philistine army see David and his men, they ask Achish, "Who are these Hebrews?" (1 Sam. 29:3). If what they mean is "Who are these *habiru*?" they could hardly have put it more accurately. David's story very closely parallels that of Idrimi, the Mitanni prince. David was once a prince, or very nearly so—he was, according to the Bible, the king's son-in-law. He was forced from his position of power into the wilderness of Canaan, where he found a group of outlaws ready to make him their leader. And now, with that same band, he was on the verge of making his triumphant return to power.

Saul's Death

DAVID'S MERCENARY CAREER WITH the Philistines was not brief. He stayed as a vassal of Achish for more than a year—sixteen months, according to the Bible (1 Sam. 27:7). That he stayed so long is testimony to the comfort and wealth that his position provided. David was in no rush to leave the Philistines. He had made a home for himself.

As we have seen, however, the lengthy periods of small-time raids were regularly broken up by full-scale battles between the Philistines and the Israelites. And David must have known that his turn for such a battle would eventually come. And indeed, the beginning of 1 Samuel 28 says that "the Philistines mustered their forces for war, to fight against Israel" (28:1). Since David had been more than a year in his service, Achish had every right to expect that David would accompany him to war. In fact, the Bible tells us that Achish made David his personal bodyguard (28:2), a role that is so anathema to the notion of David as the glorious Israelite king that it is almost certainly true.

Before turning to the description of this crucial battle, the biblical account detours with the famous episode of Saul and the witch of En-dor. Even the basic premise—Saul consulting a witch for help—lets us know that this is not a historical account. Like the anointing of David in 1 Samuel 16, it is a private event with supernatural goings-on, and like the first chapter in the David narrative, it serves to demonstrate that Saul has no further divine right to the kingship. Saul asks the witch to raise Samuel's ghost, for Saul is afraid of the Philistine armies. Samuel reminds Saul—and us, the readers—that God has taken the kingship from Saul and given it to David. He further tells Saul that in the next day's battle, Saul and his sons will die and the Philistines will be victorious. One hardly needs to go to great lengths to argue for the fictional nature of the story. But we may note that it complements the episodes of David encountering Saul unawares in the wilderness: the earlier stories point out emphatically that David would never harm Saul; the episode of the witch of En-dor makes clear that Saul's death in battle will be the work of God. Saul's time has come, just as David had predicted: "Yahweh himself will strike him down, or his day will come and he will die, or he will go down to battle and perish" (1 Sam. 26:10). But both stories make the same fundamental point: David will not be responsible for Saul's death.

The Philistines marched far to the north to confront Saul's army near the Jezreel valley at Mount Gilboa. This was likely a strategic decision on their part. After decades of fighting on the border be-

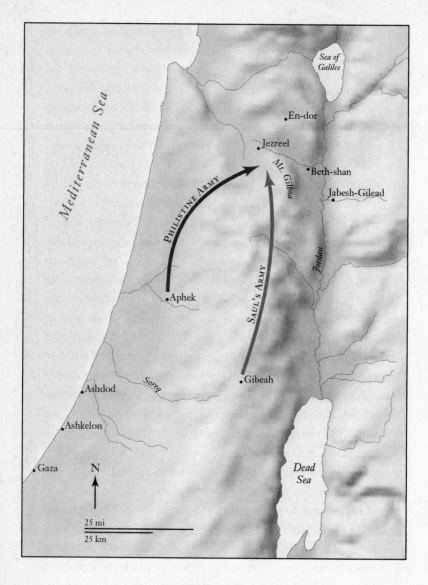

Saul's Death

tween Judah and Philistia in the south, with little to show for it, it would have made good sense to try a new tactic. By moving up the coast and swinging around near the top of the Israelite hill country, the Philistines could attack Saul from a new and unfamiliar direction. The details of the battle are lost to us, but the result is not. The Philistines won decisively and set out in pursuit of Saul and his sons when the rest of the Israelite forces abandoned the field. We may imagine that the royal family had its own private unit of bodyguards, but even these elite forces were unable to withstand the Philistine attack. Saul's three sons—Jonathan, Abinadab, and Malchishua (the latter two being unknown to us before this point)—were killed, and soon after, Saul was mortally wounded with arrows. According to the biblical account, rather than risk being tortured by the Philistines, Saul asks his arms-bearer to finish him off. The man refuses, so Saul commits suicide.[23] The Israelite inhabitants of the area, seeing the king and his sons dead and the army fleeing, abandoned the area to the Philistines.

The following day, the Philistines returned to the battlefield to collect the loot that was their due as victors. Even after his death, Saul was unable to avoid the physical abuse he had feared. The Philistines cut off his head, stripped him of his armor, and sent both throughout the Philistine territory as a means of spreading the news of Israel's defeat. As awful as it sounds, this seems to have been a common method of communication: body parts are also used as wordless messages in the grotesque story of Judges 19–20 (coincidentally set in Saul's hometown of Gibeah), in which the body of a raped concubine is cut into twelve pieces that are distributed to the Israelite tribes as a call to war.[24] Saul's body, along with those of his sons, was impaled on the wall of Beth-shean, a town near Mount Gilboa. But the Philistines permitted some Israelites from Jabesh-Gilead, a town across the Jordan from Beth-shean, to come at night and remove the bodies and give them a proper burial, in accordance with Israelite custom: "his corpse must not remain on the stake overnight, but you must bury him the same day, for an impaled body is an affront to God" (Deut. 21:23).[25]

David's Involvement

WHERE WAS DAVID DURING all this? After all, he was the Philistine king's bodyguard, so he should have been in the thick of the battle, alongside Achish. The Bible, naturally, will have none of this. Just as they were mustering to march north, we are told, some of the Philistine officers from cities other than Gath asked Achish who his bodyguard was and who the men with him were—"those Hebrews" (1 Sam. 29:3). When they learn that it is David, they demand that he be sent back to his little fiefdom of Ziklag, for they are sure that he will turn against them in the heat of battle. They even recall the Israelite women's chant: "Saul has slain his thousands, David his tens of thousands" (29:5). Achish relents and asks David to return; David protests; Achish insists; and David and his men turn back south while the Philistines continue north.

This all seems a bit too fortuitous. David had served Achish for long enough that his credentials should have been well established, even among the rest of the Philistines. It is also difficult to believe that the Philistines would have known about the songs of the Israelite women in praise of David—if such songs were ever really sung. And the back and forth between David and Achish, even as it presents David as almost desperate to fight on the side of the Philistines, serves an important purpose: it tells the reader that even if David had wanted to enter the battle against Saul, he was forcibly forbidden. Again, it is made clear that David could not have had any hand in Saul's death.

What follows upon David's return to Ziklag is equally improbable. According to the biblical account, David and his men take the prototypical three days to return to Ziklag. When they arrive, they find that some Amalekites have raided the town and captured all the women and children, including David's two wives—but, we are told, they did not harm a single one of them. David and his men, after consulting with the priest Abiathar, take off in pursuit. As they come to the Wadi Besor, the unofficial border between Philistine territory and the wasteland to the south, they miraculously encounter an Egyptian youth who happens to be an abandoned slave of the very Amale-kites who had raided Ziklag. The boy leads David to the Amalekites, and David attacks, rescuing his wives and everybody else. In another minor miracle, "nothing of theirs was missing—young or old, sons or daughters, spoil or anything that had been taken" (1 Sam. 30:19).

Many features of this story testify to its improbability. The raiding Amalekites are understood as acting in revenge for David's constant raids on their territory during his time with the Philistines—but, as we have seen, those raids are probably part of the biblical cover-up, and so this revenge should be read as a further stage of the same literary program. The chance encounter with the abandoned Egyptian slave boy who points the way forward is a typical literary flourish; it is strik-ingly similar to the episode in Genesis 37 where Joseph is sent to find his brothers and does so only by happening upon an unnamed man who overheard the brothers reveal their destination (37:14–17). And, most notably, the fact that David recovered everything the Amalekites are said to have taken is both unlikely on the face of it—not a single person dead? not a single woman raped? not a single sheep eaten?—and a remarkable stroke of evidentiary fortune. For, presented with the notion that David was not with the Philistines at Mount Gilboa because he was chasing the Amalekites, one might have wondered where the evidence of the Amalekite raid was to be found: who or what could be accounted as missing to stand as proof that such a raid really happened? Such evidence cannot be provided, however, for the Amalekites touched not a hair on a single person's head—or because the raid never happened at all. Even the biblical account admits, and tries to explain, the fact that during the battle David was absent from his home in Ziklag. But its explanation is forced.

Where was David while the Philistines were killing Saul and his sons? By all rights, he should have been right there with them. And—despite, or perhaps precisely because of, the Bible's emphatic state-ments to the contrary—we may conclude that this is exactly where he was. Now, David's simply being on the battlefield where Saul and his sons died does not necessarily lead to the conclusion that he did the deed himself. After all, the Philistines would have wanted Saul dead just as much as David did. And it is only in the movies that the hero is able to track down his nemeses in the thick of a major battle and single-handedly do them in. But by the same token, one need not pull the trigger to be convicted of murder; David may well have been responsible for the deaths of Saul and his sons.

The first chapter of 2 Samuel records the moment when David learns of Saul's death. An unnamed Amalekite man from Saul's army comes to David at Ziklag and announces the result of the battle, including the deaths of Saul and Jonathan. David asks how the man knows what he is reporting, and the man tells David that he was right there when it happened. What's more, when Saul was about to die, the king asked this very man to be the one to finish him off, which the Amalekite, obligingly, did. Then, the man says, he took the crown and armlet off Saul, which he then produces for David, saying, "I have brought them here to my lord" (2 Sam. 1:10).

Almost every bit of this story is problematic.[26] Why would someone go from the battlefield far to the north all the way south to David in Ziklag with the news? Surely David should have heard it from the returning Philistines, who had sent around Saul's head and armor precisely for the sake of spreading the message. And more important, why would a foreigner report news to a Philistine vassal in Philistine territory? What made the man think that this information would be of particular interest to a mercenary? Then there is the man's story, which directly contradicts the narrative of Saul's death given in the previous chapter. Did Saul kill himself after his arms-bearer refused to do the deed, or did this young man kill him? And, perhaps most confusingly, even if this man took Saul's crown and armlet, why, of all things, would he have thought to bring them to David, rather than to someone in Israel?

The purpose of this bizarre story is to be found in the last of these issues. Somehow, it seems, David—the man whom Saul repeatedly tried to kill, the bandit chief, the vassal of the Philistines—ended up in possession of Saul's royal insignia immediately after Saul's death.

This fact, which seems on the face of it to be quite damning, is what the narrative sets out to explain—to apologize for.[27] Some scholars have suggested that the Amalekite is lying: that he did not kill Saul but instead came upon Saul's body, took the crown and armlet, and delivered them to David because he thought that by doing so he might curry favor with Saul's nemesis.[28] The Amalekite, in this scenario, exaggerates his role, claiming responsibility for Saul's death to please David even more. Although this may be what the narrative intends us to think, it is historically unlikely. It requires us to believe that the delivery of Saul's royal insignia to David is a happy coincidence, the result of the mere chance that a random man happened to rob Saul and think to make his fortune with David. But this strains credulity. The one man in Canaan whom Saul most believed was vying for his crown can hardly have gained it, literally, in this happenstance way. If David ended up in possession of Saul's crown and armlet, it can only be because David *wanted* Saul's crown and armlet. We have to ask, then, how did this actually come to pass?

Since we are presented with two conflicting stories, we cannot be certain of how Saul died. Both texts agree that he was mortally wounded. But the story about his suicide seems to have a distinctly literary background: it is strikingly similar to the story in the book of Judges about Abimelech, who is mortally wounded and tells his arms-bearer to complete the deed, though in that case the arms-bearer complies (Judg. 9:53–54). Abimelech is presented as a villain—not least of all because he sought to become king in Shechem, in the course of which he also killed seventy of his brothers (Judg. 9:5). It can hardly be coincidence that Saul, who achieved the position Abimelech sought, dies in almost exactly the same way as his reviled predecessor. The story about the Amalekite, on the other hand, is equally a literary construction, designed to explain how David came to have Saul's crown and armlet. It, too, has a good biblical parallel, in the story of the capture of the ark of the covenant and the messenger who runs to take the news to the old priest Eli (1 Sam. 4:12–18).[29] Together, both stories about Saul's death emphasize, yet again, David's lack of involvement: whether Saul died by his own hand or by that of the Amalekite, David's hands were clean.

And yet: whoever got to Saul first, and therefore was able to take the crown and armlet off his body, must have been in league with David somehow. It seems likely enough that Saul's royal objects were taken to David, rather than that David removed them from Saul himself—for that would have signaled to all of Israel that David was a usurper. But he could well have sent someone to seize them. Indeed, if Saul fell surrounded by the Philistines closing in on him, presumably one of them should have looted the king's body for the royal treasures. And, since we have already seen that it is highly probable that David was at the battle, we may also suggest the possibility that it was one of David's men who, on his master's instructions, ran to strip Saul's corpse of the symbols of kingship.

It is theoretically possible that David had given instructions to his men to rush in and strip Saul only in the event that Saul died in battle. But in years of warfare against the Philistines, Saul had never fallen before. What are the chances that the only time Saul was wounded, the time when he died, was also the only battle that took place while David was allied with the Philistines? The coincidence is hard to swallow. David must have been involved. Perhaps David and his men acted as a separate unit, chasing down Saul while the rest of the Philistines faced the body of the Israelite army. Perhaps David and his men presented themselves to the Israelites as having double-crossed the Philistines, and thereby gained access behind the Israelite lines.[30] Most likely, it was David who gave the Philistines the idea to attack from the north rather than from the south. There was a reason that the Philistines had been unable to dislodge Saul and Israel for all those years. The Philistines were experts at fighting in the plains, their natural landscape; David, from the hill country of Judah, had a military expertise that would have been of great use to them. And David, more than anyone else in the Philistine camp, was familiar with Saul's tactics, with the way that Saul expected the Philistines to attack, and with the defenses that the Israelites typically mounted. The Philistine victory in this battle probably should be attributed to their unexpected assault from the north—and this new approach probably should be attributed to David. Everything else is a constant; David was the X factor in this military equation. The results speak for themselves. Saul was dead, and David held the royal insignia in his hand.

To say that David personally killed Saul would be going too far. It is not impossible, but it is not necessarily probable, either. What is probable, even bordering on certain, is that David had a hand in Saul's death. Everything points in this direction, from the historical probability of David's presence at the battle to the evidently indisputable fact that David gained Saul's crown to the overly vigorous biblical claims for David's innocence. And this biblical defense of David reaches its highest point just after he has finally gained the crown he sought for so long.

Once David and his men learn of Saul's death, the Bible tells us, they tear their clothes, lament, weep, and fast—the full litany of traditional mourning procedures in ancient Israel. David then turns his sharp eye on the young man who brought him the news, who wielded the sword that ended Saul's days, asking him, "How did you dare to extend your hand to destroy Yahweh's anointed?" (2 Sam. 1:14). Before the man can even respond—and what could he have said in any case?—David tells one of his attendants to kill the man, which the attendant obligingly does. And David proclaims the final word over the dead man: "Your own mouth testified against you when you said, 'It was I who killed Yahweh's anointed'" (1:16). David's words—"How did you dare to extend your hand to destroy Yahweh's anointed?"—hearken back directly to the two episodes in the wilderness in which David refrains from killing Saul: "Yahweh forbid that I should extend my hand against him, for he is Yahweh's anointed" (1 Sam. 24:7); "Yahweh forbid that I should extend my hand against Yahweh's anointed" (26:11). Not only did David not have a hand in Saul's death, but he was emphatically appalled that anyone should. By killing the Amalekite, David is ostensibly avenging Saul's death.

The lament that David recites for Saul and Jonathan reaches the extreme limits of the biblical apology. He hardly could be more effusive in his posthumous praise: "How the mighty have fallen!" (2 Sam. 1:19, 25, 27). Saul and Jonathan are presented as Israel's glory. David calls for nature itself to cease and praises the military might of the two men: "They were swifter than eagles, they were stronger than lions" (1:23). He tells Israel's maidens to weep. All this for Saul, David's mortal enemy, and Jonathan, the heir who stood in the way of David's ascent to the throne. The path has been cleared for David to ascend to the kingship—everything he ever could have wished for has come to pass. But the Bible presents David as wracked by anguish, as expressed in mourning, in murder, and in lament.

In all of this—the mourning rituals, the vengeance on Saul's killer, the lament—David is making a performance of grief. But who is he performing for? His band of outlaws, men who have been ostracized from society and have happily worked for the Philistines for more than a year? According to the story, they are the only ones who would have witnessed any of these actions. The performance, rather, is for the reader. It is for our benefit that David goes through the motions of grief, to demonstrate to the last possible moment that he had always loved Saul and Jonathan.

The Bible doth protest too much. In story after story, the biblical account strains to reject the notion that David was responsible for Saul's death. From the two episodes in which David spares Saul's life in the wilderness to the excuse for David's absence from the battlefield to David's reaction to the news of Saul's death—every episode desperately argues, each from a different perspective, for David's innocence. The only sensible historical conclusion is that David really did participate actively in the death of Saul.

THE DAVID OF THE wilderness resembles a figure out of a classic Western film. He is not the righteous sheriff, however, as we might expect. Instead, he is the unscrupulous outlaw, willing to do whatever it takes to survive and gradually gain power. This period is one of extortion, theft, homicide, and—with the death of Saul—regicide. Though David's actions are far from admirable, we may acknowledge that he is not unskilled in the art of survival. He enters the wilderness as an outcast, with nothing and no one to call his own. He is able to gain a following, avoid capture, find a safe haven among the Philistines, and even make a living—albeit by raiding the towns of Judah. And, when the opportunity finally arises to open the way to the kingship, David makes the most of it.

Yet the death of Saul did not mean that David was suddenly king of Israel, even if he did literally hold the crown. Attaining the kingship—and, just as importantly, holding on to it—would require further efforts still.

CHAPTER 4

David Becomes King

A SERIES OF TIMELY DEATHS

IN THE MODERN IMAGINATION, SAUL is succeeded directly by David. This is what we are taught in religious school, and this is what we find in most introductory overviews of the Israelite monarchy. And, given the biblical presentation, it is a natural assumption. After all, David is predestined to be king, anointed by God's prophet Samuel—and God himself is said to have stripped Saul of the kingship in order to give it to David. After Saul's death, therefore, it would seem self-evident that David—who, after all, literally held Saul's crown in his hand—would ascend the throne and begin his glorious reign over all Israel.

This version of events, however, is highly abbreviated. David would eventually become king in Saul's place, to be sure. But his path to the crown was hardly easy or straightforward. We, as readers of the Bible, are prepared for it well in advance. But the inhabitants of Israel and Judah had no such foreknowledge, no reason to assume that David was entitled to rule them. Indeed, it would have been quite the contrary: David, remember, had effectively given up his membership in the community of Judah by going over to the Philistines—and he never really belonged to Israel, the northern territories over which

Saul had ruled. He was not a member of the royal family. Indeed, as we have seen, David likely played a direct role in the death of Saul and his sons. From an Israelite perspective, David had about as much right to rule as did a Philistine.

David, King of Judah

IT IS THUS SOMEWHAT surprising, from a historical perspective, that directly after Saul's defeat and death David should be anointed king—though not over all Israel, but rather over only Judah. The biblical account of this event is startling for its brevity. In a mere four verses (2 Sam. 2:1–4) we are told that David went to Hebron with his wives and faithful followers and settled there and that "the men of Judah came and there they anointed David king over the House of Judah" (2:4). For a seminal moment in David's royal career, this report is so short as to be almost overlooked. And while the basic facts seem plausible enough, the basic facts are all the biblical authors provide here. The text raises a number of questions to be answered and gaps to be filled. Why, for instance, does David go to Hebron? Who are the "men of Judah"? How did popular acclaim function as a mechanism for anointing a king? Why did the Judahites anoint David? What were the practical implications of David's new position? The haste with which the Bible describes David's anointing in Hebron may suggest that there is more to this event than meets the eye—surely, it was not so simple as that.

David's choice of Hebron as his new residence, and in fact as his capital in Judah, was a strategic one. The city sits squarely in the middle of the hill country of Judah, in one of the highest areas of the region. Already a thousand years before David, Hebron was the most significant city in what would eventually be called Judah. It was both a cultic site and, more important, a royal city encircled by a massive wall, an administrative center from which the surrounding area was controlled.[1] The significance of Hebron in the region is evident from its prominence in the early biblical traditions: it is in Hebron that Abraham dwells and that the patriarchs and matriarchs are buried (with the exception of Rachel). When Moses sends spies to go explore "the hill country," they go to Hebron. For someone with royal aspirations, there could be no more symbolic place to be anointed than in the ancient royal city of Hebron.

What is not obvious at first glance is just how odd it is that David should have relocated to Hebron at all. Since we know he will become king there, the move seems natural. Yet this is the same David who, fewer than two years earlier, was unable to find even temporary shelter among the inhabitants of Judah. Towns and regions far less important than Hebron—Keilah and Ziph, for example—were all too happy to turn David aside. Yet suddenly, and without comment, David is able to settle himself, his family, and all of his men and their families in one of the largest and most important cities in Judah. Something has changed.

In fact, two significant transformations have occurred since David last found himself in the hills of Judah. The first is the defeat and death of Saul. When David first entered the wilderness, Saul was powerful enough both to regularly send search parties after David and to be viewed by the Judahites as the better bet, so to speak—to all appearances, Saul and his army had the upper hand in the conflict against David and his ragtag militia. Keilah and Ziph were able to refuse David's advances because they knew that Saul would support them if necessary. With Saul's death, however, there was no longer a greater force to stand behind the Judahites' denials of David. The second change is the rise in David's military power during his time among the Philistines. No longer a relatively ill-equipped gang scrounging the wilderness for supplies, David and his men now had a comfortable home base, ample supplies from their many months of raids, and almost certainly improved arms thanks to the Philistines whom they served. David did not move out of desperation any longer—now his movements were calculated. If he relocated to Hebron, it was because he had the power to maintain his presence there, especially in the vacuum created by the absence of Saul's military counterweight.

The point, then, is that it was not the attitude of the Judahites toward David that changed. Indeed, after more than a year of David's regular raids from Philistia, it was likely that their feelings had only hardened against him. What changed was their ability to do anything about it. This is all to suggest that David's move to Hebron is less a mere relocation and more an act of aggression. Note how his settlement there replicates that of the Philistines in the north. After the defeat of the Israelite army, the Philistines occupied the conquered territory. That they could settle their own people in Israel without the native populace being able to prevent it signaled Israel's complete subjugation. This is especially true in a culture like that of ancient Israel, in which familial possession of the land was of the utmost importance, protected by custom and law. It was rare enough for an Israelite to move within Israel—an outsider settling in the land would have been an indication of the people's abject weakness. Settlement equals possession; it is a mark of power. And so, too, David, in the south, moves into the very heart of Judah, to one of its oldest and most famous cities. By settling in Hebron, he makes a bold statement about his strength relative to that of the inhabitants of Judah. They once may have been able to push him away, but they are unable to do so any longer.

Hebron was the logical choice for David for another reason. It was the main city of the Calebite tribe. In the book of Joshua, when the conquered land is apportioned among the Israelite tribes, the city of Hebron is granted specifically to Caleb, the tribe's eponymous ancestor, as a reward for his faithfulness during the episode of the spies in Numbers 13–14: "So Joshua blessed Caleb son of Jephunneh and assigned Hebron to him as his portion" (Josh. 14:13). David's move to Hebron was more than merely symbolic: he was making good on his right to be the Calebite chief, a right he claimed when he killed Nabal and married Abigail. At the time, he was unable to assume the position because he had not yet amassed enough power. But that was then.

Although the death of Saul may have been the precipitating event for David's incursion into the heart of Judah, his movements were not unplanned. Saul's defeat opened the door for David, but he had been laying the groundwork for the establishment of his power in Judah for quite a while—beginning with his marriage to Abigail. Moreover, it seems likely that the entire time he was among the Philistines was intended to prepare for just this eventuality. As we have seen, David's main activity during the sixteen months of his residence in Ziklag was the regular raiding of Judahite towns. While such raids had obvious economic benefits, we should not overstate the tangible rewards that resulted from them. These towns were not major centers of commerce; they were not blessed with agricultural or material abundance. What could be captured in a raid was probably hardly enough to justify the expense of mounting the expedition in the first place. And from the Judahite perspective, the raids were not economically crippling—there is no evidence that any Judahite community was destroyed, abandoned, or even deeply harmed by these Philistine advances (we may note the example of Keilah discussed in the previous chapter). David's raids were, as such minor attacks usually are, less about tangible reward and more about the intangible message they sent. The ability to enter Judah unopposed, and to leave without being pursued, sent a clear signal of regional dominance. David's raids were aimed not at Judah's economy, but at its psyche. The Judahites would not have known where or when David might strike— they would have had to be constantly on guard, constantly reminded of their susceptibility to attack. In his time with the Philistines, David established himself as a fearsome presence.

At the same time, however, he was taking a different tack, though one that contributed to the same basic ends. In 1 Samuel 30:26–31, we are told that David sent some of the spoil he had captured to the elders of Judah. The text suggests that this spoil was from David's vengeful attack on the Amalekites who had captured Ziklag, but we have already seen that that story is a patent apology for David's participation in the battle against Saul. The notice of David sending spoil to Judah may contribute to this apologetic end: in theory, the receipt of the spoils from David would prove that he was not on the battlefield. Yet this notice seems, unlike the rest of the story, to have a ring of truth to it—in fact, it may well be further evidence of David's concerted efforts to establish himself as the power figure in Judah.

We may note the detailed list of the towns to which David is said to have sent these spoils: Bethel, Ramoth-negeb, Jattir, Aroer, Siphmoth, Eshtemoa, Racal, Hormah, Bor-ashan, and Athach, as well as the regions of the Jerahmeelites and Kenites (30:27–31). All of these Judahite towns are clustered in the south, near the top of the Negeb desert. What is notable about this list is that it matches almost perfectly the list of areas that David told Achish he had raided, when (according to the biblical author) he was in fact raiding various tribes to the south. David told Achish, in 1 Samuel 27:10, that he was raiding "the Negeb of Judah or the Negeb of the Jerahmeelites or the Negeb of the Kenites." We have already seen that David almost certainly did raid those territories—which means that he also seems to have sent spoils to precisely the same places.

This conclusion is, remarkably, confirmed by the biblical text itself, which describes the places to which David sent spoils as "all the places where David and his men had roamed" (30:31). Earlier, the biblical authors had (unconvincingly) told us that David did not in fact raid those regions but had lied about doing so to appease Achish. Here, however, we are told that he and his men actually *were* in those places. In other words, the cover-up has slipped away momentarily. This suggests that a historical account of David sending spoils to Judah—to the very towns that he was raiding under Achish—has here been reconfigured to serve as part of the apology for David's whereabouts during the battle against Saul. The question, then, becomes under what circumstances David really did send spoils to Judah, if it was not when the Bible says it was.

Before coming to the when, however, we must understand the why. How would it benefit David to redistribute to the towns of Judah the very spoils he had taken from them in the first place? As with the raids in which the spoils were captured, the sending of gifts back to Judah is important more for its symbolism than for its content. It sends a message: David has the power to take away, but he also has the power to give back. He is in complete command, able to punish or reward as he sees fit. David clearly doesn't need the spoils—he is not dependent on them for his survival; they are worthless to him. Their value is with the communities from which they were taken, and David, in controlling the spoils, is stating clearly his value to these communities as well. By taking and giving, David is saying, "This can go one of two ways: you can oppose me, or you can support me—and you can see what each choice entails."[2] If this behavior seems familiar from stories of the modern mafia, it is no coincidence. The knowledge of how to use power to control a population is as old as power itself.

This giving of favors also has a distinctly royal tone. As we have already seen, early rule in Israel, as in many other cultures, was based on both military strength and royal patronage. A ruler gained and kept the loyalty of his servants and officers by proving himself capable of doling out favors to those close to him. David seems to be doing the same, but writ large: he doesn't need to court individuals, but communities.[3] In distributing spoils to the towns of Judah, David presents himself as a monarch. All of this leads to the strong possibility that the timing of David's distribution of spoils followed on the heels of Saul's death. While Saul was still alive, such efforts might well have been wasted; whatever gifts David might have been able to offer, they hardly could match the military protection Saul offered. Once Saul had fallen, however, David was ready to fill the void. The spoils served his purpose perfectly: they demonstrated his military power—since he was the one who had taken them in the first place—and his royal patronage. In short, David was telling the Judahites, "I'm the best you've got, and I can offer you both protection and favor." Call it what you will—diplomacy, bribery, extortion—in the end, it seems to have worked. David wanted to present himself as a king, and a king is what he became.

This is how David became king in Hebron—essentially, by coercion. Less clear is the formal mechanism by which this is imagined to have happened. The biblical account says simply that "the men of Judah came and there they anointed David king" (2 Sam. 2:4). But who were these "men of Judah"? Why did they come to Hebron? And how did they "anoint David king"? To start, we should remember that there was no unified tribe of Judah, but rather a number of individual communities occupying a geographical territory independent from the northern kingdom of Israel. Thus "the men of Judah" cannot be imagined to be a collective leadership group, let alone literally all of the men of Judah. What we may imagine is that "the men of Judah" refers to a leader or leaders from each community. This conforms to the notice of David's sending spoils not to Judah as a whole, but to the elders of each town—each community had to be dealt with independently.

How, then, did these independent communities each send one or more representatives to Hebron to anoint David king at what would appear to be the same time? The biblical authors naturally want to present David's kingship as a collective, spontaneous act—the people of Judah confirming what God himself had decreed in David's youth. But concerted efforts like this require centralized leadership, which Judah did not have—or, at least, did not have until the arrival of David. If the towns and regions of Judah sent their leaders to Hebron to see David, it is most logical to assume that they did so not of their own accord, but because they were summoned. Such a summons would, in fact, reflect standard ancient Near Eastern protocol. Upon the assumption of the throne, kings would regularly require those lands subject to them to send representatives bearing tribute. By appearing before the new king, these lands demonstrated their loyalty to the new regime and explicitly marked themselves as subservient to the royal overlord.[4] This is precisely what we would expect to have happened with David at Hebron, especially because he had to ensure the loyalty not of one unified territory, but of each individual community—or at least enough of them to be certain that his control was secure.

It is even possible, though by no means certain, that the summons to the communities of Judah to show themselves before David in Hebron was sent along with the redistribution of the spoils discussed above. The function of the spoils was, as we have seen, to articulate David's power and to send an implicit either/or choice. By sending representatives to Hebron, communities publicly demonstrated their choice, and their acceptance of David's power.

Such acceptance is, in the end, what the "anointing" of David entailed. Literally, anointing refers to the pouring of oil on the head. It was typically performed by an established authority figure in the name of the deity: thus Moses anoints Aaron and his sons as priests; Samuel anoints Saul and David as king; the priest Zadok and the prophet Nathan both anoint Solomon; Elijah anoints Jehu as king and Elisha as his prophetic successor. Anointing thus marked individuals as divinely ordained in their roles. It seems likely that in the story of David's anointing at Hebron, the literal meaning is not intended—we cannot suppose that the representatives of Judah either individually or collectively poured oil over David. Rather, the symbolic import of anointing is alluded to here. By acknowledging David's power, and their subservience to him, the people of Judah elevated David to a position of authority and granted him—at least in the eyes of the biblical authors—the divine right of kingship. We may imagine that if any literal anointing occurred, it would have been by David's own hand—as a sort of ancient Napoleon.

With the acceptance of David's kingship, a new era dawned—not just for David, but for Judah. What was once a region of independent communities was now, for the first time, unified under a single leader. What Saul had accomplished in the north, David had now accomplished in the south. The creation of the monarchy in Judah was at the same time the creation of Judah itself. It is in this moment that we hear for the first time of "the House of Judah." David's achievement in this is undeniable, considering the central role that Judah would play in history, literature, and religion. Without David, there would be no Judah. Yet it should be remembered that, at least at first, Judah was still only a very minor kingdom. The acknowledgment of David as king did not suddenly make Judah into a powerful political or cultural force. It was still no more than a collection of backwater villages scattered in the wilderness among the hills. And though Judah would come to valorize David as its glorious founder, it came into being not by choice, but by coercion. It existed by force of David's will—a will that he exerted with a heavy hand and a strong arm. Judah's glory years were still to come. And, in fact, there is one further piece of the puzzle that makes the moment of Judah's creation even less triumphant.

When we think of David becoming king in Judah, we see in this the beginning of the great nation of Israel. We read the story through the lens of what followed, the history of Israel from David to the present. What is forgotten is the political situation after the death of Saul, and more important David's own position. Saul's death may have been David's doing, one way or another, but Israel was defeated by the Philistines. It was the Philistines who had the power in the region. And David was, for all intents and purposes, a vassal of the Philistines. As we have seen, he established his power from that position. The death of Saul did not change that fact, and neither did David's move to become king of Judah.

We may imagine a scenario in which David, seizing his opportunity, left the embrace of the Philistines to establish himself as the king of a new independent state of Judah. In such a case, we may also imagine the Philistines' response. They had overwhelming military advantage, especially with the collapse of the northern kingdom after Saul's death. David had been their loyal subject—they could hardly have allowed him to go off on his own and found a rival kingdom right in their backyard. In short, there would have been a significant Philistine response, and one that inevitably would have wiped Judah off the map before it even had a chance to defend itself. And yet none of this happened. David ruled over Judah in Hebron for seven years, and during that time, there is not a word of any Philistine aggression. How can this be explained?

The answer is as obvious as it is unpalatable: Judah, David's new kingdom, was effectively a Philistine territory. For his entire tenure in Hebron, David remained a loyal vassal of the Philistines.[5] This may be hard to hear, but it makes perfect sense. Without the northern kingdom to protect it, Judah was entirely at the mercy of the Philistines. David—born in Judah, though long since having abandoned any attachment to it—had been acting as a Philistine mercenary in the region for more than a year and had proved himself capable. We may even imagine that rule over Judah was David's reward for having helped the Philistines finally defeat Saul. There is no notice in the text that David turned against his Philistine masters when he became king of Judah. The Philistines seem to have accepted his kingship without complaint. In fact, the period of David's rule in Hebron seems to have been one of newfound peace—which is entirely sensible, since the Philistines had defeated the northern kingdom and were now in control of the southern region through David. Judah would one day be independent, but it was created as a Philistine territory and led by a Philistine vassal.[6]

Support for this reconstruction may be found in the Bible itself. The entire narrative of David's anointing in Hebron and reign over Judah is absent from Chronicles. If this was a high point of his royal career, as it would seem to the modern reader, why would Chronicles, which goes to such lengths to glorify David even above and beyond what we find in Samuel, not mention a word of it? Why is this period of David's career treated as an embarrassment—ignored out of existence, just like the unseemly events of his time in the wilderness? Something about this story must have seemed unacceptable to the authors of Chronicles. Whether it was the historical recollection of what David's Judahite kingdom really was or a keen reading of the story in Samuel, Chronicles seems to have understood that this ostensibly glorious moment was anything but.

The Bible presents David's kingship over Judah as almost a foregone conclusion, a spontaneous moment of popular acclamation of God's chosen monarch. The reality is far less appealing. David became king in Judah through intimidation and coercion. The towns of Judah coalesced into a nation not by choice, but by force. David's reign was based not on love, but on fear. And he ruled not as a Judahite, but as a servant of the Philistines.

The State of the North

IT IS UNCLEAR JUST how long David waited after becoming king in Judah to begin confronting Saul's former kingdom. Presumably, however, he wouldn't have waited long, for Israel would never be as weak as it was immediately after the death of Saul. It is not surprising, then, that virtually the first thing we hear after the anointing of David in Hebron is that he turned to the north.

The situation in Israel after the battle at Mount Gilboa was understandably unsettled. Not only Saul but three of his sons, the heirs to his throne, had died on the battlefield. Such a situation could hardly be planned for, especially for a first-generation monarchy like that of Israel. Jonathan, Saul's eldest son, had been primed to succeed his father by leading part of Saul's military. But of Saul's sons after Jonathan we have heard nothing to this point, almost certainly because they had no significant position in the military or administration of the northern kingdom. Even if Saul had other sons—and, it turns out, he did—their claim to the throne would be based solely on the principle of lineal royal succession, a rather tentative basis for power so early in a monarchy. The people of Israel must have been very uncertain about their future.

David tried to take advantage of the situation in the north almost immediately—not militarily, at first, but diplomatically. He sent a message to the inhabitants of Jabesh-Gilead, the town that had taken Saul's body down from the wall and given it a proper burial. The Bible records this message, though it is undoubtedly not the very words that David actually sent. According to 2 Samuel 2:5–7, David blessed Jabesh-Gilead for its act of faithfulness to Saul, hoped for God's blessing on the town, and offered David's own reward, along with a not-so-subtle suggestion: "Now take courage and be valiant men, for your lord Saul is dead and the House of Judah has anointed me king over them" (2:7). Whatever David may have really said, this last line probably sums it up fairly accurately. He suggests that with Saul no longer able to protect Jabesh-Gilead, the town would be smart—or, as the Bible puts it almost with a wink, "valiant"—to follow the example of Judah and make David their king as well. As he did with the towns of Judah, David presents Jabesh-Gilead with a choice. But unlike Judah, which was essentially defenseless and had been subject to David's displays of power for some time, the far northern town of Jabesh-Gilead was under no direct threat from him. This was true diplomacy. David had nothing to back up his words—and they seem to have fallen on deaf ears.[7]

In part, this may have been because, in the vacuum created by Saul's death, a new power figure in the north had begun to emerge. This was not one of Saul's sons but rather his general, Abner. That Saul's general should have taken up the reins of leadership—though, as we will see, not the reign itself—is unsurprising. We need not look far afield in our modern world to recognize that the fall of an established government is often succeeded by military rule. And as we have seen, royal power was predicated first and foremost on a person's ability to command the military, which is why kings like Saul and princes like Jonathan made leading the troops a priority. Without a credible military leader from the immediate line of royal descent, the most important military leader from outside that line would have been in a position of significant power. And Abner would wield his power, in sometimes unexpected ways, for the relatively brief remainder of his life.

Abner probably could have proclaimed himself king in Israel; as Saul's cousin, he was at least from the right family. And yet he did not. Instead, he put Saul's son Ishbaal on the throne. The standard royal succession notwithstanding, it is clear that this was truly Abner's doing. Even the Bible says that Abner "took Ishbaal son of Saul . . . and made him king over Gilead, the Ashurites, Jezreel, Ephraim, and

Benjamin—over all Israel" (2 Sam. 2:8–9). It seems to have been by Abner's will, communicated to Saul's former territories, that Ishbaal assumed his father's place. Abner acted as kingmaker rather than as king. This was the smarter decision. The northern kingdom of Israel was hardly a choice place to rule, given its military and political situation vis-à-vis the Philistines and David to the south. There was no guarantee that the kingdom would survive for much longer—king of Israel might be a relatively dangerous position to hold. By establishing himself as the real power behind the throne, Abner could control the kingdom to a degree while keeping himself safe. And should Ishbaal falter, Abner would be able to deflect any criticism from himself, especially as he had done the "right" thing by maintaining the expected royal succession.[8]

Who, then, was Ishbaal, the new king of Israel? We know remarkably little about him. He doesn't appear in the Bible before Abner makes him king; evidently he was of little consequence before his father and three elder brothers were killed. Almost all we know is his name—and the Bible has obscured even that, for in Samuel he is called not Ishbaal, but Ishbosheth. Like many Israelite names, his is a combination of two words. The first, *ish*, means "man." The second, at least as it appears in Samuel, *bosheth*, means "shame" or "disgrace." This is not a comment on his character but is a well-known biblical adaptation of his real name, *baal*, which is both a proper noun meaning "lord" and, more famously, the name of the main Canaanite deity, Baal—the same Baal that Elijah famously proves powerless on Mount Carmel. Thus, Ishbaal's name meant "man of Baal." Here and elsewhere, biblical scribes, perhaps embarrassed that an Israelite should have a name glorifying a foreign god, replaced the divine name with a pejorative term. To be fair to Ishbaal—or to Saul, who named him—in the early years of Israel, "Baal" seems to have been used to denote the Israelite god, Yahweh. We should not think that Saul worshipped a Canaanite deity. Later, however, any association with Baal would have been unthinkable, and hence the alteration in the text.[9]

Military confrontation between David and Israel was inevitable, and it took place at Gibeon, a town near the southern border of Israel. Given the location, it is likely that Abner led the Israelite troops to Gibeon as a defensive measure and that David's men, led by his general Joab, saw this as an opportunity to engage in combat without going too far north. The Bible presents the battle as a rout, with Joab and his men pursuing Abner until the last light of day. With the sun setting, Joab gave up the chase, allowing Abner to retreat, and returned to Hebron. This much seems likely enough.

Not quite so believable are the stories embedded in the biblical account of this battle. The first is a bizarre moment right at the beginning of the fighting, when Abner and Joab are supposed to have selected twelve men from each side to engage in single combat, almost for the entertainment of the rest of the troops. Each pair is said to have simultaneously stabbed each other, such that "they fell together." From both the "set-piece" feel of the story and the fact that it has no effect on the rest of the narrative, it is clear that this story is nothing but an elaborate etiology for a place in Gibeon called "the Field of Blades."[10] The second story is again of single combat, but of a different kind. David's leading warriors, the sons of Zeruiah—Joab, Abishai, and Asahel—are said to have been present at the battle. Asahel, according to the text, set off on a run after Abner, such that the two of them were essentially alone, streaking through the field. Abner begged Asahel to stop chasing him, warning that if he did not relent, Abner would have to kill him. Asahel refused, and so Abner, left with no choice, "struck him in the belly with a backward thrust of his spear" (2 Sam. 2:23), killing Asahel on the spot. Not only is this sort of single combat story more literary than likely—it is decidedly reminiscent of Homer—but the episode exists entirely as a means for establishing, for future use, a rationale for why Abner should die: as blood vengeance for the death of Asahel. Interestingly enough, though the other parts of this trio, Joab and Abishai, are regular figures in the David story, Asahel is never mentioned before this episode. It is not that he was invented, necessarily—in fact, he is listed as one of David's elite warriors in 2 Samuel 23:24 (well after he is supposed to have died at Gibeon). But his relationship to Joab and Abishai does seem a new creation of the biblical authors, again to justify the impending death of Abner.

This battle between David and Israel ended without a decisive victory, as most battles did. David's military forces proved their strength in driving Abner and his men away from Gibeon, though they seem not to have had the resources to capture any Israelite territory. This is the only battle between the two sides recorded in the Bible—we are told after this only that "the war between the House of Saul and the House of David was long-drawn-out, but David kept growing stronger while the House of Saul kept growing weaker" (2 Sam. 3:1). The battle at Gibeon thus may be taken as representative of the war as a whole: nothing decisive, but a clear advantage to David's side. This is to be expected, since Abner's army was probably significantly diminished after the defeat of Saul, and David's army substantially stronger both by controlling all of Judah and by virtue of Philistine support. The course of the war, tilting slowly but inexorably in David's favor, would have made Abner's decision not to become king look better and better. At the same time, it made Ishbaal weaker and weaker. Eventually, the power dynamic in the north would come to a head, with unpleasant consequences for both the king and his master.

Abner's Betrayal

EVERYONE SEEMS TO HAVE seen where things were headed. Ishbaal, however, was stuck—he was the king of Israel, and like any good captain, he had to go down with the ship. Not so, Abner. The biblical story of how Abner broke with Ishbaal is a strange one. Ishbaal accuses Abner of having slept with one of Saul's concubines—a seemingly trivial matter, but in fact one with significant symbolic import, as we have seen already in the case of David and Ahinoam. For Abner to sleep with one of Saul's concubines was as good as Abner declaring himself king. Abner's response to Ishbaal's accusation is equivocal: he

castigates Ishbaal for doubting his loyalty to Saul's family and kingdom, yet doesn't quite deny the charge. But Abner's anger leads him
to change sides, to "do for David as Yahweh swore to him—to transfer the kingship from the House of Saul, and to establish the throne
of David over Israel and Judah" (2 Sam. 3:9–10). That the dialogue
between Ishbaal and Abner is not historically accurate is proved by
the reference to God's promise to make David king, which Abner
could not have known about. And some have argued that the entire
episode is an invention, simply a mechanism for explaining Abner's
disloyalty.[11] Yet it seems a strange story to invent. Given all the possible ways for the break between Abner and Ishbaal to have happened,
this accusation and nondenial, complete with the details of the concubine's name, is not the most obvious. Thus while we may set aside
Abner's speech as a literary construction, the episode may well have
a historical basis. Abner was, after all, the real power in Israel, and he
may have felt himself entitled to some of the perks that came with
that power. He also may have been testing Ishbaal's resilience—would
the king have the courage to oppose him? As it turned out, the answer
was no: after leveling the charge, Ishbaal "could say nothing more in
reply to Abner, because he was afraid of him" (3:11). All of this would
have been reasonable preparation for Abner's next step: full betrayal.

Abner sent a message to David: "Make a covenant with me and
I will lend my hand to bring all Israel over to your side" (3:12). The
Bible gives us no details of what this "covenant" may have been, but
we may reasonably conjecture. Abner would not have simply given up
his power for nothing. It seems likely that he would have supported
David's nominal kingship in the north, but with himself as a vassal
king, ruling over Israel—just as David was a vassal king of the Philistines, ruling over Judah. Abner would maintain his power in the north
while preventing any further military advances by David. With the
war going badly for Abner, this would have been a prudent move to
make. Note, however, that in sending this message, Abner has taken
on the role of the king, even without the official title. He feels himself empowered to present Israel on a platter to David. It seems quite

possible that Abner's dalliance with Saul's concubine was his way of establishing that authority, at least in his own eyes.

Even without specifics, David would have recognized Abner's overture immediately for what it was. Across the ancient Near East, a population on the verge of being conquered commonly relinquished its independence to maintain some internal stability. Given the options of putting up a fight and risking wholesale destruction on the one hand and accepting the yoke of vassaldom on the other—which frequently meant only paying regular tribute and providing troops for military actions—the choice was a fairly easy one. For the conquering nation, such a deal would spare the significant expense of full-fledged military preparations and war.[12] For much of their history, both before and after David, Canaan and Israel took this subservient role, being vassals of the Egyptians during the second millennium BCE, of the Assyrians during the eighth to seventh centuries BCE, of the Egyptians and Babylonians during the seventh to sixth centuries, the Persians during the sixth to fourth centuries, the Greeks during the fourth to second centuries, and finally the Romans beginning in the first century BCE and culminating with the destruction of the temple in 70 CE. Periods of Israelite independence were the exception, not the rule, and usually coincided with the decline of the previously dominant foreign empire.[13] Revolts against the foreign overlords were occasionally successful, as with the Maccabees, but more often they ended in defeat and significant punishment—as was the case with the destruction of the northern kingdom in 722 BCE and of the southern kingdom in 586 BCE.

David would have received Abner's message in this light. He would have known that Abner was offering himself as a vassal, hoping to avoid further military conflict and willing to recognize David's power and perhaps maintain some of his own, even if in a limited capacity. David's response was positive but came with an interesting condition: that Abner come before him in person and bring along Michal, Saul's daughter. We have already discussed the probability that the story of David marrying Michal while he was still in Saul's service is fictional.[14] This moment, however, seems eminently plausible. Whether they were married in the past or not, David's summons of Michal is a highly charged symbolic gesture. He is establishing his kinship right to Saul's throne, as son-in-law of the deceased king. David is removing an avenue of objection from the north and simultaneously following the established ancient tradition of using royal marriage for diplomatic ends. Now, however, the marriage is truly between two royal houses, for David is an acknowledged king. The marriage to Michal consummates the joining of the two houses into one, with David at its head.

If, however, David was in fact not married to Michal previously, then this is more than mere diplomacy—it is yet another demonstration of David's incontrovertible power over the north. He felt himself strong enough to demand that Saul's daughter be stripped from her rightful husband—who is portrayed pathetically as weeping while following her out of his house—and, evidently, he was right. Even more interesting, David made his demand not only of Abner, but also of Ishbaal. In some ways, this was the more logical avenue, since Ishbaal was the king, at least nominally, and more important was Michal's brother. In the end, according to the Bible, it was Ishbaal who sent Michal off to David. And this, too, would have had political significance: though Abner was the one who approached David to relinquish the rights to the Israelite throne, Ishbaal, in sending Michal, signaled his complicity in the decision. And, in the end, what choice did he have? His general had just offered to turn his nation over to David, and he could do nothing to stop it. Denying Michal to David would have been inviting military retribution at a moment when Ishbaal had no power to withstand it. The defection of Abner meant the practical dissolution of Ishbaal's kingdom. Perhaps "man of shame" is an appropriate name for him after all.

When Abner arrived in person before David, the meeting seems to have been relatively brief. In part, this is because the visit was mostly symbolic: the subjugated vassal presenting himself before his new overlord, presumably bearing some sort of gift and pledging his fealty. However, the meeting was brief also because it came to a rather abrupt end. Abner never made it back to Israel, because Joab, David's general, struck him down and killed him. The question that both the biblical text and the modern historian need to answer is why.

The Bible, as already mentioned, suggests that Joab killed Abner as revenge for Abner's murder of Joab's brother Asahel. Since, however, it seems that Abner did not really kill Asahel—and even, perhaps, that Asahel was not really Joab's brother at all—this explanation must be rejected. But it ties into the larger theme of the David story that we have already seen over and over: the exoneration of David for the deaths of his enemies. This case is a particularly tricky one, however, as even the Bible admits that it was David's own general who killed Abner. To deal with this, the Bible gives Joab a personal motivation for the murder quite apart from any connection with David, and David is portrayed as being appalled at Joab's actions: "May the guilt fall upon the head of Joab and all his father's house. May the House of Joab never be without someone suffering from a discharge or skin disease, or a male who handles the spindle, or one who falls by the sword, or one lacking bread" (2 Sam. 3:29). And later: "Those men, the sons of Zeruiah, are too savage for me. May Yahweh requite the evildoer for his evil!" (3:39). Yet, for all his talk, David takes no action against Joab; he remains David's commander for the entirety of David's reign. The over-the-top condemnation of Joab is exceeded only by David's own proclamations of innocence: "I and my kingdom are forever innocent before Yahweh of shedding the blood of Abner son of Ner" (3:28). As he did with Saul and Jonathan, David intones a dirge over Abner—the man he had been fighting against for years. And as with Saul and Jonathan, David puts on a public display of mourning, rending his clothes, wearing sackcloth, lamenting, and fasting. David even personally walks behind Abner's body as it is taken to be buried, and he weeps aloud by Abner's grave.[15] If all of this weren't enough, the biblical narrators remind us again and again that David had nothing to do with Abner's death—that when Abner left David's side, he was absolutely fine: "David dismissed Abner, who went away unharmed" (3:21); "Abner was no longer with David in

Hebron, for he had been dismissed and had gone away unharmed" (3:22); "Joab was told, 'Abner son of Ner had come to the king, was dismissed by him, and went away unharmed,'" (3:23); "That day all the people and all Israel knew that it had not been the king's will to kill Abner son of Ner" (3:37)—and if "all Israel" in the story knew it, then "all Israel," the story's audience, is expected to know it, too. This defense of David, reformulated and reiterated in almost every verse of the narrative, is simply too much to believe.

Far more likely is the simpler solution: that David instructed Joab to kill Abner, perhaps after Abner had left his meeting with David so as to avoid suspicion.[16] This is the counternarrative that the Bible is trying to defend against, and it is also sensible from David's position—if, by this point, we have come to accept that David regularly finds murder to be a sensible solution to a problem. At first, it does not seem like a wise choice on David's part: wasn't Abner about to turn all of Israel over to David? Isn't this what David wanted, in the end?

David did want control of the north, but he was smart enough to see that Abner was negotiating from a position of weakness. After years of war, Abner's overtures signaled that the Israelite forces were on the verge of complete defeat. This was a last-ditch effort, though it was probably the best move Abner had. David hardly needed or wanted to share power with anyone. Tribute and military service are valuable substitutes for warfare when the dominant party is far away and the cost of moving troops to the conquered territory is high. But David was close enough that he could enter Israel at a moment's notice, and even return to Judah in the same day, as in the battle at Gibeon. In short, Abner could not offer anything that David could not take for himself. What's more, if Abner really was the power in Israel, then David would have recognized that the best way to slay the beast is to cut off its head. Without Abner to lead Israel, the northern kingdom would be utterly lost, with only the figurehead Ishbaal in place—and Ishbaal, by sending Michal, had already effectively signaled his abdication of the throne. With Abner's death, the north lay open to David.

The Death of Ishbaal

THE EFFECT OF ABNER'S death on the north was precisely what David would have anticipated: "When the son of Saul heard that Abner had died in Hebron, his courage failed and all Israel was terrified" (2 Sam. 4:1). The killing of Abner would have been most terrifying to Ishbaal, for through it, David signaled clearly that he was not interested in concluding this conflict by diplomatic means. David would give no consideration to Ishbaal, who had been willing to relinquish his throne in the name of peace. That option was now clearly off the table. Ishbaal had rendered himself a nonentity—and now he was about to realize that fate in the most tangible of ways.

Without a figure of power at the head of Israel—Abner being dead, and Ishbaal being ineffectual—any last attempt to save the north would logically come from the remaining national institution: the military. But there was little the military could do to spare Israel from being overwhelmed by David's army. Only one path remained, only one option for avoiding the inevitable. And so it should not be a surprise that two of Ishbaal's officers, Rechab and Baanah from the tribe of Benjamin, entered Ishbaal's house at night and killed him, removing his head and taking it to David with an obsequious message: "Here is the head of your enemy, Ishbaal son of Saul, who sought your life. This day Yahweh has avenged my lord the king upon Saul and his offspring" (2 Sam. 4:8). Their intentions are clear enough: by killing Ishbaal and taking his head to Hebron, Rechab and Baanah would have been presenting the kingdom to David. They had performed the dirty work, leaving David free to enter the north without further bloodshed.

The two officers also had personal motives: they displayed their loyalty to their new sovereign, and they may have hoped for some preferential treatment as a result. They also may have been motivated by their tribal affiliation. Benjamin was the territory farthest to the south in the northern kingdom, directly bordering on David's kingdom of Judah. If David did decide to engage in a full-out assault on the north, Benjamin would be the first area to bear the brunt of the action. What's more, Saul was from Benjamin, and therefore Ishbaal was also. It thus may have been Benjamin's responsibility to take care of the Ishbaal problem. Or at least Rechab and Baanah may have thought that David would trust that all of Israel supported the decision only if it was Saul's own tribe that did the deed.

Unfortunately for Rechab and Baanah, they did not realize the depth of David's concern for appearances. The death of Ishbaal was all to David's good, but if it looked as if David had happily accepted Ishbaal's head, won not in battle but by cowardly subterfuge, the ramifications for public perception would be unacceptable. Rechab and Baanah died on the spot, struck down by David's men, their bodies mutilated and publicly displayed as if to say, as usual, "David did not approve of this."[17]

This episode should be very familiar to the reader of the David story, its course almost predictable: it is a nearly perfect parallel to the story of the Amalekite who claimed before David responsibility for Saul's death and was killed for it. Indeed, the Bible even refers directly to that earlier episode in this one. David says: "The man who told me that Saul was dead thought he was bringing good news. But instead of rewarding him for the news, I seized and killed him in Ziklag. How much more, then, when wicked men have killed a blameless man in his bed in his own house?" (2 Sam. 4:10–11). Since we have already seen that the story of the Amalekite looks very much like a literary invention, we may be tempted to think the same in this case: that David was in fact responsible for Ishbaal's death and that this story is a cover-up by the biblical authors.[18] Yet this story has certain features that suggest it might be more believable than would first appear.

Unlike the story of the unnamed Amalekite, this narrative clearly identifies Ishbaal's killers by name and by tribal affiliation. If the story were invented, then this would be akin to biblical slander: the families of Rechab and Baanah, and the entire tribe of Benjamin, would be tagged with the guilt of having killed the rightful Israelite king. But there is no obvious justification for such slander—unlike in the case of the Amalekite, Israel's constant enemy and a common target for the biblical authors. Furthermore, whereas in the story of Saul's death there seemed to be no good reason for the Amalekite to have gone to David—as David was merely a Philistine vassal at the time—now that David is king of Judah, and embroiled in a lengthy war against Israel, the taking of Ishbaal's head to him makes perfect sense. Finally, the motivation of Rechab and Baanah is understandable on every level: personally, tribally, and nationally. They were simply trying to accomplish what Abner had been unable to do.

When we come to this story in the biblical text, we read it in light of the earlier narrative of Saul's death. But in fact, we should do the reverse: this story is the historically accurate one, and the story of the Amalekite is constructed on the basis of the story of Rechab and Baanah. This is a clever move by the biblical authors: since Ishbaal's death does actually appear not to have been David's direct responsibility, then by the literary parallel it is made to appear as if the same is true of the death of Saul.

We are accustomed at this point to expect that every death that accrues to David's benefit is to be laid at his feet: Nabal, Saul, Jonathan, Abner, and now Ishbaal. But though Ishbaal's death did benefit David, it also benefited Rechab and Baanah and the northern kingdom they intended to represent. For the murder of Ishbaal had precisely the desired effect: David did not have to enter Israel with military force.[19] With the death of Ishbaal, David's reign in Israel was assured. Rechab and Baanah paid for it with their lives, but on a national scale the price was worth paying. David would have recognized the value of the gift when Ishbaal's head was presented to him. But this is one death for which he probably did not bear direct responsibility.

David, King of Israel

THE NORTHERN KINGDOM HAD no choice. Its leading power, Abner, was dead by the hand of David; its king, Ishbaal, was dead by the hands of its own people. The only path was to acquiesce to David's power. The biblical notice of David's anointing as king of Israel is almost a complete parallel to that of his anointing in Hebron: "All the elders of Israel came to the king at Hebron, and King David made a covenant with them in Hebron before Yahweh. And they anointed David king over Israel" (2 Sam. 5:3). We may imagine the details of this episode to be essentially identical to those of the earlier anointing. After the death of Ishbaal, David summoned the elders of Israel—in this case, probably tribal leaders—to Hebron, where they were made to offer tribute and swear loyalty to their new monarch.

With this crucial moment, David achieved something entirely new: the consolidation of the kingdoms of Israel in the north and Judah—which he himself had created out of nothing—in the south. For the first time in history, a single kingdom spanned the length of Israel, from Dan in the north to the Negeb desert in the south. For the first time, Israel was united. This was a moment of truly world-changing import. The idea of the people and land of Israel that we find throughout the Bible and beyond, and that is realized to this day in the modern state of Israel, is authentically due to the person of David. There can be no denying the extraordinary change that David wrought on the history of Western civilization. But as in the case of Judah, the glory we attribute to this unification hardly would have been felt by those who lived through it. For them, this was not unification—it was conquest. And at no point in David's long career on the throne would Israel ever think of it otherwise.

There was another party that recognized David's enthronement over Israel as an act of aggression. It is one thing for a vassal to rule over a backwater region. It is equally fine for that vassal to cause trouble for the longtime enemy to the north. But when David became king over Judah and Israel, he crossed the line from useful mercenary to potential threat, and the Philistines were less than pleased.[20] "When the Philistines heard that David had been anointed king in Israel, all the Philistines went up in search of David" (2 Sam. 5:17). The sudden reemergence of the Philistines, entirely absent from the

scene since David had become king in Hebron, reinforces the conclusion that David's kingdom of Judah was a Philistine vassal state.
The idea of a resurgent Israel—now even combined with Judah—was
impossible for the Philistines to accept, and they were intent on doing
something about it.

Possibly the Philistines were putting on a show of force to remind
David of his obligations to them, to see whether he would treat Israel
as a Philistine vassal state as he had Judah. If so, they were to be
disappointed, for David met them with force. Quite probably, the
Philistines were trying to drive a wedge between Judah and Israel,
thus preventing David's access to the north.[21] In this too they would
fail. But even David knew, having just taken the throne, that he was in
no position to meet the Philistines in the open field. So he returned
to his old established ways and retreated to the wilderness. There, he
waited for the Philistines in the hills, where their chariots and war
machines were more an encumbrance than an advantage. The Bible
reports that David delayed attacking until the Philistines had entered
the forest—until he heard "the sounds of marching in the tops of the
baca trees" (2 Sam. 5:24). David, in other words, took advantage once
again of his knowledge of the rough terrain and of the Philistine difficulty fighting in the hills, just as he had under Saul. In repulsing the
Philistines, David was simultaneously declaring—for the first time in
almost ten years—his independence. He had been a loyal vassal, but
his time had come. And with command of both Judah and Israel, he
finally had the resources to stand up for himself.[22]

David's victory against the Philistines was, like every other such
Israelite victory, defensive. He was able to push them back to their
territory, but not to do anything more than that. Yet, as was always
the case, the mere ability to fend off the Philistines was of major
symbolic significance for Israel. David knew what he was doing on
this front, both militarily and politically. Even if Israel saw him as a
foreign conqueror, he was still performing the most important role
of the monarchy: keeping his newly acquired kingdom safe from its
great nemesis.

But he was, nevertheless, a foreign conqueror. Although we think of David as emblematic of Israel, we should remember that he was not an Israelite by any contemporary definition of the term. He was born and reigned in Judah, a non-Israelite territory. That the two regions spoke basically the same language (though with dialectical differences) and worshipped the same deity did not make them the same. Judah was not Israel, as Canada is not the United States. David may be identified with Israel today, but he was an outsider, and he ruled only by imposing his will on the unwilling north.

Saul's Descendants

WITH SAUL AND JONATHAN dead, the war between David and the north decisively concluded in David's favor, and with Israel subjugated, it might seem that David could turn to the task of building up his new kingdom without any further concerns about the legitimacy of his kingship. After all, who could possibly pose a challenge to him at this point? But David was keenly aware of how the Israelites perceived him. They might have no choice now—but they surely would not miss any future opportunity to remove him and replace him with one of their own. No people willingly accepts foreign domination indefinitely, and especially in a culture so centered on kinship ties, a nativist movement was bound to arise as soon as it was feasible. The northern kingdom had known only one family as king, that of Saul, and so it was likely enough that, should any steps be taken to throw off David's yoke, the hopes of the people would rest with someone from Saul's lineage. (This may be contrasted, perhaps ironically, with the constant desire of the Israelites after the exile in 586 BCE that the Davidic kingship would one day be restored.) No matter how spectacular David's reign, he would never be from the royal family of Israel. It was thus imperative that he find a way to remove the potential for a Saulide uprising, and do so as soon as possible.

In the ancient Near East, royal dynasties had an inherent staying power. The patronage system ensured that there would always be those in high positions who remained loyal, even after a king and his family had been deposed. Any faltering on the part of a royal usurper would inevitably lead to calls for the restoration of the old dynasty. Even though kings were often seen as repressive forces by much of society, better the king you know than the king you don't. There was a comfort in familiarity, in tradition. It was harder to maintain a theology of kingship—that the monarch and his descendants ruled by virtue of the divine will and were the earthly stewards of the deity—when there was no continuity.

For all these reasons, it was commonly understood that a usurper would try to eliminate as much of the surviving royal family as possible. We may mention Jehu, the ninth-century BCE king of Israel, who murdered all seventy sons of his predecessor Ahab—and who is praised for it by God: "You have acted well and done what was right in my eyes, having done all that was in my heart toward the House of Ahab" (2 Kings 10:30). Any remnant of the former dynasty was a potential threat to the new regime. This principle would have been familiar to anyone in the ancient Near East, and even into more recent times, as Machiavelli knew: "To possess [dominions] securely it is enough to have eliminated the line of the prince whose dominions they were."[23]

David was therefore in something of a bind. He wanted to ensure that Saul's line would never challenge his rule in Israel, but at the same time he did not want to give the Israelite populace any reason to detest him further. He was already established as king—to eliminate Saul's remaining descendants at the height of his new powers would appear to be an act of unprovoked cruelty. What David needed was an excuse to get rid of Saul's descendants. And, eventually, he found one.

Later in David's reign, according to 2 Samuel 21:1, there was a famine in the land. Famine was not an uncommon occurrence in ancient Israel.[24] The agricultural system hung by a thread on what little rain fell in the region, and it was a precarious situation: any reduction in rainfall had disastrous consequences. Just a few fewer inches of rain per year, and what was once marginally fertile land was transformed into virtual desert. For the ancient Israelites, as for people through-out the ancient Near East, rain, like everything else, was controlled by the deity. And the deity's decisions regarding rainfall were, in turn, tied to Israel's behavior. Thus in the Bible we find passages explaining that the reward for Israel's obedience is "rains in their season, so that the earth shall yield its produce" (Lev. 26:4); "Yahweh will open for you his bounteous store, the heavens, to provide rain for your land in season" (Deut. 28:12). But if rain was considered a blessing, then drought—along with its inevitable result, famine—was a curse: "I will make your skies like iron and your earth like copper. . . . Your land shall not yield its produce" (Lev. 26:19–20); "Yahweh will make the rain of your land dust, and sand shall come down upon you from the sky" (Deut. 28:24). Once obedience was tied to climate, climate was necessarily tied to obedience. Thus if there was famine, it was only logical to look for the reason among the Israelite people.

The most obvious place to look first, however, was the king him-self. When the nation suffered, who could be to blame but the nation's sole representative, the individual in whose name the nation acted?[25] For David more than most, the famine represented a potential crisis. His claim to the kingship was tenuous enough; now it might appear as if God too had turned against him. Remarkably, however, David—or at least the Bible—found a way to turn this crisis on its head and use it to justify the destruction of what remained of Saul's line.

According to the biblical story, David asked God what had caused the famine and received a startling reply: "It is because of the bloodguilt of Saul and his house, for he put the Gibeonites to death" (2 Sam. 21:1). Immediately, we know that the famine is not David's fault—remarkably, it is Saul's fault. To understand why, we have to understand who the Gibeonites were and what the Bible has told us of them to this point.

The inhabitants of Gibeon were not considered ethnically Israel-ite. They seem to have been an enclave of a native Canaanite popu-lation that was not absorbed by the emerging Israelite people when the Israelites settled in the central hill country of Canaan.[26] As Israel developed traditions about the conquest of the land under Joshua, in which it was declared that they would wipe out all of the native populations, the presence of these foreigners in their midst required explanation: why were they permitted to survive? The answer came in the story now found in Joshua 9. The Gibeonites saw that Joshua and Israel had razed the cities of Jericho and Ai, the first two towns destroyed in the conquest, and hatched a plan to avoid the same fate. They sent messengers to Joshua presenting themselves not as native Canaanites, but as outsiders, who were therefore not subject to the same destruction visited upon the Canaanites. They offered to be Israel's servants, and so Joshua made an agreement with them that their people would be spared. Soon enough, the truth was revealed, and Israel realized that it had made an oath of friendship with one of the peoples that it had been instructed to obliterate. But the oath was sworn, and it could not be undone. This, then, is the story of how Gibeon came to live among Israel even though it was not really an Israelite population.

Fast-forward to David's time: if Saul had truly tried to wipe out the Gibeonites, perhaps in some moment of nativist zeal, he had thereby violated the oath that Joshua had made centuries earlier and thus brought about God's wrath in the form of the famine. David therefore asked the Gibeonites what he could do for them to make restitution for Saul's actions. Their answer was predictable: hand over Saul's remaining descendants so we can kill them. David had no choice but to acquiesce—the fate of the nation was at stake. Two of Saul's children, through his concubine Rizpah—the same concubine whom Abner had been accused of sleeping with—and five of his grandchildren through his eldest daughter Merab were killed in Gibeon, thus eliminating all of Saul's descendants (all but one, to whom we will turn presently).

This story is pure literary invention. Its roots are found in a different biblical book, in a different biblical story, one that was itself invented to explain the anomaly of Gibeon's ethnic distinction from the rest of Israel. It depends on laws from Deuteronomy and narratives from Joshua. It is fiction built upon fiction. And its coincidences are too hard to overlook. Why should Saul's crime be punished with famine only now, years after Saul supposedly oppressed the Gibeonites? Why do we learn only at this point that Saul did so, instead of during the account of his reign?[27] Is it believable that the Gibeonites should independently ask for the one thing David most desired? Is it believable that David's one course for saving Israel was the murder of Saul's family?

Reconstructing what actually happened, however, is not a simple matter. We can posit at least one basic aspect: it was David who was responsible for the deaths of Saul's descendants. But was Gibeon really involved? Was there really a famine? Did the story occur when the Bible says it did?

Gibeon may have had a part to play—not because Saul had tried to eliminate the Gibeonites, for there is no record of this having actually happened, but perhaps because Gibeon was never loyal to Saul.[28] Nowhere is it said that Gibeon was part of Saul's kingdom. The city was an independent territory within Israel's borders. This being the case, the Gibeonites' assistance in this matter may have been a means of currying favor with David. We may even imagine that this story is the real explanation of how Gibeon became part of Israel: in order to ensure that David would not try to conquer them by force, the Gibeonites agreed to dispatch Saul's descendants and become part of David's kingdom peacefully. Others had recognized that eliminating David's enemies might be a way to win his good graces. Gibeon may have had the same idea. It is also possible that Gibeon had made some sort of deal with David even earlier. The battle between Abner and Joab mentioned above took place at none other than Gibeon—which, if it was an independent territory, is something of a strange place to fight. Note, however, how the Bible presents the setting of the battle: Abner "marched out from Mahanaim to Gibeon," after which Joab came to confront him (2 Sam. 2:12–13). It is thus conceivable that Abner went to Gibeon not to meet David's forces, but to attack Gibeon itself, to make it part of Ishbaal's kingdom—and that

Joab went not only to fight Abner, but to protect Gibeon and keep it out of northern hands. Thus Gibeon's part in the deaths of Saul's sons may have been a way of thanking David for his support.

As for the famine, it seems a bit of a contrivance. The famine is part of the literary and theological framework of the narrative. It is the precipitating event for the entire narrative, found in the first verse of the story, and the relief from the famine forms the story's conclusion: "They did all that the king had commanded, and thereafter God responded to the plea for the land" (2 Sam. 21:14). There is no question that famines occurred in Israel, but one that begins because of Saul's actions and ends because Saul's descendants were killed by the Gibeonites is a dramatic event, not a climatic one.

If the famine is discounted, then we are left to wonder when Saul's descendants really died. The Bible is unclear on this count: rather than date the famine relative to other events in David's reign, it says only that "there was a famine in the days of David" (2 Sam. 21:1). We may be meant to understand that this occurred late in David's kingship, as the story comes almost at the end of 2 Samuel, but we may also conjecture that the authors' lack of a specific timeline indicates otherwise.[29] In fact, it strains credulity to imagine that David would leave Saul's descendants alive, as a lingering threat to his kingship, for any significant length of time. In the other biblical examples of a new ruler eliminating the previous royal family, the murders take place immediately. Of all people, David was not one to permit any challenges to remain, especially ones that could be so easily resolved. It is most likely, then, that David had Saul's descendants killed shortly after he became king in Israel. But it was one thing to have participated in the battle that led to Saul's and Jonathan's deaths, where blame could be cast on the Philistines. The killing of Saul's remaining descendants would be much harder to attribute to anyone but David, as he would be the only one to benefit. Thus the invention of the story of Saul's attempt to conquer Gibeon. David had Gibeon take responsibility for eliminating Saul's descendants, probably in exchange for a peace treaty. Now, finally, David could be confident that, whatever else might come his way, he no longer had anything to fear from Saul. Many years after he had first entered Saul's service, the battle between Saul and David was finally concluded. David stood alone.

Meribbaal

TO BE MORE ACCURATE, David stood nearly alone. One descendant of Saul remained alive—not by chance, but very much by David's choice. Jonathan, Saul's eldest son, had a son of his own. His name was Meribbaal, probably meaning "the lord is my master." At least, this is how he is known in Chronicles. In Samuel, his name has been changed, just as Ishbaal's was. We know him as Mephibosheth.[30]

Meribbaal may have been Saul's grandson, and thus in line for the throne, but he almost certainly would never have held it, even in the absence of David. For Meribbaal was disabled, his feet having been crushed in an early childhood accident. Modern notions may abhor the idea that such a disability should prevent someone from achieving high office. But it was less than a century ago that Franklin Roosevelt felt compelled to hide the fact that he needed to use a wheelchair because of the debilitating effects of polio. In the ancient world, it was even less thinkable that a physically impaired person should rule. Kings were, in ancient Israel and everywhere in the Near East, servants of God, divinely ordained and anointed. For Israel, which saw God as the perfect power behind all creation, imperfections in that creation were a problem. Though people with such imperfections obviously could not be eliminated, they could be withheld from positions where they would remind others of God's creative mistakes. Thus priests, who served before God in the sanctuary, could have no physical impairments (Lev. 21:17–23). Sacrificial animals, brought before God as offerings, could not be blemished in any way (Lev. 22:17–25). So too the king, who stood before God as the leader of God's people, was expected to be physically perfect. Consider the description of Saul, who "stood a head taller than all the people" and of whom Samuel said, "There is none like him among all the people" (1 Sam. 10:23–24). Or consider David, who, even though God tells Samuel to "pay no attention to his appearance or stature" (16:7), is described as "ruddy-cheeked, bright-eyed, and handsome" (16:12).

It is not that a physically impaired person was of no use to society. An ancient Sumerian myth called "Enki and Ninmah" tells of the creation of humans by the god Enki.[31] Rejoicing in his accomplishment, he and the goddess Ninmah relax with some beer and find themselves playing a drinking game: Ninmah creates imperfect humans, and Enki finds a place for them in the new human society. The blind man becomes a musician, the eunuch becomes a courtier, and the one whose feet are crippled becomes a metalsmith. This is essentially the same notion that we find in Greek mythology, in which the physically impaired deity Hephaestus spends his days forging the weapons of the gods. These myths, distant from each other in both time and place, agree not only on what the disabled man's role is, but also on what his role is not: he is no king, even if he might be a deity. In large part, this was probably due to the fact that the disabled man could not perform the most important task of the king: to lead the nation to war. Meribbaal may have been of royal descent, but he could never take on the practical duties of being king.[32]

The situation could hardly be more perfect for David. He did not need to eliminate Meribbaal, for Meribbaal posed no real threat. Quite the contrary: it was entirely in David's interest to keep him alive. After Meribbaal, the next in line could well be someone with the physical ability and ambition to challenge David. As long as Meribbaal remained safe, however, the royal succession would be in a holding pattern: Israel might desire that one of Saul's descendants reclaim the throne, but the sole remaining heir was incapable of doing so.

Keeping Meribbaal alive also would provide David with another opportunity to score political points with his new kingdom. With the deaths of Saul and his descendants, David must have seemed not only cruel, but also deeply insensitive to the attachment that Israel felt for its only royal family. Meribbaal provided an opportunity for David to demonstrate the opposite: that David had never been anti-Saul, but that the previous deaths were merely the result of circumstance. Given the chance to display royal generosity, David could point readily to Meribbaal. Thus the Bible presents David as asking, "Is there anyone still left of the House of Saul with whom I can keep faith for the sake of Jonathan?" (2 Sam. 9:1). No one could accuse David of seeking to obliterate Saul's name from history. His care for Meribbaal would prove his affection for the traditions of the north.

David summoned Meribbaal to him, an invitation that undoubtedly would have been terrifying for the young man. After all, the last northerner to be personally invited to see David was Abner, and the previous heir to the throne was Ishbaal—both now dead. Meribbaal could have no idea what David's intentions were. Thus he made his fealty to David as clear as possible. Upon arriving, he "fell on his face and prostrated himself" (2 Sam. 9:6), in the standard Near Eastern gesture of subjugation.[33] When David spoke his name, Meribbaal's response was equally abject: "At your service" (9:6). But Meribbaal need not have worried. David had no intention of harming him and told him, "Don't be afraid, for I will keep faith with you for the sake of your father Jonathan" (9:7). Then, in an act of ostensible generosity, David laid out the terms of this faithfulness: "I will give you back all the land of your grandfather Saul, and you shall always eat at my table" (9:7).

Most readers understand this as true kindness: David is promising to care for Meribbaal, even perhaps to treat him as part of the royal court. David's actions are, however, less altruistic than they appear. By decreeing that Meribbaal would eat with David "always," David was in essence confining him to house arrest in the palace. Though Meribbaal would not die, he would be a glorified prisoner, kept constantly under David's watchful eye. This practice of royal house arrest is known from elsewhere in the ancient Near East. In fact, ironically, it is precisely what happens at the end of the Davidic dynasty. In the very last verse of the books of Kings, after the kingdom of Judah has been destroyed by the Babylonians and its leaders killed or exiled, we hear of the fate of the last surviving Davidic monarch, Jehoiachin. Jehoiachin, who had long been imprisoned in Babylon, was released from his cell and brought to the court of the Babylonian king Evil-merodach. There, "he ate before [the king] always, all the days of his life" (2 Kings 25:29). The parallels between that story and the story of Meribbaal are apparent. The Babylonians had conquered Judah, just as David had vanquished the north. There was no surviving administrative structure to support the return of the Davidic monarchy, just as there was no structure to support the return of Saul's family to power. And just as the Davidic monarchy would never resume after the house arrest of Jehoiachin, so Saul's line would never regain the throne after the confinement of Meribbaal. In both cases the historical status of the royal line is acknowledged, but at the same time a firm statement is made that that royal line's time has passed. David's actions toward Meribbaal are only an outward show of generosity. In fact, they are a death sentence for the House of Saul.

What should we make, then, of David's promise to grant to Meribbaal all of Saul's land? This appears to be a kindness, as Saul's royal lands would have been quite considerable, at least by the standards of ancient Israel. Yet this too is deceptive. After all, Meribbaal, confined to David's court, could hardly take advantage of the property. In fact, David did something quite clever here. He struck a deal with a man named Ziba, Saul's former steward: "You and your sons and your servants shall work the land for Meribbaal and shall bring in its yield to provide food for your master's grandson to eat" (2 Sam. 9:10). That is, Saul's landholdings may belong nominally to Meribbaal, but they will be worked by Ziba and his family, who are thereby indebted to David. What's more, this arrangement means that even though Meribbaal is eating at the king's table, he is not eating of the king's food. He is, in effect, paying for his own imprisonment.[34] Again, David has turned an ostensibly kind gesture to his own benefit.

The fact that David had the authority to grant Saul's former lands to Meribbaal is also revealing. Traditionally, Israelite property was inviolable, held in perpetuity by the family, clan, and tribe. Even if it was necessary to sell the land, it was to be returned to its original owners after a time (Lev. 26:10–34). Israel's territories were considered to have been granted to them by God himself at the moment of Joshua's conquest. This was a cultural understanding that Saul never violated—nowhere is it intimated that he claimed any authority over the landholdings of his subjects. David, on the other hand, arrogated this authority to himself, in line with the regular practices of other ancient Near Eastern monarchies.[35] This must have been a shock to the Israelite population, who would have felt that their ancestral lands were suddenly in jeopardy of being seized by the crown.[36] But David's power was such that he could overturn this long-standing tradition without fear of retribution.[37]

Given David's well-established tendency to dispatch by the sword those who stood in his way, it is revealing that he took another path with Meribbaal. The value of Meribbaal's life must have been higher for David than his death. And indeed, David's treatment of Meribbaal is a stroke of brilliant diplomacy. With one deft move he elevated to prominence an heir who could never become king, kept under close watch his most obvious opponent (even if Meribbaal was only a symbolic threat), financed Meribbaal's imprisonment with Meribbaal's own land, created a dependent in charge of Saul's property in Ziba, and in all of this displayed to Israel his implicit loyalty to the memory of Saul's kingship.

But one final step needed to be taken with regard to Saul's family, now that they were no longer a threat. David collected the bones of Saul and Jonathan from Jabesh-Gilead, where they had been resting since the battle at Mount Gilboa, and the bodies of Saul's other descendants killed at Gibeon and buried them in the family tomb of Saul's father, in the territory of Benjamin. This postmortem repatriation was highly symbolic. Family tombs were of great significance in ancient Israel. They formed a major part of a family's title to the land: if one's descendants were buried there, then no one else could claim possession. The family tomb was effectively a deed of ownership. The tomb was also a locus for religious observance. In early Israel, there was a well-established cult of the dead. Living descendants offered sacrifices and poured libations at the gravesites of their ancestors, in the hopes that the deceased would protect them from the great beyond.[38]

It was thus of utmost importance that those who died be returned to their family tombs. At the same time, it meant that David had every reason to want to prevent Saul and Jonathan (and Ishbaal, who was buried in Hebron) from being buried in Benjamin. Without the body of the king there, the claim of Saul's descendants to their land was weakened. And, more important, there could be no cult of the dead on Saul's behalf. As long as the king remained elsewhere, there would be no place for anyone to rally to Saul's memory. The one physical location where Saul could be venerated would be empty.

For David to be willing to return the bones of Saul and his descendants to the family tomb, then, signals his growing sense of security. The threat of a Saulide uprising had passed, permanently. Returning the bones would have no adverse consequences and might just score David some points on the political front. It was a prudent and gracious move.

FROM THE MOMENT OF Saul's death to the moment his bones were returned to Benjamin, David had come a remarkably long way. He began as a vassal of the Philistines, a servant of foreigners, and ended as the king of a newly united Judah and Israel. At every step, David took advantage of his changing situation. He used the powerful support of the Philistines to consolidate his rule over Judah. He used his new power over Judah to confront and wear down Abner and Ishbaal. He used the increasing weakness of the north against itself, driving Abner to defect and Ishbaal's killers to turn traitor. He used Ishbaal's death to become king in Israel. He used the combined forces of Judah and Israel to declare his independence from and to fend off the Philistines. He used both murder and diplomacy to control the remainder of Saul's line.

David was a brilliant and ruthless tactician. Nothing he did was unexpected or particularly innovative within the larger standards of the ancient world in which he lived—he was simply good at what he did. Of course, attaining the throne and removing the threat of Saul's descendants was just the beginning. We now turn to the question of what David actually achieved while he was on the throne. How did he create his new kingdom in his image?

CHAPTER 5

David's Kingdom

THE MYTH OF NATIONAL AND RELIGIOUS ORIGINS

To be remembered as a glorious king, one must have reigned over a glorious kingdom. In Israel's cultural memory, no kingdom was more glorious than the united Israel and Judah under David. This was an easy period to glorify—not only was it the only time when the northern and southern kingdoms were ruled by a single monarch, but it lasted for only two generations, under David and then Solomon, before disintegrating. The best times are always those of the irrecoverable past, largely because that past can be reshaped in our memory, made finer than it ever really was or could have been.

David is credited with the creation of the nation of Israel. He established the eternal capital, Jerusalem, where he inaugurated the worship of Yahweh. And he expanded Israel's borders through the conquest of many neighboring nations. Some of this is true; some is false. Much of it is either exaggerated or misunderstood. It is our task to understand what David actually accomplished, and why.

The New Capital

ONE OF DAVID'S FIRST acts upon becoming king of Israel was to conquer Jerusalem and establish it as his new capital. It was a smart choice. Jerusalem was an ancient city, and in fact an ancient capital city.[1] Archaeological discoveries have revealed that the city was probably inhabited as early as the fourth millennium BCE.[2] Its location, atop one of the higher hills in the area and fed by a reliable water source, made it a natural place to settle. There are references to Jerusalem in Egyptian texts from the twentieth century BCE, and in the fourteenth century BCE Jerusalem was the capital of a significant territory in the hills of Judah, complete with a king (albeit a vassal of Egypt). As with his choice of Hebron in Judah, David's choice of a capital had historical and cultural resonance.

Before David arrived, however, Jerusalem and its surrounding area had fallen under the control of a people known as the Jebusites. Like the Gibeonites, the Jebusites were a non-Israelite population. They were well enough ensconced in Jerusalem that the expansion of the Israelites throughout the surrounding region was not sufficient to displace them. This is reflected in the biblical account of the conquest, in which, among the lists of the many regions Joshua conquered, we find the notice that "the people of Judah could not dispossess the Jebusites, the inhabitants of Jerusalem" (Josh. 15:63). Thus Jerusalem goes unmentioned in the stories of Saul's reign, because, like Gibeon, it was not part of Saul's kingdom. For David, this presented an opportunity: rather than make his capital in part of Saul's former territory, or in the backwater of Judah, he could establish his own place, one with historical power but without any baggage from the Saulide legacy. Moreover, David could capture Jerusalem with his personal militia, rather than with any Judahite or Israelite help, and thereby turn the city into something of a private royal fiefdom—rightly called the "City of David."[3]

Jerusalem was also well located for David's purposes. As David was the first king to rule both Judah and Israel, it was important that he choose a capital that would not appear to show favoritism toward either. Jerusalem is situated almost directly on the border between the two. The obvious modern analogy is the choice of Washington, D.C., as the new capital of the United States, positioned as it is on the line between the northern and southern states. We see David's choice of Jerusalem as almost divinely inspired, since we know that the city became the spiritual capital of the Judeo-Christian faith. The Bible, written after Jerusalem was well established as the holy city of Israel, takes the same perspective. But for David, the choice was purely tactical, a considered political move.[4]

The actual conquest of the city is narrated quite briefly in the Bible. As David and his forces were strong enough to withstand the attacks of the Philistines, it is reasonable to assume that the capture of Jerusalem was a relatively straightforward affair. What is perhaps lost in the brevity of the narrative is the way that David undid centuries of Jerusalem's independence. We are accustomed to thinking of the Jebusites as the enemy—after all, they are frequently listed as one of the indigenous nations that the Israelites were to dispossess during the conquest and are therefore aligned with the Canaanites. Yet in reality, the Jebusites had lived peacefully among the early Israelites for generations, and Jerusalem had been a proud and independent city for millennia. It is not surprising that David should have wanted it as his capital, nor that he would have taken what he wanted. But if we put ourselves in the place of the Jebusites, we may recognize just how sudden and violent an upheaval the conquest of the city was. It is hard to mourn a people who no longer exist. But the Jebusites, like every other ancient populace, had their own culture, their own history, their own narratives that had been cultivated for centuries. The mutual understanding between the Jebusites and the Israelites was undone in the flash of an eye. The creation of David's kingdom meant the destruction of the Jebusites. In fact, the Jebusites would become a metaphor for an obliterated people. In the book of the prophet Zechariah, the destruction of the Philistine cities is predicted, and of Ekron it is said, "Ekron shall be like the Jebusites" (9:7). David

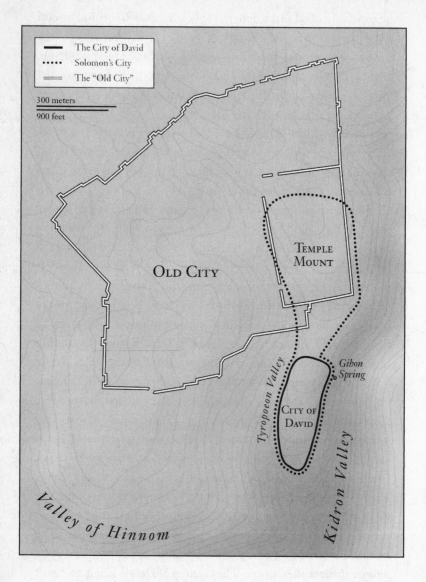

Jerusalem

created a new nation, but in doing so he wiped another clean off the map. The Bible, and the traditions that emerged from it, consider this justified by the results, by the transformation of the city into Israel's glorious capital. But if it happened today, we would call it genocide.

The modern tourist walking the streets of Jerusalem's old city can still feel the power of the ancient site. As one passes through one of the seven gates embedded in the mighty walls, a few short turns lead to the Temple Mount, where the Wailing Wall supports the enormous platform on which the temple once stood, now dominated by the Dome of the Rock. From the top of the Temple Mount one can see the full panorama of hills and valleys all around, and one can sense how this place would have been the center of the kingdom. It all appears utterly befitting the capital city of the great David.

What most people do not realize, however, is that the Jerusalem they visit and worship in today has virtually nothing to do with the Jerusalem of David. The Wailing Wall is from the first century BCE, built by Herod the Great. The walls and gates are from the sixteenth century CE and were constructed by the Muslim conqueror Suleiman the Magnificent. The tourist site known as David's Tomb is a medieval building in very much the wrong location for David's actual burial site. The old city is not David's city.

David's city does remain, however, though few visitors find their way there. David's capital comprised what is now known as the City of David, a small spur to the southeast of the Temple Mount, outside of Suleiman's walls. It doesn't have the appearance of a great capital. For one thing, it is covered with private Israeli and Arab homes, with archaeological excavations only gradually revealing the ancient structures beneath. What's more, from top to bottom it is little more than half a kilometer in length, and from side to side, no more than a quarter of a kilometer. It is a tiny area. This was the Jerusalem that was settled and fortified in the millennia before David, and it was from here that a large swath of the hill country was governed in the second millennium BCE. Compared with the great imperial capitals of Egypt and Mesopotamia, or even with the relatively enormous cities of the

Philistines, the Jerusalem of David's time was incredibly small. Its size reminds us that the sort of magnificence we associate with kings and capitals today was not necessarily a feature of early Israel.[5] After all, Saul ruled from underneath a tree in his hometown.

One of the major reasons that capitals both ancient and modern tend to be larger than the average city—or tiny village—is that they need space to house and support all of the officials required for the task of governing. The more extensive the administrative structures, the more expansive the physical structures. Thus the tininess of David's capital tells us something important about the nature of his administration. Despite ruling over a far larger territory than any Israelite before him, David did not fundamentally change the nature of Israelite leadership in a single generation. He imposed no national programs of taxation or construction—the types of programs that require robust centralized oversight. Such programs were foreign to Israel, literally: Israel's only experience with enforced taxation and labor would have been during its very early history, even before it was truly Israel, when Canaan was a vassal state of the powerful Egyptian empire.[6] Since it had come into its own, however, Israel had survived without that sort of centralized authority, and even after the monarchy was instituted this did not change. At most, Saul would on occasion require the towns under his authority to provide troops for military actions. David was very much in the same mold.

Indeed, like Saul, David maintained a limited administrative structure, surrounding himself with only a handful of people whom he felt he could trust (2 Sam. 8:16–18; 1 Chron. 18:15–17). Just as Saul's army commander was a relative, his cousin Abner, so too David chose a kinsman, in this case a nephew, as his commander: Joab, the son of Zeruiah, who according to Chronicles was David's sister.[7] Choosing a family member as chief military officer was prudent: as we have seen, the most likely source of a coup was from the ranks of the army, and so having a relative in that position assured some degree of loyalty. At the same time, by selecting a kinsman who was not in the direct line of succession, David could also be secure in the knowledge that Joab would never have a rightful claim to the throne. Aside from Joab, David's cabinet consisted of Jehoshaphat, a "recorder," probably something of a foreign minister; Shausha (also known as Seraiah), a scribe; and Benaiah, the head of David's personal bodyguards. There was also Adoram, who was in charge of forced labor—though this probably refers to the labor performed by foreigners David defeated, rather than by Israelites. Rounding out the list were David's two main priests, Abiathar and Zadok, both of whom had joined David back when he was living in the wilderness.

As in the case of his kinsman Joab and his old supporters Abiathar and Zadok, when it came to his most important military forces, David stuck to people he knew and trusted and who had been with him for some time. His bodyguards, known as the Cherethites and Pelethites, were probably of Philistine origin, as their titles, derived from Greek, suggest.[8] They were joined by six hundred soldiers from Gath under the leadership of a man named Ittai, who had been with David since his days in Ziklag. David's core soldiers, in other words, were his old Philistine compatriots, trustworthy perhaps precisely because they were foreigners. David's administration was minimal, which accords with the lack of any major national projects attributed to him.

The structures of government would change, in fact, only with Solomon, who seems to have recognized the opportunity that David's newly created united kingdom offered for the imposition of centralized authority. It is Solomon who created a taxation system for the nation and who imposed forced labor on the populace for the construction of new monumental buildings—with, as we will see, disastrous consequences. If it was a conscious decision at all, David was undoubtedly right to maintain the relatively simple mode of authority with which Israel had long been familiar. His power was an imposition upon the people no less than Solomon's, but David's kingship, like Saul's, probably did not affect the everyday life of most Israelites.

Still, David had achieved something beyond Saul, and he was not content to rule from beneath a tree as Saul had. Thus, according to the Bible, his first decision after conquering and refortifying Jerusalem was to have a palace built for himself.[9] This is described in a single verse: "King Hiram of Tyre sent envoys to David with cedar trees, carpenters, and stonemasons; and they built a palace for David" (2 Sam. 5:11). We know nothing of the dimensions of this palace, though given the relatively restricted space in the City of David, it could not have been very large. We are also unsure of its exact location within David's Jerusalem, though recent archaeological excavations have uncovered what may be part of it.[10] What separated a palace from a normal residence was its size and, perhaps more important, its mode of construction. Whereas the usual Israelite home was basically four rooms with walls made of mud-brick, a royal building was made of cedar and stone and required advanced knowledge of carpentry and masonry. This explains the perhaps unexpected appearance of the king of Tyre in the middle of the David story.

David's palace was the first Israelite palace to be built. The Israelites had no experience with monumental construction; they had never had either a need to build anything on such a scale or the centralized administration to bring such a project to fruition. The nearest culture with such expertise was the Philistines—David may have come up with the idea of a palace from seeing the one in Gath when he had been a vassal of Achish—but it probably would have been bad form for David to ask them for help in this particular matter. Thus the next closest would have been the Phoenicians, living on the coast north of Israel. Tyre, an ancient and exceptionally wealthy seaport, was one of the great Phoenician cities and the closest to Israelite territory. If David wanted a palace, Tyre was the place to turn. Though the Bible suggests that Hiram sent supplies for the palace to David out of the goodness of his heart, or perhaps in recognition of David's newly acquired status, it is certain that David paid for Hiram's services. The Phoenicians were merchants, after all—they were not about to give their services away for nothing.

Every palace is a symbol, and David's was no exception. Israel had entered a new era under him, and he was very aware of it. He was not a king like Saul, accepted by the people as a military leader. He was a conqueror, ruling by force, and his power required a physical manifestation unlike anything Israel had seen before. He would not live as everyone else lived; his dwelling would be that of a foreigner. By building himself a royal home, David announced, again, his distinction among all of Israel. Saul was merely an elevated Israelite. David was a monarch.

David and the Ark of the Covenant

JERUSALEM IS FAMOUS, HOWEVER, not for being the administrative center of Israel, but for being its religious center. And perhaps David's most significant achievement as king, at least in terms of the lasting effects of his actions, was to turn this former Jebusite city into the heart of Israel's faith.

The Israelite landscape in David's time was dotted with sanctuaries, local shrines serving the needs of one or more communities. There was little sense of a "national" religion. Though Israel's sanctuaries were devoted to the same god, and probably shared many similar cultic practices, they were not outlets of a centralized cult, but rather independent "mom-and-pop" operations, with priestly lineages stretching back into the distant past.[11] Many of these sanctuaries were very ancient and had their own legends attached to them. The shrine at Bethel, for example, claimed that its sanctity derived from having been the spot where God spoke to the ancestor Jacob, a claim that has found its way into the Bible in multiple places.[12] Others told different stories, and some relied merely on their long standing in the community. And one shrine laid claim to a physical object that was understood to be God's very throne: the ark of the covenant.

For all of its importance, we know remarkably little about the ark. Though it is described in some detail in the Bible, it is described in contradictory ways. In Exodus, it is depicted as a gold-plated box with a golden cover, mounted by golden cherubim (not pudgy babies, but fearsome winged lions). In Deuteronomy, by contrast, it is described as a plain wooden box without adornment. Its function is also differently conceived: in Exodus it is the physical seat of God, the center of God's literal dwelling-place, the Tabernacle, and it is from atop the ark that God communicates with Moses. In Deuteronomy, it is merely the receptacle for the tablets of the Decalogue (the Ten Commandments), kept in the innermost sanctum of the temple. In yet a third passage, in Numbers, the ark is used as a palladium, a sort of military standard that went before the Israelites on their march through the wilderness.

In truth, the ark is most easily understood as the Israelite equivalent of an idol. That is, it is the physical representation of the deity—not the form of the deity, but its presence in the midst of the people. Like an idol in a non-Israelite temple, the ark stood in the innermost sanctum, the place where the deity was understood to dwell. Just as copies of ancient Near Eastern treaties were placed in the temples of the respective parties so that the gods could act as witnesses, the ark—at least in Deuteronomy—was the location of the most fundamental covenant between God and Israel. And just as non-Israelites took their idols out to battle with them to guarantee victory, so too the Israelites took the ark with them. Obviously, it was not really an idol—it was not worshipped as if it were God himself. But in its function it was the symbolic equivalent.

The ark belonged originally to the sanctuary at Shiloh, a major cultic site in the hills of Ephraim. It is likely that its presence there played a significant role in the importance of Shiloh's sanctuary, investing it with special sanctity and probably making it a center for pilgrimages. In the book of Joshua, Shiloh is where the Israelites assembled to apportion the newly conquered promised land (18:1). It is to Shiloh that Elkanah and his wife Hannah went annually to offer sacrifices, where Hannah prayed for a son, and where Samuel spent his youth and received his call from God (1 Sam. 1:3). As the ark was a physical manifestation of God's presence, it was natural for Shiloh to be a center for oracular inquiry, like an Israelite Delphi. Shiloh was not the only sanctuary in Israel, but it was a central cultic site and the only one to lay claim to the ark. For most purposes—for the usual offerings and priestly inquiries—a local sanctuary would suffice. Shiloh would have served as a sanctuary for exceptional occasions.[13]

Among these occasions would have been those rare times when the Israelite tribes came together to defend themselves against external threat—like an attack by the Philistines. At such moments the priests of Shiloh would bear the ark into battle, as a sign that the God of the Israelites was fighting on their behalf. In the battle of Eben-ezer, however, described in 1 Samuel 4, the ark was captured. Though it eventually found its way back into Israelite hands, it would never again reside at Shiloh. It was kept for about a generation in the Gibeonite town of Kiryath-jearim, just east of Jerusalem.[14] And there it remained until David became king and found himself in possession of a capital with no religious significance.[15]

Jerusalem had a cult before David, but it was not an Israelite cult because Jerusalem was not an Israelite city. As the very name of the city shows, Jerusalem—"Foundation of Shalem"—was devoted to an old Semitic deity, Shalem, a god of dusk or of the evening star.[16] To make his capital an Israelite cultic center, therefore, David had to start afresh. But this was not as easy as, say, building a church or synagogue is today. Cultic sites had long histories and associations stretching back into the past that justified their sanctity. David's new capital had none of this. He could hardly get away with making up a story explaining how Jerusalem, a well-known foreign city, was actually of great Israelite religious significance; there could be no founding legend like that of the Bethel cult. What he needed was something tangible, something everyone would recognize as marking God's presence. And the ark was just a few kilometers away.[17]

As with so many other parts of the David story, when we read it in retrospect we take it for granted that the ark should have been brought to Jerusalem. But, as with so much else, this hardly would have been obvious to an Israelite in David's time. If the ark was not to remain in Kiryath-jearim, its rightful place would have been at Shiloh, its traditional home, or at the very least at another established

Israelite sanctuary.[18] The ark did not get to Jerusalem of its own accord. David took it—and it is likely that he took it by force. According even to the biblical account, before going to Kiryath-jearim David "assembled all the picked men of Israel, thirty thousand strong; then David and all the people that were with him set out" (2 Sam. 6:1–2). The biblical authors may want us to understand this as a show of honor, or as a sign of the ark's role in military affairs. But in practical terms, the effect of David and his entire army descending on the town where the ark was held would have been one of implicit, if not explicit, threat.[19] As we have seen, David always took what he wanted whenever he could. What he wanted now was the most important religious emblem in Israel, and he had more than enough men to ensure that he got it. Whatever benefits the inhabitants of Kiryath-jearim enjoyed during the ark's stay in their small town were gone in an instant. Whatever ancient rights Shiloh may have had to the ark were ignored. As with so many other things, the changes that David made to the long-established fabric of Israel's society were unilateral and abrupt.

The biblical story of the ark's journey from Kiryath-jearim to Jerusalem describes quite reasonably how it was loaded onto a cart and conveyed by oxen, accompanied by music and dancing. Where it turns unlikely is in the moment when a man named Uzzah reached for the ark to steady it and was struck down by God on the spot. This episode is nothing more than an etiology for a place named Perez-uzzah, "the breach of Uzzah," and has no historical significance. It does, however, speak to a well-established Israelite tradition that the ark was so holy that it was in fact dangerous. And this tradition explains why it was not immediately taken to Jerusalem but stayed for three months in the house of one Obed-edom. In the biblical narrative, David commanded that the ark be kept there after witnessing the death of Uzzah. In reality, it seems more likely that David wanted to ensure that the tradition of the ark's inherent danger was not one that he needed to fear. Obed-edom was essentially a guinea pig, a royal taster, making sure that the king would not suffer any harm.

One can imagine that the poor man was terrified of his responsibility, though it turned out he had nothing to fear. When it was clear that Obed-edom had experienced no adversity because of the presence of the ark in his home, it continued its delayed procession into the City of David.

The final leg of the ark's journey was accompanied by grand ceremony. After every six steps taken in the procession, David sacrificed an ox and a ram.[20] The symbolism of this ritual would not have been lost on any observer. On the one hand, David was positioning himself as priest—he was taking on the cultic role of sacrificial officiant, making it clear that the ark was now a royal object. Though this confusion of roles may seem unusual from a modern standpoint, in the ancient world, including Israel, it was very common for kings to play a priestly role on special occasions.[21] Doing so was a way to explicitly connect the monarch and the deity, to demonstrate not only that the deity had special care for the king, but that the cultic apparatus was under royal control. By leading the sacrifices before the ark himself, David turned an ethnic and national cultic symbol into a royal cultic symbol. On the other hand, the sheer volume of the sacrifices—an ox and a ram every six steps—would have sent a clear message regarding David's personal wealth. For the average Israelite, an ox or a ram would have been enormously expensive, and sacrifices of such animals would have been rare and reserved for only the most important moments.

It is also noteworthy that these sacrifices were rather unlike any commonly known in Israel. There were essentially two types of sacrifice: burnt offerings, during which the entire animal was burned on the altar, and well-being offerings, during which part of the animal was burned and part consumed by the offerer. Each sacrifice had a specific function: burnt offerings to curry God's favor or express thanks, and well-being offerings for communal celebration in a cultic context.[22] David's offerings, however, fit neither category. It is impossible that the animals should have been burned, for they were offered every six steps—and besides, there is no indication that an altar was available on which to burn them. But if the sacrifices weren't burned, then no part of them reached God—for it is the smoke that conveys the sacrifice to the deity. In other words, David's sacrifices were pure show. His ostentatious offerings again would have reminded the people that he was not one of them, that he was different not only in title, but in kind.

Upon the ark's arrival in the City of David, further sacrifices were offered—this time the appropriate ones, a burnt offering and a well-being offering—after which David "blessed the people in the name of Yahweh of Hosts" (2 Sam. 6:18). This again reinforces David's position at the head of the cult: aside from the regular blessing of sons by fathers, blessing is an act generally reserved for the deity and his appointed human messengers, be they priests or prophets. David claimed possession of the cultic symbol of the ark, and now he firmly claimed the religious role appropriate to that possession.

The final ceremonial act of the ark's procession into the City of David was a purely secular one. David distributed to all the people present—according to the Bible, unrealistically, "the entire multitude of Israel, man and woman alike" (6:19)—bread and cakes. This is a transparently political move. David had already established his unique wealth with his sacrifices. Now he did so again, with offerings not to God, but to the people. David had long known the power of a well-timed gift, as he showed with his redistribution of spoils to Judah. At that time, he was illustrating the benefits of military and administrative subservience. Now his gifts demonstrated the benefits of religious adherence to the newly established royal cult.

From start to finish, the procession of the ark into Jerusalem was constructed so as to elevate David to new heights in the eyes of the people. He endowed his new capital with religious significance by laying claim to the most prominent symbol of God's presence in all of Israel. He made himself out to be the central officiant of the new Jerusalem cult. And he both displayed his personal wealth and made clear the rewards that were available to those who accepted the new religious reality at the heart of the new Davidic kingdom. The bringing of the ark to Jerusalem is often viewed as a sign of David's great piety, but it was in fact a shrewd political move. David had claimed the political leadership of Israel by force. Now he had done the same with Israel's religion.

In our modern age, with its common notion of a transcendent God who is accessible from anywhere through the intangibles of prayer and faith, the material realities of ancient religion are easy to overlook. In early Israel, God was not transcendent, but very much physically present, even if invisibly so. God had said to Moses, "I will come to you and bless you" (Exod. 20:21) at every sanctuary; "For there I will meet with you, and there I will speak with you, and there I will meet with the Israelites. . . . I will dwell among the Israelites" (Exod. 29:42–43, 45). Sanctuaries were divine places where the deity was literally present. And though prayer was a means of communicating with God, it was not generally sufficient by itself. Sacrifice—the burning of a slaughtered animal on an altar, the bringing of raw or cooked grains, the pouring of wine libations—was the primary mode of appeal to the divine. When we put these two elements together, it becomes clear that the cult was not only a spiritual enterprise, but also an economic one. The ritual laws written by the priestly class of Israel, those found in Leviticus, not only invent new types of sacrifices previously unknown in Israel—the guilt offering and the purification (or sin) offering—but also institute rules about purity that require abundant sacrifices when none was needed in the culture before.[23] Almost every sacrifice (with the exception of the burnt offering) required that the offerer give some portion of the animal to the priests. Often, sanctuaries kept their own herds and flocks so that offerers, rather than bringing their own animals, could simply buy one from the sanctuary and offer it instead.[24] Tithing and offering the first fruits of the harvest or the firstborn of the herd and flock were ways to ensure the continuity of God's favor on the part of the offerer—and were ways for the priests to ensure the continual growth of the sanctuary's finances. The priesthood was a lucrative job, and sanctuaries were the most well-established economic cornerstones of Israelite society.[25]

Moreover, three times a year, on the major agricultural festivals, it was common practice for Israelites to make a pilgrimage to a sanctuary. As the great pilgrimage sites from medieval Europe demonstrate, significant ancillary economic advantage could be gained from these visits: pilgrims need shelter, food, and other supplies, and the local economy booms as a result.[26] In practical terms, this meant that there was some competition for the faithful, at least among the largest and most important sanctuaries. An entire community could be sustained on the strength of a local sanctuary. Thus an ambitious sanctuary needed a "draw," something to make its altar more attractive than the one a few towns over. The same combination of cult and economy carried forward into Christianity, for which the cult of the saints, centered on the possession of relics, served as a major source of income for shrines throughout the Christian world from the fourth and fifth centuries to the present day.[27]

In ancient Israel, physical objects—such as the ark—could also do the trick. This sort of competition is behind the story in 1 Kings 12 of Jeroboam's golden calves. Having split Israel off from Solomon's united kingdom, Jeroboam needed to draw the religious economy back away from Jerusalem. So he made two golden calves—symbols of Yahweh—and put one in Bethel, a town near the southern border of Israel, and one in Dan, to the north, saying, "You have been going to Jerusalem long enough" (12:28).

All of this is to say that in bringing the ark to Jerusalem, David was after more than the Israelites' faith—he was after their wallets as well. To make Jerusalem a viable center for sacrifice, one key element was required: a public altar on which to offer the sacrifices. The biblical story of how David came to build this altar, in 2 Samuel 24, is complex and decidedly theological. God, rather bizarrely, incited David to take a census and punished him for it by bringing a plague on Israel. When the plague reached Jerusalem, God stopped it just as his messenger of destruction was at the threshing floor of Araunah the Jebusite. In thanks, David chose this spot as the place where he would build an altar and bought the property from Araunah.

There is undoubtedly a kernel of historical truth in the notion that David took a census. The census in Israel existed solely for the purposes of identifying men of fighting age; it was the first step in military conscription.[28] For this reason, the census was generally viewed negatively by the majority of the Israelite population, including the biblical authors, who describe it as instigated by God for the purpose of punishment: conscription was yet another means by which the monarchy, an untrustworthy institution to begin with, could impose itself on the freedom of the people. Given the military function of the census, however, and David's understandable need to know what sort of fighting force he could muster from his new kingdom, it is reasonable to assume that he did indeed take a census, probably relatively early in his kingship. The story of the plague, however, appears to be no more than an etiology for why the altar was built where it was. Yet no such narrative is really required—David's motivations for building the altar and his choice of the threshing floor of Araunah are logical in and of themselves.

As we have already seen in the story of Keilah, the threshing floor was among the most prominent public spaces in every community. It needed to be large enough to accommodate a good number of people, for everyone would have been harvesting and threshing at the same time each year. It also needed to be in an open space, where the wind could blow away the chaff. As noted earlier, for walled cities—like Jerusalem, which had been fortified since at least the Jebusite era—this meant that the threshing floor would be outside the city walls. As Jerusalem was built on a hillside, the natural location for the threshing floor would have been the flat area to the north—what is now known as the Temple Mount.[29] There hardly could be a better location for the altar. It would be prominent above the city, as close to the heavens as the landscape could allow. And the transformation of an agricultural area into a cultic one would signal that Jerusalem was a distinctively religious center, with enough open space to serve the needs of the pilgrims who would come to sacrifice before the ark. By taking over and repurposing the threshing floor, David made certain that his capital would no longer be an agricultural community, but an urban one, dependent on royal income—both political and sacrificial—rather than on the land.

Who was Araunah the Jebusite, the man from whom David purchased this property? Most likely he was actually no one at all. Though Araunah is commonly understood, even by the biblical authors, as a personal name, it is almost certainly a Hittite title, *ewrine*, meaning "lord."[30] That is, this threshing floor originally belonged to the previous Jebusite ruler of Jerusalem and was a sort of state-owned property. If this is the case, then we can also dismiss the notion that David bought the land from "Araunah." Although the Jebusite community may not have been completely eradicated when David conquered the city, it is certain that the Jebusite ruler would have been subject to David's hungry sword. When David began his reign as the new king in Jerusalem, this royal property would have devolved directly to him. He would have had no need to purchase it—it was already his.

From the perspective of the biblical authors, however, it was important that David purchase the land—indeed, they depict Araunah as trying to give it to David as a gift, and David refusing. The depth of Israel's connection to the site of its temple was such that no possibility could be allowed for anyone else to make a rightful claim on the property. This same impulse is at the root of the story of Abraham's purchase of the cave of Machpelah in Genesis 23 (where, as in our passage, the property is first offered as a gift): the land is fully Israelite only if the claim to it is undeniable by both its previous and its current owners. It was thus important for the biblical authors to make certain that the site of the altar in Jerusalem—which would become the site of the temple—was authentically and incontestably Israelite. David, however, would not have had such qualms. Taking the property of others was never a difficulty for him.

The threshing floor of the Jebusite city thus became the cultic center of David's new capital, and it is to this spot that he also moved the ark, protected by its traditional tent. Just as the threshing floor was the economic center of most Israelite communities, so now the ark and its altar would become the economic centers of David's Jeru-salem, a communal space not only for the surrounding area, but, in theory, for the nation as a whole.

The establishment of Jerusalem as a religious center may have been a shrewd economic move by David, but it also served a greater symbolic purpose. Throughout the ancient Near East, the king and the deity were closely intertwined.[31] In Mesopotamia, kings were un-derstood to have been divinely appointed to rule; they engaged in divine rituals such as the "sacred marriage," in which they symboli-cally slept with a goddess; they are depicted in art as taking the form of a deity.[32] Among the Hittites, the king was also the chief priest of the land; one shrine shows the king being embraced by a god; and upon his death, the king was said to "become a god."[33] In Egypt the equation was simple: the pharaoh was himself a living god.[34] Such explicit deification was an impossibility in Israelite religion—but it would have been natural for David to want to demonstrate God's ap-proval of his reign.[35] The presence of the ark in his new capital ac-complished this end.

What we have in David's bringing of the ark to Jerusalem, then, is the beginning of Israelite royal theology: the notion that Israel's king was akin to God's steward on earth. Saul, David's sole predeces-sor on the throne of Israel, ruled by consent of the people, his reign legitimized by his ability to protect Israel from its enemies. David, by contrast, positioned himself as divinely legitimized—a position he was more in need of than Saul, for David ruled not by popular consent, but by force. This claim of divine approval, and even selec-tion, was a common technique for establishing power. When Baby-lon was briefly captured by the invading Chaldean people in the late eighth century BCE, the conquering king claimed that Marduk, the chief god of Babylon, had personally selected him to rule.[36] Cen-turies later, when the Persian emperor Cyrus the Great conquered Babylon, he made the same claim.[37] This is royal propaganda at its best: an attempt to persuade a defeated enemy that their new over-lord came to power by the choice of their own deity. Though there is no reason to doubt that David authentically worshipped the Israelite deity Yahweh, his possession of the ark in Jerusalem sent much the same message.

In time, this royal theology would come to encompass not only David's reign, but that of his entire dynasty. It is therefore understandable that in the seventh to sixth centuries BCE a biblical author would explicitly link the arrival of the ark in Jerusalem to God's promise of an uninterrupted Davidic lineage on the throne. This is the famous passage in 2 Samuel 7, following directly on the ark's entrance into the city, in which God promises David through the prophet Nathan that God "will establish a house [that is, a dynasty] for you. When your days are done and you lie with your fathers, I will raise up your offspring after you, one of your own issue, and I will establish his kingship. . . . Your house and your kingdom shall ever be secure before me; your throne shall be established forever" (7:11–12, 16). This is the fundamental statement of the royal Davidic ideology, projected back onto the beginning of the dynasty by authors who had known uninterrupted Davidic kingship for the previous three hundred years.[38] The text is pure theological invention, but its roots are in the reality of David's establishment of Jerusalem as a royal cultic site.

This chapter in 2 Samuel seeks not only to justify David's dynasty as divinely ordained, but also to address a well-known fact that must have pressed heavily on the minds of the later pro-David authors: David, the great king, did not build the temple in Jerusalem. According to 2 Samuel 7, David is promised his dynasty because he wanted to build the temple, but was dissuaded by God himself: "I have not dwelt in a house from the day that I brought the people of Israel out of Egypt to this day, but have moved about in tent and Tabernacle" (7:6). This text explains, then, why David did not build the temple; but it fails to explain why, if God was uninterested in such a dwelling, David's son Solomon would be allowed to construct one. In the fourth-century BCE books of Chronicles, this logical inconsistency is recognized, and it is explained that David did not build the temple because he was a man of war, whereas Solomon was a man of peace. Both explanations are apologetic. What is commonly agreed is that David did not build the temple. The question that the biblical authors seek to answer is, why not?

In truth, this question is relevant only from a later perspective, when the temple was the center of Israel's religious existence and David was recognized as the greatest king in Israel's history. Modern scholars have fallen sway to the same forces, often going to lengths similar to those of the biblical authors to explain why David didn't build the temple. From the historian's perspective, the question may be answered relatively simply: David did not build the temple—or, better, *a* temple—because he had no need to do so. He had the ark and an altar, and thus both the enticement for pilgrims and the means by which they could offer their sacrifices. A physical temple was unnecessary, and, what's more, David may have seen a temple as potentially drawing the revenues from the cult away from the royal court. Without a physical temple, the priesthood in Jerusalem was under David's control: appointed by him and maintained by him. And, at least according to one passage, David's own sons served as priests—a common reality in the ancient world but an embarrassment to later biblical texts such as Chronicles, for which the idea of anyone from a nonpriestly lineage serving in the cult was unthinkable.[39] The Jerusalem cult was a family business, and David had no reason to create any structures that might take on a life of their own. The Bible wants us to believe that David would have built the temple if he could have. The real question should not be "Why didn't David build the temple?" but rather "Why *would* David build a temple?" If David didn't build the temple, it is because he had no desire to.

By inaugurating the Israelite cult in Jerusalem, David accomplished something of lasting value, an achievement that still resonates today. Like the unification of the northern and southern tribes, the establishment of Jerusalem as the religious center of Israel changed the course of history. All of the emotions tied up in the city—from the exilic cry in Psalm 137, "If I forget thee, O Zion," to the medi-

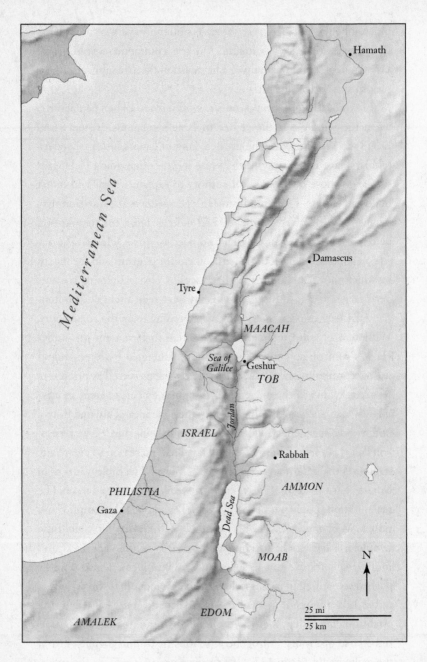

Israel's Neighbors

eval zealotry of the Crusades, all the way to the present conflicts over the status of Jerusalem as a joint Israeli and Palestinian capital—are grounded in David's vision for his capital. It is tempting to apply our own feelings about Jerusalem back into David's time, to ascribe to him the passion and the piety that the city inspires in us. The biblical authors themselves succumbed to this temptation. But David acted for far more mundane reasons. The choice of Jerusalem as his capital and the decision to make it a religious center for Israel were primarily political and economic. They were grounded in the realities of David's seizure of the throne and his need to establish himself and his government in the eyes of a conquered and resentful populace. The results, centuries on, may have benefited the entire nation, but the motivations were self-serving.

David's Empire

FROM THE CENTER OF David's kingdom, Jerusalem, we may look outward to the peripheries. For David is lauded not only for his piety, but also for his military conquests; he is credited with expanding the borders and influence of Israel to virtually all the surrounding nations. David's kingdom is often described as an empire, collecting tribute from the vanquished foes all around. The biblical claim to such an empire has remained a fundamental aspect of Jewish self-definition for millennia—so much so that when the state of Israel was founded in 1948, it was understood by many that, since David had conquered most of what is now Jordan and Syria, Israel was, in accepting a partition of Palestine that gave it a rather small territory, generously relinquishing its traditional rights to more than half of David's empire in the name of peace with its neighbors. David's conquests are an important touchstone for the history of the land of Israel. Yet virtually everything we know about these victories comes from a single chapter in the Bible, 2 Samuel 8. It is our task to evaluate these biblical claims and the picture of David's kingdom that they present.[40]

The first Israelite victory recorded in 2 Samuel 8 is over the Philistines. It is natural enough for the biblical authors to emphasize David's battles against the Philistines by placing them at the head of the chapter, for victory over Israel's longtime nemesis was one of the basic rationales for both Saul's and David's kingships in the first place. The extent of this victory is ambiguous, however. It is usually assumed that David actually defeated the Philistine heartland along the coast, thereby establishing Israel's right to that fertile territory—including what we now call the Gaza Strip. The text, however, says only that David attacked "Philistines," not "*the* Philistines." It seems that this battle was not a full-fledged assault on the Philistine homeland. Gezer, the Philistine-controlled town closest to Israelite territory, was still in Philistine hands into the reign of Solomon. David never conquered the Philistines in any substantial way. They remained firmly in control of their coastal cities for the duration of his life.

The second verse of 2 Samuel 8 records David's victory over Moab, the nation across the Jordan to the east of Judah (present-day Jordan). Unlike the long-established Philistine enemy, in David's time Moab had barely coalesced into a meaningful political entity.[41] It is therefore somewhat unclear what it even would have meant for David to conquer the entire nation of Moab. Then again, the text never quite makes that claim explicitly, though it tries to imply it. On the contrary, just as in the case of the Philistines in the previous verse, the Bible provides no detail whatsoever about the scope of David's victory. Not a single town or region is mentioned—which strongly suggests that not a single town or region was taken, for the biblical authors would be sure to say so.[42] This may have been a border skirmish, perhaps the result of some small band of Moabites testing the strength of the new kingdom to their west. Regime change was often the occasion for such adventures in the ancient Near East. It was never obvious how powerful a new ruler would be, and thus the rise of a new king often coincided with external attacks or internal revolts.[43] Such may have been the case here, too. Most important, there is no record of Moab having been subjugated by David. In the monumental inscription of the Moabite king Mesha from the end of the ninth century BCE, the subjugation of Moab is attributed to the Israelite king Omri, who ruled a century after David.[44] Thus we have here another example of the biblical authors suggesting that David controlled territory that he did not.

From the Philistines in the west and the Moabites in the east, 2 Samuel 8 turns north, to describe David's defeat of the Arameans led by Hadadezer, the king of Zobah—territory that now belongs to Syria. Here again, however, the text implies more than it proves. The battle described in 2 Samuel 8:3–13 did not take place on Aramean soil, but rather in Ammon, the Transjordanian nation north of Moab. Ammon had been Israel's enemy during Saul's reign—in fact, some if not all of Saul's authority derived from his ability to successfully defend the town of Jabesh-Gilead from the advances of the Ammonite king Nahash (1 Sam. 11). Saul's enemy, however, was David's friend: David refers to the fact that Nahash "kept faith" with him, using a technical term for treaty partnership. After the death of Nahash and the rise of his son Hanun to the Ammonite throne, however, David recognized an opportunity to test the limits of his power—again, regime change and international renegotiations went hand in hand. The war against Ammon also served a political purpose for David within Israel. His rejection of his former treaty obligations to Ammon would have been popular with the Israelites, especially those in Gilead, the region most directly threatened by Ammon.

Upon David's aggression, Ammon turned for help to its allies in Aram, and soldiers came from Zobah, Maacah, and Tob, city-states just to the north of Israelite territory. It is the sequence of battles against these armies, detailed in 2 Samuel 10, that is referred to in 2 Samuel 8 as the defeat of the Arameans. David did not extend Israel's borders to the north, into Aram—he extended them east, across the Jordan into Ammon. The Arameans he defeated were not even in Aramean territory.[45] There is thus no record of David campaigning in Aram, to the north of Israel. He never occupied Aramean territory— nor does the text ever say that he did. The text implies it, perhaps, but had David really taken this territory, the biblical authors would have proclaimed and celebrated it.

Ammon, on the other hand—the actual object of the battles in which David fought the Arameans—was authentically subjugated. It is striking to note the difference between the reports that imply conquest where there was none and those that describe real conquests. Whereas details of territory taken and cities captured are lacking in those texts that can be classified as exaggerations, the notice of the conquest of Ammon is detailed. "Joab attacked Rabbah of Ammon"—the capital—"and captured the royal city" (2 Sam. 12:26). We cannot find this sort of explicit statement in any other account of David's conquests, from his early days in Saul's service to his time on the throne of Israel. This is a factual statement of victory over a foreign capital. It is the only one—and it is therefore the only one that can be trusted. We are further told that David gained possession of the royal crown of Ammon and carried off booty from the city. Moreover, he subjected the inhabitants of Rabbah to forced labor, "with saws, iron threshing boards, and iron axes, or assigned them to brickmaking" (12:31)—and here is where Adoram, who is in charge of forced labor for David, probably made his living, as there is no evidence that David ever subjected Israelites to labor.[46] This description is again in contrast to what we find elsewhere, where references to booty and forced labor are generic at best. When the biblical authors have details to give, they give them—and when they don't, they don't.

The last victory mentioned in 2 Samuel 8 is over the Edomites, the nation to the southeast of Israel. Early in its existence, Edom's territory was confined mostly to the southern Negev, as we know from the biblical story in Numbers 21 of the Israelites' wandering in the wilderness: they are prevented from moving straight up into Canaan by the Edomites, whose territory they are forced to circumvent.[47] The value of this territory was mostly for its trade routes, which brought rare goods—spices and precious metals—into Israel from Arabia.[48] Although the notice of David's subjugation of Edom is brief ("He stationed garrisons in Edom—in all of Edom he stationed garrisons—

and all the Edomites became vassals of David" [8:14]) it may be trustworthy. Solomon controlled Edomite territory, as he kept his fleet in the Edomite city of Ezion-geber (1 Kings 9:26). But the fact that in Solomon's time this area was still referred to as Edomite suggests that it was not annexed to Israel, but rather controlled by Israel. It seems most likely, then, that David's conquest of Edom consisted mostly of his seizure of the southern Negev and the establishment of garrisons to protect the trade route. Remarkably, archaeological evidence supports this process: an unusually high number of settlements in the Negev appeared out of nowhere in the tenth century BCE.[49]

In 2 Samuel 8, then, we have the biblical argument for the creation of a Davidic empire. The text is arranged geographically, with the conquest of the Philistines to the west, the Moabites to the east, the Arameans to the north, and the Edomites to the south. The artfulness of this construction is telling, especially when we recognize that those in the north, the Arameans, were really defeated in Ammon, to the east. The chapter is not a straightforward historical account, but a piece of propaganda, intended to magnify David's conquests and give the impression of a mighty empire stretching in all directions. Notably, it appears to be yet another piece of pro-David one-upmanship regarding Saul, for we may note the verse that describes Saul's military triumphs: "He waged war on every side against all his enemies: against the Moabites, Ammonites, Edomites, the kings of Zobah, and the Philistines, and wherever he turned he worsted them" (1 Sam. 14:47). This is precisely the list of nations we find in 2 Samuel 8, even down to the kings of Zobah. David hardly could be made to seem less powerful than his unworthy predecessor when it came to military success, and 2 Samuel 8 is the biblical authors' attempt to ensure David's legacy. Scholars have further argued that this chapter is of a piece with royal propaganda from elsewhere in the Near East, especially monumental inscriptions relating the victories of kings over their many enemies.[50] The text, like its parallels from elsewhere, implies great achievements without quite stating them explicitly. As a piece of propaganda, it has been remarkably successful. Even the later biblical

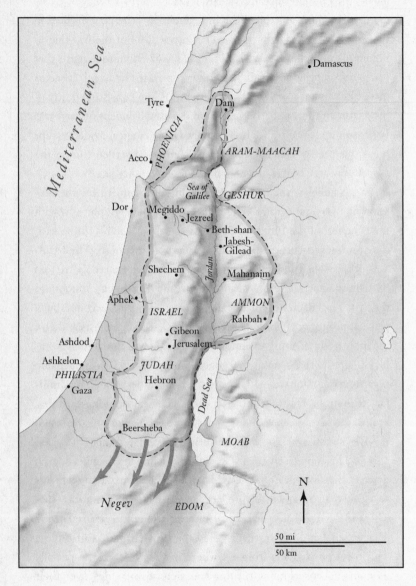

Damascus

Tyre

Dam

PHOENICIA

ARAM-MAACAH

Acco

Sea of Galilee

GESHUR

Dor

Megiddo

Jezreel

Beth-shan

Jabesh-Gilead

Shechem

Jordan

Mahanaim

Aphek

ISRAEL

AMMON

Rabbah

Gibeon

Jerusalem

Ashdod

Ashkelon

JUDAH

PHILISTIA

Hebron

Gaza

Dead Sea

Beersheba

MOAB

N

Negev

EDOM

50 mi

50 km

Mediterranean Sea

David's Kingdom

authors of the two books of Chronicles accepted the story as presented here: Chronicles says explicitly that David captured Gath from the Philistines (1 Chron. 18:2), a claim made nowhere in Samuel.

In the end, then, what can we say about the extent of David's kingdom? To the west, it was no larger than it had been in Saul's time. The Philistines still controlled all of their traditional territory. David's kingdom never reached the coast of the Mediterranean. To the north, Israel also maintained its previous boundaries, with the northernmost point still being the city of Dan. This is reflected in the Bible in the typical description of Israel's territory: "from Dan to Beersheba," a phrase used to describe Israel in the time of Samuel (1 Sam. 3:20), at the time of David's census (2 Sam. 24:2), and in the time of Solomon (1 Kings 5:5). The Arameans remained a formidable power to the north, becoming Israel's main rival and even overlord in the ninth century BCE. To the south, David made inroads into the Negev territory of the Edomites, though this was less a conquest than a transfer of influence. This area was virtually uninhabited before David installed garrisons there to protect the trade routes. The traditional phrase "from Dan to Beersheba" reflects the fact that Beersheba remained the southernmost major settlement in Israelite territory, even after David.

It was only to the east, in his conquest of Ammon, that David expanded with any real force. Yet this was really not such a great distance—Rabbah is only about twenty miles from the Jordan valley, and there was little of Ammon to the east of that, as the mountains give way to uninterrupted desert. What's more, the territories just to the east of the Jordan were probably already Israelite, or at least pro-Israelite, rather than Ammonite, for these are the regions in which the tribes of Reuben, Gad, and part of Manasseh are said to have settled (Num. 32). Consider, for example, Jabesh-Gilead, the town oppressed by the Ammonites, the town that rescued Saul's body from the wall: it is on the Ammonite side of the Jordan. This diminishes even further the Ammonite territory to be conquered by David. The conquest of Ammon was a real conquest, and a real subjugation—

perhaps the only one of its kind in all of David's reign. But it was hardly a major expansion, nor was Ammon a major power like the Philistines or the Arameans.

The largest view we can realistically maintain of David's kingdom, then, is not very different from what it was at the beginning of David's reign. It could hardly be called an empire—it was no stronger than the Philistine and Aramean peoples to its west and north. And compared with Egypt and Mesopotamia, it remained a virtual nonentity—note that David is never said to have had any diplomatic contact with either of those two great superpowers at any time during his reign, nor is there any record from those civilizations of David's reign. Israel under David remained what it had always been: a minor state, largely confined to the central hill country of Judah and Israel.

The current area of the modern state of Israel, small though it may be, is in fact perhaps larger than that of David's Israel. Certainly the coastal plain, almost all the way up to Jaffa, would not have been under David's control. On the other hand, the West Bank would have been David's heartland, even extending a little into what is now Jordan. But the Davidic empire of tradition, stretching from the border of Egypt up to the Euphrates, is a gross exaggeration. The biblical account is propagandistic, and that propaganda has been accepted as fact for thousands of years.

To give David credit where it is due, however, simply maintaining the newly expanded borders of his kingdom was achievement enough. He left a territory secure enough that it could endure, at least for the most part, for many generations. For a small kingdom with few natural resources at its disposal, a widely scattered populace, and no tradition of statehood, this is impressive. But it is not the Davidic empire of tradition. Such an empire never existed.

CHAPTER 6

David Under Attack

DESPERATE TIMES CALL FOR
DESPERATE MEASURES

THE POPULAR DEPICTION OF DAVID'S reign as gloriously successful is based largely on the memories of David preserved by later biblical authors. Those who wrote the books of Kings established David as the ruler against whom all others were judged. Those who wrote the books of Chronicles whitewashed David's story to remove all traces of embarrassment or potential wrongdoing. But in the earliest material in the books of Samuel, even as the authors try to glorify David at every turn, they are forced, by virtue of their proximity to the historical events, to reckon with reality. The events that truly could be described as glorious—the capture of Jerusalem, the entrance of the ark into the city, and David's victories against the neighboring nations—are narrated in only two chapters of Samuel. Almost the entire rest of the history of David's kingship describes not a glorious reign, but rather a constantly troubled one.

In some respects, it is not surprising that David's reign would not be an easy one. It was hard enough for rightfully chosen kings to maintain their grip on power. How much more difficult for a man who had taken the crown against the popular will and who had in addition spent years fighting on the side of the enemy, been responsible for the death of the previous and well-liked monarch, and appropriated a national cultic treasure for himself. If anyone knew the dangers of being king, it was David. But even David was unprepared when threats to his kingship came from an unexpected source: his own family.

David's Family

To UNDERSTAND THE CHALLENGES David would face, we need to be familiar with those closest to him. According to 2 Samuel 3:2–5, David had six sons by six different wives while he reigned in Hebron. His first wife, Ahinoam—the former wife of Saul—bore Amnon, David's firstborn and a significant part of the story to come. His second wife, Abigail—the former wife of the Calebite chief—bore a son named Chileab according to Samuel, but Daniel according to Chronicles.[1] The discrepancy in the son's name is curious, but ultimately irrelevant, for neither Abigail nor her son is ever mentioned again. This may seem odd: after all, an entire chapter was devoted to the story of how Abigail became David's wife. Yet her absence from the rest of the narrative is telling. As suggested above, this marriage had nothing to do with love and everything to do with replacing Nabal as chief of the Calebites. Once David had become king of Judah, Abigail and her offspring were of no use to him. Her job was done.[2]

It is possible, even probable, that David's first two sons were born not in Hebron as the Bible says, but before David had become king in Judah. David had been married to both Ahinoam and Abigail for more than a year and a half before going to Hebron, and it seems unlikely that he would have waited to have children with them. In the case of Ahinoam, it is even possible that her son, Amnon, was conceived with David when she was still Saul's wife. The biblical authors, however, would not have been pleased with the idea that David's sons were born in Philistia, as this would make them practically foreigners. The authors have probably condensed the chronology of the births, at least for the first two sons.

David's third son was Absalom, the central figure in the coming narrative. His mother, we are told, was Maacah, the daughter of King Talmai of Geshur. Geshur was an independent territory to the northeast of Israel, just to the east of the Sea of Galilee.[3] According to the conquest narrative in the book of Joshua, Geshur was one of the regions that the Israelites were unable to dispossess, thus explaining the Geshurites' continuing presence on the borders of Israel (Josh. 13:13). We are never told when or how David came to marry the princess of Geshur, but given the standards of the time, we can make an educated guess. As noted above, marriages between royal houses were common in the ancient Near East as a way of cementing diplomatic relations between nations. It therefore seems improbable that David should have married the daughter of the king of Geshur before he took the throne in Hebron, as the Geshurites would have had little to gain from an alliance with a mere Philistine mercenary. We can thus date David's marriage to Maacah at least to the Hebron period, though we may not be able to be more precise than that.[4] The marriage itself demonstrates that David was seen from the outside as a legitimate ruler, and one secure enough on the throne to warrant diplomatic ties. As Geshur was supposedly part of Ishbaal's kingdom, David's connection to it also was probably intended to weaken Ishbaal politically in advance of David's seizing the northern throne.[5]

Of David's remaining sons listed in 2 Samuel 3, only the fourth, Adonijah son of Haggith, plays any further role in the story—though not until the very end. Shephatiah son of Abital, and Ithream son of Eglah, the fifth and sixth sons, never appear by name again. In this regard they are like the eleven sons said to be born to David once he became king in Jerusalem, listed in 2 Samuel 5, only one of whom is known to us: Solomon. What about Solomon? We will treat David's successor fully in the next chapter. After he is born in 2 Samuel 12, he disappears from the narrative until the beginning of the first book of Kings. It is there, at the end of David's life, that Solomon's story, including his birth, is properly told.

One other figure is prominently missing from the list of David's family presented here: Michal, the daughter of Saul whom David commanded to be brought to him when he became king in Hebron. Why isn't she mentioned? Second Samuel 3 preserves a list of David's sons—and Michal had no children with him. The biblical authors created an explanation for this: when David brought the ark into Jerusalem, Michal was embarrassed by David's dancing, during which he evidently "exposed himself" in front of everyone. As a result of her verbal abuse, the text tells us, "to her dying day Michal daughter of Saul had no children" (2 Sam. 6:23). The Bible implies that this was divine punishment for Michal's behavior. But there is a far simpler explanation. David took Michal as his wife as a show of strength, to demonstrate his power over even the royal family of the weakened northern kingdom. Being married to Saul's daughter was also further justification for David's rule in Israel, as it placed him in the legitimate line of succession. As was the case with Abigail, this was a marriage purely of political convenience. Having Michal as a wife served a clear purpose for David. Having children with her, however, did not. In fact, it would have been against David's interests because Michal was a descendant of Saul, and any offspring she had with David would continue Saul's line into the next generation.[6] As we have seen, David did everything possible to destroy Saul's lineage, so having children with Michal would run counter to his program of eradicating the Saulide legacy.

There is another reason to believe that David probably never even slept with Michal, much less had children with her. He was already married to, and had a son with, Michal's mother: Ahinoam. In Leviticus we read, "Do not uncover the nakedness of a woman and her daughter" (18:17). Though this law was written well after David's time, and though David was not one to adhere strictly to the law in any case, it is a reasonable guess that it reflects a cultural norm in ancient Israel, a known abhorrence of such semi-incestual relationships.[7] Just as today we need no law proscribing such an arrangement, it is likely that even David would have recognized that sleeping with both Ahinoam and Michal was forbidden. But it may not have even entered David's mind to do so. He married Michal not for her potential offspring, but for her political utility. And, like Abigail, once she serves her purpose, she disappears from the story.

The cases of Abigail and Michal remind us that David's familial relationships were fundamentally political in nature.[8] He married to gain the kingship, in Judah and in Israel. It was not only his wives who had political importance, however. David's sons were lined up to succeed him on the throne: first Amnon, then Absalom. And the question of succession would be the driving force behind the most significant challenge David faced while king—one that would, in fact, temporarily force him off the throne.

Amnon and Tamar

THIS STORY BEGINS WITH the narrative of Amnon and Tamar, the sister of Absalom.[9] Amnon, the story goes, became infatuated with his half-sister. His cousin Jonadab, in a misguided effort to improve Amnon's mood, suggested that Amnon pretend to be sick and ask that Tamar bring him some food. So Amnon did, requesting that David send Tamar to him, and so she went to Amnon's bedside. After she had prepared the meal, however, Amnon sent everyone out of the room. When Tamar brought the food close to him, he grabbed her and demanded that she sleep with him. Tamar pleaded with her half-brother, even suggesting that if he just asked David for her hand in marriage, he could have her—but to no avail. Amnon raped her. Afterward, he no longer desired her; in fact, he loathed her and ordered her to leave. Again she pleaded with him, that the shame this would bring upon her would be unbearable, but again to no avail. She was forced from his chambers, screaming and tearing her garment in dismay. She encountered her brother Absalom, who immediately discerned what had happened but told her to keep it quiet for the moment. David also heard about it and was upset, but did nothing. Absalom said nothing to Amnon, but hated him for having violated Tamar.

Such is the biblical account. In assessing its historical veracity, we must begin by noting that, as with many other parts of the David story, the events described here are fundamentally private in nature. The story could be told only by one of the participants, for no one else was privy to what happened in Amnon's bedroom. This alone is cause for doubt.

More striking, however, is the way that elements of this story find parallels in other biblical narratives of sexual misconduct, particularly those from the semimythical patriarchal era. There are two well-known women named Tamar in the Bible: David's daughter, and the daughter-in-law of Judah, whose story is told in Genesis 38. Both stories revolve around the question of sexual propriety within a family. Both stories have an element of deception: Amnon's faked illness, and Tamar's disguising herself as a prostitute. Both Tamars are treated callously by the men around them. And both are connected with David: the Tamar of Genesis bears Judah twins, one of whom, Perez, was traditionally believed to be David's direct ancestor.[10]

There are resonances also with the story of Joseph and his Egyptian master's wife from Genesis 39. Both stories feature infatuation that turns into sexual aggression, in both cases specifically when no one else is present. In both stories the infatuation eventually turns to revulsion and leads to the debasement of the victim. In both a garment plays an evidentiary role: Absalom recognizes that Tamar has been raped by her torn garment, and the Egyptian's wife holds Joseph's garment up as proof that he had tried to rape her.[11]

The closest parallel to the story of Amnon and Tamar, however, is the narrative of Dinah in Genesis 34. Both the Tamar and Dinah stories are, most obviously, about rape. In both the brother(s) of the victim is given the lead role in responding—both Jacob and David, the fathers, are mysteriously passive, even though they are fully aware of what has transpired. Both stories address the issue of marriage—Amnon refuses Tamar's proposal, and Jacob's sons offer a disingenuous proposal to Shechem.[12]

The similarities between the story of Amnon and Tamar and these three chapters from Genesis strongly suggest that what we have in 2 Samuel 13 is not a historical account, but rather a mixture of older traditional stories. In short, the narrative seems to be a literary creation.[13] There is no reason to believe that Amnon ever raped Tamar—in fact, there is no reason to believe that David actually ever had a daughter named Tamar at all. What the story seeks to establish is a reason for Absalom to hate Amnon, for that hatred appears to be the motivating factor behind what happened next.

Amnon's Death

IN THE SPRING, ABSALOM threw a party, a festival to celebrate the annual sheep-shearing. Exactly when this took place is unclear—the Bible says that it was two years after the rape of Tamar, but dating events on the basis of fictional stories is, needless to say, a risky proposition. Whenever it happened, Absalom invited David, who excused himself; he then asked David whether Amnon could attend, and after some reticence on David's part, the king relented. So Amnon joined Absalom at Baal-hazor, a town a few miles north of Jerusalem. Absalom instructed his servants: "When Amnon is merry with wine, and I tell you to strike down Amnon, kill him! Don't be afraid, for I myself command you" (2 Sam. 13:28). His servants dutifully obeyed and killed Amnon. Thereafter, David heard a false report that Absalom had actually killed all of David's sons. This, we are told, devastated him, but Jonadab, his nephew, assured him that Amnon alone had died and that this was Absalom's revenge for the rape of Tamar.

If we accept that the story of Tamar and Amnon was a literary invention, then Jonadab's rationale for the murder of Amnon can't be true. But without it, the question is glaring: why did Absalom kill Amnon? The answer is obvious: because with his half-brother Amnon gone, Absalom would be next in line for the throne. If this seems an unthinkable crime, consider that in 2 Chronicles we are told that Jehoram, a ninth-century BCE king of Judah, killed all of his brothers upon taking the throne—and this even when Jehoram was already king (21:4). If Jehoram could kill his brothers only because of the potential threat that they posed to his rule, it is not so difficult to imagine that Absalom might have killed Amnon to move up in the line of succession. Absalom may not have felt especially close to Amnon in the first place—they were only half-brothers and likely did not know each other particularly well, as they would have been raised apart by their mothers. To Absalom, Amnon may have been a virtual stranger—but he was standing in Absalom's way.

The more pressing question from our perspective has to do, as always, with David's involvement. The biblical narrative goes to some lengths to make clear that David was ignorant of everything. We are told, somewhat unnecessarily from a narrative perspective, that David did not attend the sheep-shearing party—in other words, he was (as usual) not present for the murder. We are also told, equally unnecessarily, that he had to be persuaded to let Amnon go to the party—in other words, David tried (albeit unknowingly) to protect Amnon. We are told that David initially thought all the princes had died at Absalom's hand, which is narratively useless, as this mistaken impression is immediately corrected and never comes up again—in other words, David was so ignorant of what was happening that he actually got the facts mixed up. Every aspect of this narrative that has to do with David points toward the conclusion that David had nothing to do with Amnon's death. But none of these elements is necessary for the story—which suggests that they are included precisely to lead the reader to that conclusion. And that, in turn, suggests that exactly the opposite is the case. If the Bible tries so strenuously to persuade us that David wasn't involved in Amnon's death—just as it did with the deaths of Nabal, Saul, Jonathan, Abner, and Saul's remaining descendants—then we must reckon with the possibility that, in fact, he was.

But why would David want Amnon, his firstborn son, dead? It is helpful to ask the question in political terms: why would David not want Amnon to succeed him on the throne? The answer has less to do with Amnon, and more to do with his mother: Ahinoam. Amnon was the product of David's failed coup, his sleeping with Saul's wife. At the time, this had been a necessary step, even if it turned out badly. But now that David had secured the kingship over all Israel, Amnon was yet another link to the Saulide legacy. David had done everything possible to ensure that no one with any connection to Saul would ever threaten his kingship—and yet the one person in the country with a rightful claim to succeed David was none other than the child of Saul's wife. There is no reason to think that David had any affection for Ahinoam—like Abigail and Michal, she was a pawn in his political game—and, hard though it may be to imagine, there is no reason that David would have had any special affection for Ahinoam's son, either. Amnon was a living reminder that David had taken the kingship by force.

We need not doubt that it was really Absalom who killed Amnon. As we have seen, he too had his reasons for wanting Amnon dead. But David must have been involved as well. What seems most probable is that he and Absalom conspired to have Amnon killed. David could have played on Absalom's desire for the throne. He probably made a deal with Absalom: if Absalom had Amnon killed, David would promise Absalom the right to succeed him on the throne.[14] Absalom, after all, was no descendant of Saul but the product of a legitimate royal marriage between David and the daughter of the king of Geshur—indeed, this was the first legitimate marriage David had participated in, after Ahinoam and Abigail; it was the first marriage David entered into when he was a king. Absalom would have been, in David's mind, a legitimate and desirable successor.

Thus a conspiracy between David and Absalom to have Amnon killed served everyone's interests—except Amnon's. David could eliminate the last vestiges of Saul's line and ensure that his preferred son would succeed him; Absalom could overcome the disadvantage of his birth order and attain the royal status held by both his father and mother. Amnon died for no fault of his own; once the Tamar story is debunked, there is nothing to suggest that he deserved his fate. But he was born to the wrong mother, and he died for it at the hands of his father and his half-brother.

Absalom's Flight

AFTER THE MURDER OF Amnon, Absalom fled to the territory of Geshur for three years. At first glance, this looks like an admission of guilt, as if Absalom were afraid of David's retribution. In reality, his flight was a necessary part of the conspiracy. He hardly could just return to Jerusalem and resume his life as it had been before—if he did, everyone would understand that David condoned Amnon's murder. If Absalom returned, David would be forced to punish him, probably with death. The two conspirators required a mechanism by which Absalom would be "punished" but eventually regain his position in the court. A false exile would serve this purpose well: Absalom could be understood as having been forced out of the country but could, in time, be allowed to return.

It is no coincidence that Absalom should have fled to Geshur. He would not be safe anywhere in Israel because everyone would have known that he had committed fratricide. Most foreign nations would have no use for a runaway Israelite prince. But Geshur was sure to take him in, for Absalom's mother was the daughter of the king of Geshur. Absalom fled from his father into the arms of his grandfather. The situation was perfect for everyone involved. Absalom would be safe, and David would know it. David would also have a ready-made excuse for why he was unable to capture Absalom and bring him to justice: he was being sheltered by his family in an independent foreign kingdom.

The biblical story of Absalom's return from Geshur to Jerusalem is somewhat convoluted. Joab, David's general, sets the story in motion when he tricks David with the help of the famous wise woman of Tekoa. This woman disguises herself as a mourning mother and comes to David with a tale: one of her sons killed the other, and now her clan is demanding that the killer be put to death, even though this would wipe out the only remnant of her husband's name. David's response is just what Joab expected: he promises that the woman's son will return to her safely. At this, the woman pulls back the curtain, telling David that he is guilty of the same crime, depriving himself of his own son and elevating legal principles over paternal love. David immediately suspects Joab, and the woman confirms it. David agrees to let his son return and sends Joab to fetch Absalom from Geshur. But David instructs Joab to have Absalom go straight to his own house, and not come to David. After two more years, David finally relents and brings Absalom to the palace, where they embrace.

The story of the wise woman from Tekoa—another private conversation, complete with a parable—is fictional. The question is why it would be necessary for the authors to invent such an elaborate account. Why not simply present David as having a change of heart? As is the case with so many of these overly involved biblical narratives, the story serves to obscure the historical truth. It is a continuation of the cover-up of the David and Absalom conspiracy. David must be seen as disinclined ever to forgive Absalom in order to persuade the reader that he had no hand in Amnon's death. It is only in a display of royal beneficence to the woman of Tekoa that David unwittingly acquiesces to Absalom's return. In other words, David did not want to see Absalom again, the story tells us, but he was such a deeply good person that he allowed the wise woman to force his hand. The typical biblical program of elevating David while covering his tracks is evident.

The same agenda is at work in the prominent role Joab plays in the story. David, we are to understand, would never on his own have taken the initiative in welcoming Absalom back. It is Joab who wants Absalom to return, not David. It is Joab who goes to fetch Absalom, not David. Everything that David wanted in reality is ascribed by the biblical authors to Joab. The two further years that Absalom spent without coming to see David are the final piece of the cover-up, yet another indication that David was deeply reticent about Absalom regaining his position in Jerusalem. Probably this was all worked out well in advance. It was the price Absalom and David had to pay for their determination to eliminate Amnon: five years of separation, of exile and virtual house arrest for Absalom. In the long run, this seemed a fair price to pay for getting the right son on the throne.

Absalom's Revolt

DAVID HAD EXECUTED HIS plan perfectly. In fact, since his early failed attempt to seize Saul's crown, David had experienced an unbroken string of successes. What happened next, however, was unexpected and marked the beginning of his long decline.

The Bible tells us that Absalom was exceedingly attractive—that "no one in Israel was so praised for his beauty as Absalom; from the sole of his foot to the crown of his head he was without blemish" (2 Sam. 14:25). What's more, he had a remarkable head of hair. Physical descriptions of biblical characters are rare and always meaningful. What is the purpose of describing Absalom this way? Physical gifts went beyond mere appearance; they were seen as a sign of divine favor. Joseph is described as handsome. The infant Moses is beautiful. In the right circumstances, one could be considered fit to be a king if one only looked the part: Saul, we may recall, was chosen because he was taller than everyone else; David himself is described as handsome. Absalom's appearance may have planted in him and in others the thought that he was particularly fit to be king. At the very least, the biblical authors provide this information as foreshadowing for Absalom's subsequent actions.

Absalom, some time after David had welcomed him back into his arms, "provided himself with a chariot, horses, and fifty men to run before him" (2 Sam. 15:1). The import of this may be lost on the contemporary reader, but it would have been very apparent to the ancient Israelite audience. Chariots and horses were distinctly royal possessions. In fact, they are almost always associated in the Bible with foreign kings: Pharaoh in pursuit of the Israelites after the Exodus; the coalition of Canaanite kings who engage Joshua in battle; the Philistines who confront Saul early in his reign, and again at Mount Gilboa; the Arameans whom David defeats in the battle against Ammon; and others.[15] Solomon, famous for his wealth, is said to have had thousands of chariots and horses. These were so strongly associated with kingship that they are the first item in Samuel's list of reasons why Israel will be unhappy with a king: "He will take your sons and appoint them as his charioteers and horsemen, and to run before his chariots" (1 Sam. 8:11). Absalom, in other words, has begun accumulating the trappings of kingship.

Absalom took one further step toward the kingship. He would go to the city gates and meet those who came there to plead a judicial case. In Israel, the city gate was the traditional locus for judicial proceedings.[16] The city elders would sit on benches by the gate, those with a case would come before them to have it heard, and the elders would render judgment.[17] But ultimately, justice was the responsibility of the king. This was a common understanding throughout the ancient Near East. It is the principle behind the famous Mesopotamian legal code of Hammurabi, which begins by explaining that the gods had chosen Hammurabi from among all men "to make justice prevail in the land, to abolish the wicked and the evil, to prevent the strong from oppressing the weak."[18] The same sentiment is found in 2 Samuel 8, at the conclusion of the record of David's victories: "David executed true justice among all his people" (8:15).

Absalom, however, seems to have felt that David's justice was not quite good enough, that David was neglecting his judicial responsibilities.[19] He would say to everyone who appeared at the gate with a case, "there is no one assigned to you by the king to hear it" (2 Sam. 15:3). But he went further, not only denigrating David, but suggesting that he, Absalom, could do better: "If only I were appointed judge in the land"—that is, king—"and everyone with a suit or a claim came before me, I would rule in his favor" (15:4). Absalom played on what must have been a popular sentiment that David was ignoring his subjects. Just in case this wasn't convincing enough, however, Absalom also effectively promised everyone who showed up that he would decide in their favor: "It is clear that your claim is good and right" (15:3), he said to each person. He did not allow people to bow to him—instead, he embraced and kissed them. In this way, the Bible says, "Absalom stole the hearts of the men of Israel" (15:6).

After four years of building up his image among the Israelite populace, Absalom made his final move. He told David that, when he was in exile in Geshur, he had made a vow to worship Yahweh if he ever returned, and now he wanted to fulfill that vow in Hebron. David, in a sure sign that he had no inkling what was going on, permitted Absalom to go. Had David had any idea that Absalom was planning a coup, he hardly would have allowed the prince to go to Hebron, of all places—the very city where David himself claimed the kingship. Sure enough, Absalom sent word to all the tribes of Israel, announcing that he had become king in Hebron. The Bible tells us that "the conspiracy gained strength, and the people supported Absalom in increasing numbers" (2 Sam. 15:12).

That Absalom was able to amass enough popular support to declare himself king is a clear indication that David was unprepared for the insurrection.[20] David had proved himself to have a remarkable gift for reading the political winds and riding them to success after success. Undoubtedly, he thought that he had settled the issue of his succession by making a deal with Absalom at Amnon's expense. He would have had no reason to suspect that Absalom would be impatient. We should also be surprised, because no rationale is provided in the biblical narrative for why Absalom decided to stage a coup. What motivated him to take such a bold step? Perhaps he was irritated at having had to wait five years to return to his former position. Perhaps he realized that a man who could have his firstborn son murdered was not the most trustworthy of co-conspirators. Perhaps he thought that he would be relatively old by the time he gained the throne, should David have a long life. But perhaps the simplest answer is that shown by the course of events: Absalom declared himself king because he could. The real question is why Absalom was successful.

For all of the praise that the biblical authors and subsequent tradition lavish on David, the main accomplishment that the Bible attributes to him as king is the conquest of foreign nations in 2 Samuel 8. Although their claims are exaggerated, as we have seen, they are not to be dismissed—David was undoubtedly a fine military leader. But if expanding Israel's territory was worthwhile from a royal perspective, from the standpoint of the people David was not so admirable. He had claimed power by force in both Judah and Israel—in Judah disrupting the long-established independence of the various clans, and in Israel destroying the only royal line the people had ever known. He had seized the ark, a popular cultic symbol, and appropriated it for himself and his new capital. Military victories may have added to the nation's glory, but most Israelites, farmers and shepherds for generations, hardly would have cared much. What was important to them was that their traditional way of life be preserved. They placed a high value on military protection; they were much less interested in military conquest.[21] David had a vision for himself and the nation, but it was not one that played well in the hinterland.

What Absalom promised was a return to the "good old days"—to the way things had been before David changed everything.[22] This is the symbolic import of Absalom's promise to restore justice at the city gates. His revolt was a populist movement, and David was anything but a populist. Absalom also may have represented for the Israelite people a chance to have a king of their own choosing again. Even though he was a son of David, he could be *their* son of David, a king acclaimed by the people, as Saul had been, and as David had not.[23]

For the biblical authors, of course, the impression that David's subjects did not love him or that his behavior on the throne in any way justified Absalom's rebellion would have been unpalatable. They had tried to establish just the opposite throughout the account of

David's life. How, then, could they deal with the indisputable fact of Absalom's uprising? If God had placed David on the throne, then only God should have been able to remove him from it. And so the authors claim. They found one crime in David's life that they could admit really happened: his affair with Bathsheba and murder of her husband Uriah (to which we will return at length in the next chapter). Of all David's sins, this one was perhaps the least objectionable. Although a man died, that death was ostensibly a result of David's all-too-human lust. And in the end, David's affair with Bathsheba led to the birth of Solomon. In short, this was a place where the biblical authors could accept a depiction of David as less than perfect—and it gave them an opportunity to explain Absalom's revolt. For when the prophet Nathan confronts David after Uriah's death, the punishment he lays on David is none other than this: "I will make evil rise against you from within your own house" (2 Sam. 12:11). Absalom's rebellion is divine retribution, and even as David is punished for one sin, he is absolved of having been hated by his subjects or of having been deficient in any way as a king.

David's Flight

DAVID MAY NOT HAVE SEEN Absalom's actions coming, but he knew a successful coup when he saw one—he still knew how to read the political winds. Upon hearing the news of Absalom's self-coronation, David realized that he had no choice. He and his entire court packed up and fled the capital, leaving behind only ten concubines "to mind the palace" (2 Sam. 15:16).[24] David stopped at the edge of the city and watched as those who remained loyal to him paraded past—not in victory, but in flight. He greeted his courtiers, his bodyguards the Cherethites and Pelethites, and the six hundred Philistines under the command of Ittai who had been with him since his days in Ziklag. When David's priests showed up bearing the ark, however, David turned them back. The Bible presents this as an act of faith, of David not wanting to remove the ark from its rightful home. In fact, however, in Zadok and Abiathar David had two perfect spies: men who were faithful to him but who had every reason to remain in Jerusalem to tend to the cult.

To his priests David added one more crucial loyal servant to serve as a spy: his advisor Hushai. Across the ancient Near East, kings relied on a retinue of advisors, usually men of an older generation, who counseled the monarch on all matters related to the royal administration.[25] The word of a trusted advisor was taken with the ultimate seriousness. If David could plant a high-ranking advisor in Absalom's court, one whose advice would be to David's advantage, the rewards could be enormous. Thus Hushai was instructed to present himself to Absalom as having defected from David. Hushai's undercover work on David's behalf was especially necessary because, much to David's chagrin, another of his well-respected wise men had authentically gone over to Absalom's side: a man named Ahitophel. With his best men remaining in the city as spies, and with his loyal militia at his side, David crossed the valley to the east of Jerusalem to enter, once again, the wilderness of Judah.

In one fell swoop everything that David had built was torn down. He had abandoned the capital that he had conquered and established, and with it the kingship that he had fought so hard for so long to attain. He was right back where he had started. David had experienced two coups in his life: his own against Saul, and his son Absalom's against himself. Both ended with David fleeing into the wilderness, which, as before, was a refuge for those on the run from the authorities. It must have been shocking to David to realize that he was no longer that authority. He had fallen from the greatest heights any Israelite had ever known. By entering the wilderness, David recognized that, for the first time in many years, he was powerless.

This sensation was driven home by the sudden appearance of a man named Shimei in a small village to the east of Jerusalem. Shimei threw stones at David and his men, shouting at him, "Yahweh is returning upon you all the blood of the House of Saul, in whose place you rule" (2 Sam. 16:8). As David and his men continued to walk, Shimei continued to insult him and throw stones and dirt. The David of old hardly would have tolerated such outrageous behavior, as his warrior Abishai reminded him: "Why let that dead dog curse my lord the king?" (16:9). But David understood that he was in no position to fight back. The people had turned against him, and Shimei was merely their mouthpiece. David had been rejected, but the focus for the moment was on the rise of the new king, Absalom. To kill Shimei would be to arouse the wrath of the nation against David—far better to take the abuse and flee in relative safety.

Shimei's insults do more than prove David's powerlessness. They also confirm for us David's role in the deaths of Saul and his descendants. Shimei's speech is the historical truth that the biblical authors have tried to counter. That his words have been preserved even by these same authors is explainable by the situation: unlike many of the stories and conversations that we have identified as apocryphal, Shimei leveled his charges against David publicly, and therefore undeniably. Shimei says what everyone must have known and been thinking for all of these years: that David had no right to the throne, that he had murdered Saul and all the other Saulides in cold blood to achieve the kingship. It is no wonder that the people sided with Absalom. Anyone was preferable to David, against whom they had harbored a deep-seated hatred every moment that he sat on the throne.

As David leaves Jerusalem for the wilderness, Absalom arrives in the capital to formally take up his new kingship over Israel. The first man he encounters is Hushai, David's trusted advisor and spy. Hushai acclaims Absalom as king, but Absalom is rightfully wary. Hushai convinces him, however: "I am for the one whom Yahweh and this people and all the men of Israel have chosen" (2 Sam. 16:18). This speech is telling. David is also said to have been chosen by Yahweh to rule, but nowhere is it said that the *people* of Israel chose David as their king. This is the difference between Absalom's kingship and David's—this is why Absalom's coup was a success. The people's voice was heard, for the first time since David went to Hebron. And Hushai's speech was convincing, for Absalom allowed him to remain in Jerusalem as one of his counselors.

The final act of Absalom's coup was one that we will recognize. Absalom slept with the concubines whom David had left behind in the palace, in fulfillment of the second part of Nathan's punishment for David's affair with Bathsheba: "I will take your wives and give them to another man before your very eyes and he shall sleep with your wives under this very sun" (2 Sam. 12:11). What David had tried and failed at in his coup against Saul, Absalom accomplished with ease. David's downfall was complete: the entire nation now knew that David's power had vanished, and Absalom was the unquestioned monarch.

Absalom was truly his father's son. Like David, he knew precisely how to go about achieving his desired results. Just as David had slowly gathered power, taking a series of well-calculated steps to become king, so too Absalom: his chariots and horses, his promises of justice, his call to the populace to join him—all were thought out and executed over a matter of years. David initially had been impatient and had suffered for it at the hands of Saul. Absalom did not make the same mistake. He had all of his father's political gifts—including unvarnished ambition—and added to them a sensitivity to the desires of the people who would be his subjects. The combination was unstoppable.

Absalom's Downfall

ONLY ONE THING WAS left for Absalom to do to cement his place on the throne. He had to kill David. As David knew when he murdered Saul's descendants, it was impossible to rule in security when another legitimate claimant for the kingship was still alive. Eliminating David was the only way for Absalom to be certain that his father would not one day try to take back the throne. And Absalom could be sure that David would not rest until he had regained control—David had already invested too much in gaining the kingship to let it go so easily.

Considering David's state—with only a few hundred men by his side, all weary from flight—capturing and killing him should not have been a particularly difficult task. Absalom had the resources to pursue David. A quick strike with overwhelming force—an ancient campaign of shock and awe—and David's men would be unable to resist. This, in fact, seems to be precisely what Ahitophel, Absalom's chief advisor, recommended. Ahitophel even offered to lead the charge in Absalom's stead, guaranteeing David's death at his own hands.

But Absalom wavered—once, and fatally—asking to hear also from Hushai, David's former counselor. And here David's sole advantage over Absalom—his web of loyal servants, those who had been with him and benefited from his patronage for so many years—came into play. Hushai was left behind for this exact reason: to provide Absalom with harmful advice. And Hushai played his part beautifully. The plan he suggested sounded perfectly reasonable: remembering that David was at his best in the wilderness, he said, it would be safer to call up troops from all the tribes, as many as possible, and attack him in an orderly fashion, leaving (in theory) no room for error. There was only one catch: if the tribes were all to be mustered for war, then their new commander in chief would have to march at their head.

There were many reasons for Absalom to like Hushai's plan. He could take up the traditional royal role of military leader. He could physically stand before his people as their king. And he could personally ensure that David was really dead. Hushai's argument was convincing, but in accepting it, Absalom sealed his fate.

With Hushai's plan in place, David's spy network went into action. Hushai passed the word to David's priests, Zadok and Abiathar, who passed it on to a slave girl, who relayed it to Zadok and Abiathar's sons, Ahimaaz and Jonathan, respectively. These latter two were staying at a spring just outside the eastern walls of the City of David, and they ran the news to David in the wilderness. The instructions they gave David were clear: David had to get out of the wilderness and across the Jordan. So David did, arriving at the city of Mahanaim.

Why did David have to cross the Jordan? Under Hushai's plan, he would be pursued not only by a selection of troops, but by the amassed forces of all the Israelite tribes. This would include Judah, the territory in which David was hiding. Nowhere in Israel, even the wilderness, would be safe. And further, with so many troops set to take the field, David would need a place to regroup and resupply. We remember that the one significant non-Israelite territory that David had authentically managed to subjugate was to the east, across the Jordan. It was to these vassals that David went, and they dutifully supplied him and his men with food and a place to rest. This may, however, have had less to do with their treaty obligations to David—after all, he was no longer king—and rather more to do with the fact that he and hundreds of his best soldiers had just arrived at their door requesting provisions.[26] Whatever the reason, the Transjordanian supplies probably made a significant difference. And, more important, David's move across the Jordan shifted the field of battle out of Israel and into a terrain that David knew better than anyone.

The battle is described very briefly in the Bible. David split his men into three divisions: one under Joab; one under Abishai, Joab's brother; and one under Ittai the Philistine. David himself remained away from the field of battle for his safety (as Absalom, in his pride, did not). Absalom and his forces, the army assembled from the various Israelite tribes as per Hushai's advice, engaged David's men. Much of David's military success, starting back in his days as an officer under Saul, was predicated on the advantages he gained from the terrain, and this battle was no different. The two sides met in the forest of Mahanaim. It is difficult enough for a regular trained military company to maintain order and position when fighting in the woods. Absalom's army—a patchwork of men convened from the various Israelite tribes, virtually none of whom had any battle experience or practice fighting alongside one another—was undone by the landscape. David's men, by contrast, were well trained, had fought together for years, and had experience particularly in the hills and forests of both Judah and the Transjordan. The biblical authors put it aptly: "the forest consumed more troops that day than the sword" (2 Sam. 18:8).

There is something symbolic about David's victory in Mahanaim. Absalom's rebellion was grounded in a popular appeal, a promise to return Israel to its old ways before David. Yet when it came to military matters, this battle proved that the old ways, of each tribe contributing men to fight together against a common cause, were no match for the royal militia of the centralized monarchy. If Absalom's revolt pitted populism against elitism, it was the elite who came out on top.

As for Absalom, the biblical description of his death is highly literary. We are told that his hair got caught in a branch, and when his mule rode out from under him he was left hanging in midair. It was while Absalom was in this very unroyal position that Joab supposedly came upon him and stabbed him in the chest, after which ten of Joab's men hacked him to death, threw his corpse into a pit, and covered the pit with stones. The last part of the story—Absalom's death and ignominious burial—seems plausible enough. But the dangling in midair by his hair is the biblical authors' way of communicating Absalom's comeuppance: his beauty, which, it is implied, had something to do with his popularity and perhaps desire for the throne, was the very thing that ended up causing his death. This is a morality lesson, not a history lesson. Exactly how Absalom died is unknowable, but it is as likely as not that Joab personally made sure that Absalom perished.

David's reaction to hearing the news of Absalom's death is among the most famous parts of the biblical story: "My son Absalom! O my son, my son Absalom! If only I had died instead of you! O Absalom, my son, my son!" (2 Sam. 19:1). No reader, especially one with children, can help but be moved by David's cries. This is perhaps the emotional high-water mark of the entire Bible, among the most authentic representations of grief in all ancient literature. And in its emotional authenticity, it rings true. After all, David really did want Absalom to succeed him, he was truly shocked by Absalom's revolt, and thus he very well may have been devastated by the news of Absalom's death.

Yet David surely knew that one of them, either he or his son, would die as a result of this battle. David understood why Absalom was pursuing him—he knew Absalom could not allow him to live. But by the very same logic, if David were ever to reclaim his throne, Absalom had to be eliminated. It is therefore curious that the biblical authors maintain otherwise—that David explicitly requested that Absalom not be killed. More telling is the way that they describe this request. David told Joab, Abishai, and Ittai, his three generals, to "deal gently for my sake with the boy, with Absalom" (2 Sam. 18:5). Crucially, "all the people heard when the king gave the order about Absalom to all the officers" (18:5). We have seen this type of statement before. It is similar to what the biblical authors say about the death of Abner: "all the people and all Israel knew that it had not been the king's will to kill Abner son of Ner" (2 Sam. 3:37). When the biblical authors say that everyone in the narrative knows something, what they are really communicating is that we, the audience, should accept it as absolute truth. And, as often happens when the Bible wants to persuade the reader, the point is hammered home. The first man to encounter Absalom hanging by his hair refuses to kill him because of David's words; the two messengers who bring news of the battle to David are each greeted with the question, "Is my boy Absalom safe?"; David continues crying as the troops return from the combat, "and the victory that day was turned into mourning for all the troops" (2 Sam. 19:3). David is represented as caring virtually nothing for the result of the battle—the battle that would determine his fate, whether he would die or return to the throne—but only about the preservation of Absalom's life.

David's mourning continues so long, according to the Bible, that Joab has to intervene and put an end to it. He castigates David for seeming to care more about Absalom than about all of the soldiers who fought so bravely for him and for his kingship. He threatens David, suggesting that if the king refuses to present himself to the troops, they will abandon him. And so David—reluctantly, the Bible implies—stops mourning and stands before his men as victor. This episode is the conclusion of the apology regarding Absalom's death.

It claims that David was so distraught over his son's demise that he would have been willing to relinquish even the kingship just to grieve. This is moving stuff—but it hardly sounds like the David we have come to know.

Joab's significant involvement in the story should be a clue for us as to what may have been happening. At almost every point where Joab appears, the biblical authors position him as the counter to David's desires. It was not David who wanted Abner dead—it was Joab. And it was not David who killed Abner—it was Joab. It was not David who wanted Absalom to return from exile—it was Joab. And it was not David who brought him back—it was Joab. So too here. It was not David who wanted Absalom dead—it was Joab. And it was not David who recognized the great victory he had won over Absalom—it was Joab. Joab is a central element in the pro-David apology. Historical events that incriminated David were deflected onto Joab. As the biblical authors have David himself say: "those men, the sons of Zeruiah"—Joab's mother—"are too savage for me!" (2 Sam. 3:39). In effect, the authors are saying that David was constitutionally incapable of doing the things it appears that he did; it must have been his cruel general. And yet the authors could do nothing about the fact that Joab not only went unpunished, but remained David's right-hand man throughout his reign.

What this tells us is that in the case of Absalom, despite the high emotion of the episode, the truth is that David ordered Absalom's death. Indeed, he had no other choice. He may well have been saddened by it, and he may well have mourned in his way. But he was responsible.

An intriguing question is why the biblical authors felt the need to persuade us that the opposite was true. After all, it would make perfect sense for David to defend himself, even to the death. There seems to be little here to apologize for. The best guess is that, at the time the biblical authors were writing their David story, substantial pro-Absalom feelings remained among Israel's populace, the audience for the narrative. The thrust of the apology is that David would have allowed Absalom to live if he could, and, we may assume, to take the throne either in David's place or after him. The biblical authors are proclaiming that the loss of Absalom as Israel's desired king is not to be blamed on David, their actual king. Such a claim would make no sense generations later, when the memory of Absalom, the momentary monarch, had faded in Israel. The Absalom apology thus serves as another indication that the David story should be dated to a time very close to David's own.

Absalom's coup, though a failure, dealt a severe blow to David, as regarded both his power and his image. David had clawed his way to the top, using every possible advantage he could find, destroying lives and traditions without regard or remorse. He controlled the nation as no one had before him. And yet it all came undone, the mighty king forced into the wilderness and then out of the country altogether, in need of foreign assistance to defend himself against his own former subjects. David would return to his throne in Jerusalem, but his reign would never quite be the same.

The Aftermath

The change in David's power is evident from the immediate aftermath of Absalom's death. The rebel son was dead, and the throne empty—it was David's for the (re)taking. But David remained in Mahanaim. The man who had brought all of Israel to its knees was incapable of returning, for the people who had reluctantly accepted his rule in the past had been empowered by the momentary success of Absalom's revolt. And yet, at least according to the biblical text, the Israelites—the inhabitants of the north—were uncertain of what to do next. David was in exile, Absalom was dead, and the original royal family of Saul had been wiped out—someone had to sit on the throne, someone had to protect them. For if any of Israel's enemies realized that no one was in charge, the nation would be open to easy conquest. Their tribal armies, defeated at Mahanaim, had returned to their homes and were in no position to be raised again any time soon.[27] David, for all his faults, had successfully protected Israel from the Philistines and the Ammonites, the longtime antagonists of the northern tribes. It seemed that there was little choice. For the north, the fall of Absalom meant a return to David.

Judah was another matter. This had been the heartland of Absalom's rebellion—he had been a Judahite, born and crowned in Hebron, the original capital of Judah under David.[28] The northern and southern tribes were not so deeply intertwined that the decision of one was necessarily that of the other. While the north had effectively acquiesced to David's return to power, David still had to deal with the south. Until the situation in Judah was settled, he would not be able to return to Jerusalem as king.

David had taken control of Judah through diplomacy once; he could do it again. He sent word to his priests, Zadok and Abiathar, who had ostensibly maintained their neutrality throughout the Absalom rebellion by staying with the ark in Jerusalem and who were therefore credible in the eyes of the people. David told them to speak to the elders of Judah, appealing to David's old Judahite origins and requesting that Judah unite to return David to the throne. At the same time, Zadok and Abiathar were known to be two of David's oldest compatriots. To add an extra level of force to his request, David turned to someone who was known not to have any affection for him and whose credibility was therefore unimpeachable: Amasa, Absalom's general.

Amasa is introduced in the Bible for the first time as Absalom's personally appointed army commander. But his lineage is also provided, and it turns out that he is Joab's cousin—and therefore David's nephew. In retrospect, this makes sense. Absalom's coup was from within—as a member of the royal family, he wouldn't have had access to anyone outside David's administration. This is why his main advisor, Ahitophel, was David's former counselor. And it seems more than likely that his general, Amasa, had also been a high-ranking officer in David's military.[29] After all, David's commanders were, like Saul's, family members. But whatever role Amasa may have played in David's army, he had sacrificed it when he threw his allegiance behind Absalom. It was thus significant that David approached Amasa for support in his return to the throne. And it also required that David give him something in return. So David told Zadok and Abiathar to send a message to Amasa: "Are you not my own flesh and blood? May God do thus and more to me if you do not become my army commander permanently in place of Joab" (2 Sam. 19:14). Although the appeal to kinship ties may have struck Amasa as somewhat disingenuous—David had just had the second of his sons killed—the appeal to Amasa's ego in the offer of Joab's position was no doubt hard to refuse.

Zadok and Abiathar are never said to have fulfilled their mission to the elders of Judah. But Amasa did his job. It no doubt made a major impression to have Absalom's general supporting David. Not only did it indicate that the Absalom establishment had shifted its support to David—which surely helped with the popular perception of David's power—but it also meant, more practically, that Israel's anti-David army was no more. Just as Abner's defection had signaled the end of Ishbaal's ability to fight David, Amasa's defection did the same for Absalom's supporters. Like the army in the north, the army of Judah had dispersed after the defeat at Mahanaim, and now its commander, himself from Judah, had announced his allegiance to David. Judah was hardly in a position to refuse Amasa's overtures on David's behalf. The message from Judah was sent to David: "Come back with all your followers" (2 Sam. 19:15). David had won again.

The royal procession back across the Jordan was both a grand symbolic moment and an opportunity for some individuals to make personal gestures of support—or self-abasement—before the returning king. The first of these was Shimei, the northerner who had hurled stones and insults at David during the flight from Jerusalem. His appearance before David confirms for us that the north had agreed to have David back as king. Shimei therefore had reason to ask for David's forgiveness, now that the man he had tarred as a murderer was returning to power. David, however, swore not to kill Shimei, much to Abishai's astonishment (again). David's rare show of leniency is readily explained—not as the Bible does, as a display of grace, but rather in simple political terms. David's rule in the north was hanging by a thread, the result not of his great power, but of the Israelites' need for someone, anyone, to protect them. The murder of an Israelite—even before David had made his way to Jerusalem—likely would have incited a fresh wave of resentment. David was in no position to make more enemies now. He had to let Shimei live.

Ziba, Saul's former steward whom David had given control of Meribbaal's royal estate, also appeared before the king. He had more personally at stake in David's kingship than most, as he controlled his property (Meribbaal's property) entirely by David's word. A new king would have no reason to uphold David's agreement with Ziba. A show of respect and heartfelt welcome was therefore appropriate. But along with Ziba came Meribbaal himself, who had more to account for. For Meribbaal had not gone into exile with David alongside the rest of the royal court, choosing instead to stay in Jerusalem and await the arrival of Absalom (2 Sam. 16:3). Meribbaal's decision may be chalked up to his infirmity—it would have been physically difficult, if not impossible, for him to have made the trek through the wilderness and across the Jordan. But Ziba explained it to David differently: Meribbaal, he said, stayed in Jerusalem hoping that, somehow, he might attain the northern kingship that was rightfully his. Meribbaal declares Ziba to be a liar, but of course he has every reason to say that. It is possible that Meribbaal hoped Absalom might really return things to the way they were before David, including the restoration of an independent northern kingdom of Israel. Absalom would rule in Judah, where his rebellion was centered, and Meribbaal, naturally, would rule in the north. As Absalom hardly ruled long enough to effect any changes at all, we will never know what his intentions were—though it is hard to believe that he willingly would have relinquished the command of the north won by his father.[30]

In any case, Meribbaal had to explain his stay in Jerusalem, and thus his apparent support for Absalom. All he could do was beg for mercy. David, upon learning that Meribbaal would not accompany him, had formally transferred all of Meribbaal's estate to Ziba (2 Sam. 16:4). Now that Meribbaal was before him asking for forgiveness, David, so the story goes, declared that Meribbaal and Ziba would split the royal estate equally between them. This decision seems almost Solomonic, and perhaps it is too neat to be true. The authors want to show David as gracious, but at the same time they must have known that he did not in fact divide Saul's estate but gave it in its entirety to Ziba. Thus they have Meribbaal responding to David's division of the property by formally renouncing his claim to it: "Let him take it all, since my lord the king has come home safe" (2 Sam. 19:31).[31] In other words, David did the gracious thing—and if Saul's estate ended up entirely in Ziba's hands, it was Meribbaal's own decision. But Meribbaal would be allowed to live, for the same reason that Shimei was pardoned. Any Saulide death was politically impossible.

The last person to present himself to the king was Barzillai the Gileadite, who had provided David with supplies during the stay at Mahanaim. He was not obligated to David in any way, nor did he need David's forgiveness. He accompanied him merely as a show of respect, made all the more remarkable by his advanced age. David requested that Barzillai spend his final years in Jerusalem as David's honored guest, but Barzillai refused. Instead, he offered Chimham— most likely Barzillai's son—as one whom David could honor in that way. This was effectively an international treaty between David and Gilead, and one that reaffirmed that it was the Transjordanians who were vassals to David, and not the other way around.

With the formalities out of the way, David and his men continued across the Jordan and back into Israel. At this point the Bible describes a remarkable debate. All the men of Israel, we are told, came to David and complained that Judah had been given the right to invite the king back. The men of Judah replied that David was their kinsman, and they had every right to be the ones to welcome him home. The Israelites responded that, as they had ten tribes, they had ten shares in the kingship, and they claimed that they were the first to suggest that David return at all. In the end, we are told, "the men of Judah spoke more powerfully than the men of Israel" (2 Sam. 19:44). This episode is faintly ridiculous. A dialogue between "the men of Israel" and "the men of Judah" can hardly be taken at face value. The presentation of the north and south bickering over who had more right to honor David has no historical veracity. It serves, rather, to suggest that Israel and Judah were each desperate to bring David back, a notion at odds with the reality: that Israel had no other options and that Judah was, once again, coerced into accepting David as king.

There seemed to be little to prevent David from finally making his way to Jerusalem to resume his reign. One man, however, was displeased by David's return. Before David could even reach his capital, a man named Sheba from the tribe of Benjamin declared Israel's independence: "We have no portion in David, no share in the son of Jesse—every man to his tent, O Israel!" (2 Sam. 20:1). Sheba pointedly used the terminology of kin-based landholding: "portion" and "share." This language is cleverly doubled-edged. It states that the northern tribes do not consider David's kingship to be an authentic part of their patrimony; at the same time, it reminds the Israelites that David is originally from Judah and is their problem to deal with. The final phrase—"every man to his tent"—has military overtones and signals the dispersal of the army and the return to traditional tribal life.[32]

The Bible presents Sheba as a significant threat to David's kingship in the north. In reality, Sheba was always a lone revolutionary, and in the end a rather pathetic one. Even if he had been able to rouse Israel to rebellion, David had just defeated Israel's army at Mahanaim with only his private royal army. Now that Israel's troops had returned to their homes, they would have to be mustered again to face David's same victorious warriors—but this time without Judah, which had returned its allegiance to David. Sheba's revolt never would have had any chance of success. In the end it hardly mattered, since the rest of Israel had no idea that Sheba had declared a rebellion on their behalf. Thus when David sought to quash the uprising, he needed to do no more than simply hunt down Sheba. Even this, however, is an indication of how insecure David must have felt his kingship to be. At the height of his power, he would have had nothing to fear from a nobody like Sheba. But his control was so tenuous now that he needed to commit his weary troops to ensure that Sheba's call would go unheeded.

Along with Sheba, David still had one outstanding issue to deal with: Amasa, who, David had promised, would take over for his cousin Joab. If we remember the story of Abner, we can predict how this story will turn out. Amasa may have been family, but he had sided with Absalom against David. Having survived the battle at Mahanaim, he still could be of some momentary use—but once Judah had accepted David as king, Amasa had no further value.

During the pursuit of Sheba, David, we are told, gave Amasa instructions to muster the troops of Judah. This seems a rather bizarre decision. The troops had just returned home; being immediately called up again, this time to fight not against David, but for him, would have been cause for significant resentment.[33] Moreover, David was pursuing a single individual, Sheba—he hardly needed an entire tribal army to chase down one man. To compound matters, David is said to have given Amasa only three days to muster Judah's forces, an impossible task even under the best of conditions. When Amasa was unable to gather his assigned forces in time, according to the narrative, David sent Joab and Abishai with the Cherethites and Pelethites to find Sheba. The two forces, the Judahites under Amasa and David's warriors under Joab, are said to have converged in Gibeon—an inauspicious location for an enemy of David. It was there that Amasa would meet his end. The manner of his death, according to the Bible, was predictable. As in the case of Abner, Joab approached Amasa, ostensibly for private conversation, and stabbed him through the abdomen. The story then tells us that the Judahite army stopped short upon seeing Amasa's corpse in the road, which was quickly moved into a field and covered. At this point Judah's army, in a declaration of allegiance to David, continued to follow Joab after Sheba.

There is much about this story that doesn't ring true. It seems impossible for David to have mustered Judah's troops, even under Amasa. There would be no need to do so in any case. The three days Amasa is given has a distinctly literary ring to it, as we have seen elsewhere. David hardly needed an excuse to send his private army after Sheba—it would have been the obvious choice from the beginning, with its smaller numbers, greater mobility, and experience. It is equally unlikely that Amasa's troops ever would have caught up to Joab's, since the tribal army would have moved far more slowly than David's militia. The siting of the meeting at Gibeon is so inauspicious as to be suspicious. And the death scene is all too familiar. Finally, the denouement of the episode, Judah's declaration of allegiance to Joab, appears to be a transparent attempt to have the people ratify Amasa's death and David's kingship.

There is no question that Amasa died, but everything else in the story is open to doubt. It is almost certain that David never sent Amasa after Sheba, but rather sent only Joab and Abishai and their men. Whether Joab killed Amasa, wherever and whenever the death took place, is impossible to know. Joab is constantly made out to be the murderous one in the Bible for the sake of preserving David's reputation—as in this case—but it is possible that he really was willing to act as David's personal hit man. However it may have happened, Amasa's death would have been David's decision. No one who had commanded a rebel army against David could be permitted to survive.

Joab and Abishai eventually caught Sheba at the far northern city of Abel in the land of Maacah. To get there, David's men had to pass through the entire northern territory of Israel; that they were able to do so without any difficulty suggests both that Sheba's rebellion had no broader effect and that the north had officially returned to David's side. As for the city of Abel itself, it stood outside Israelite territory, at the source of one of the major tributaries of the Jordan. We have already noted the kind of treatment that a city housing a rebel would expect to face, and this case was no different, even if the city was in a foreign land. Joab besieged Abel and began battering its wall, intent on killing Sheba even if it meant also destroying the city. But the residents of Abel had nothing at stake in this conflict. They didn't care about Sheba or his revolt. They were, in fact, perfectly happy to hand Sheba over—and they even did the dirty work for Joab, since all they handed over was Sheba's head, unceremoniously tossing it over the wall. With Sheba's death, his revolt ended, for he was its only member.

Once David had returned to power in Jerusalem, he had to deal with only the matter of his concubines, with whom Absalom had slept in the standard pronouncement of a coup. Had Absalom survived, no doubt they would have been sent away with him, just as Ahinoam had been sent away with David. But with Absalom dead, the concubines were of no use to anyone. They were merely a living reminder of Absalom's rebellion. David imprisoned them within the palace for the rest of their lives.

ABSALOM'S REBELLION REVEALED MUCH about David's power in Israel. In victory, David had proved, once again, that he had the military prowess to maintain his authority. Even against the tribal armies of all Israel, David and his personal, professional militia were dominant. The basis for his rule remained the same as it had when he first took power: David still ruled as a conqueror. At the same time, the fact of a popular uprising demonstrated that despite anything he had accomplished during his years on the throne, David remained deeply disliked. Over the generations, Israel would come to venerate David as the ideal king, but in his own time, he was never loved.

David would never again reach the heights of power that he had attained before Absalom's revolt—perhaps because of the strain of trying to maintain power in the face of subjects whom he now knew despised him; perhaps because of the realization that with Absalom's rebellion and death, his legacy was in question; perhaps simply because of the fatigue of decades of hard fighting to gain and keep the throne in Israel. Perhaps all of these factors contributed to the fact that the rest of David's reign—what little of it remained—witnessed a king in inexorable decline. The man who had once controlled everyone and everything around him would find himself being the one controlled. And, most humiliating for David, who had always used his wives as mere pawns—Ahinoam, Abigail, and Michal—his final fall from power would be at the hands of a woman. Her name was Bathsheba.

CHAPTER 7

David in Decline

WHAT GOES AROUND COMES AROUND

THE ROOTS OF DAVID'S FINAL fall from grace can be traced back to much earlier in his reign, to a time when he was at the height of his considerable power and it seemed that nothing could stand in his way. David hardly could have foreseen the long-term consequences of his actions, but the end of his kingship over Israel began when he decided to take Bathsheba as his wife.

David's affair with Bathsheba is one of the most famous parts of the David story. His lust for her, his murder of her husband Uriah, his condemnation by Nathan the prophet, his realization of his guilt— the episode humanizes David in a way seldom seen elsewhere in the biblical narrative of his life. The story is a model of the biblical doctrine that sin must be followed by punishment and repentance. Even the great David made mistakes—and suffered the consequences. Everyone can relate to this, which is why the story has had such an effect on readers over the centuries.[1] But as we saw in the case of the legendary battle against Goliath, sometimes the most famous stories are the most open to doubt.

David and Bathsheba

THROUGHOUT THE DAVID STORY, we have seen that when the biblical authors go to great lengths to emphasize that something must be the case, we have reason to suspect exactly the opposite. We saw this sort of emphasis in the claims that David was completely loyal to Saul and that David had no hand in the deaths of Nabal, or of Saul and Jonathan, or of Abner, or Amnon, or Absalom, or Amasa. The literary clue in all of these instances is the attempt to establish the Bible's case from as many angles as possible. In all of Saul's confrontations with David, we are told repeatedly that David is innocent and Saul's wrath is unjustified. For every death, not only is someone else to blame—Joab, an unnamed Amalekite, even God himself—but David is always somewhere else when the death occurs. The biblical authors want to leave nothing to chance, to allow no room for misunderstanding. Ironically, it is their very insistence that, for the suspicious reader, undermines their case. And we find this same insistence at work in the story of David's affair with Bathsheba.

In the Bathsheba story, the point to which the biblical authors want to lead us—and they do successfully, as is evident by how universally accepted the story has been over the millennia—is that Solomon was David's son. To get us to this point, they tell the story of David seeing Bathsheba, lying with her, and impregnating her. He arranges for her husband Uriah to be killed in battle, and then he marries her. A child is born, but dies a few days later. Bathsheba becomes pregnant again, and this time she gives birth to David's son Solomon.

The biblical account begins with the notice that David witnessed Bathsheba bathing. This is not merely a voyeuristic element in the narrative. We are told that "she had just purified herself after her period" (2 Sam. 11:4). Thus she was not merely bathing; she was undergoing the ritual bath to cleanse herself after menstruation, a common ancient Near Eastern practice, the details of which are found in the Bible in Leviticus 15.[2] The key to understanding the import of this notice is that such purification took place approximately seven days after a woman's period had ended—in other words, when she would be at her most fertile. This, in turn, makes inevitable the result of David's sleeping with Bathsheba: "the woman conceived, and she sent word to David: 'I am pregnant'" (11:5). We may wonder, however, at how the biblical authors would have known this detail about Bathsheba's most private life. Women did not bathe only for the purpose of postmenstrual purification. And how would the authors know in the first place that David saw her when she was bathing? These details are unverifiable, but they are necessary for establishing Bathsheba's fertility at precisely the moment that David slept with her.

The Bible then tells us that David actually tried to extricate himself from this potentially embarrassing situation. He had Bathsheba's husband, Uriah—one of David's army officers—sent back from the battle against Ammon, where Joab and the military were besieging the Ammonite capital, Rabbah. When Uriah arrived, David encouraged him to go spend some time at home, to "bathe his feet"—a euphemism for sex. But Uriah, despite David's repeated urgings, refused to go anywhere but to the military encampment near the palace. This episode too suffers from an excess of seemingly private information. David's instructions to Uriah to go sleep with his wife—as well as Uriah's refusals—should, in theory, have been known only to David and Uriah. But these details are needed for the reader to appreciate the point of the story. David wanted Uriah to sleep with Bathsheba so that Uriah would think himself to be the father of the child that Bathsheba was carrying. Thus the Bible presents David as trying to preserve Uriah's honor, but failing. The biblical story tells us that Uriah did not go home. Instead, he spent his time in a very public place, among the other military officers in front of the palace. In this way the authors announce that there were plenty of witnesses who could testify to the fact that Uriah never went home. The child could not be his.

Here, as elsewhere, the biblical authors are trying to put a particular spin on an event for which the basic facts are not in dispute. In this case, the facts are that Bathsheba was once Uriah's wife, was now David's wife, and that she bore a son, who (though no one knew it yet) would one day become David's successor on the throne. This is the essence of the biblical narrative, but it has been overlaid with details that betray their nonhistorical origins. As with other episodes from David's life, the aspects invented by the biblical authors are identifiable by both the insistence on a particular interpretation and the introduction of unverifiable private moments. These two features are present in almost every verse of the story we have examined so far. Whatever the underlying truth may be—and we will get to that shortly—the biblical story appears to be a literary creation.[3]

As the story continues, Uriah returned to the battlefront and David took the pregnant Bathsheba into his harem. This meant that when Uriah came home from battle, he would find that his wife suddenly belonged to another man. David knew only one solution to most of life's problems, and it was the obvious choice here as well: Uriah had to die. The Bible presents David's decision to have Uriah killed as the result of Uriah's refusal to sleep with Bathsheba, and as if it were the only option David had left. Yet the two do not logically follow. The authors had already established beyond a doubt that Bathsheba's baby was David's child—what difference did it make now if Uriah lived or died? The child would still be David's, and Uriah, who had not slept with Bathsheba, would know that something was amiss. Uriah's death has nothing to do with paternity and everything to do with marriage. We understand this from the prophet Nathan's famous encounter with David. Nathan approaches him and recounts the parable of the rich man who takes the poor man's only lamb, even though the rich man has so many of his own. David, when he hears the story, is angry, because the rich man has committed a great wrong. Nathan then retorts with the dramatic accusation: "You are the man!" (2 Sam. 12:7). David's crime is spelled out for him: "You have put Uriah the Hittite to the sword; you took his wife and made her your wife" (12:9). There is nothing here about the baby in Bathsheba's womb.

We may imagine that Uriah's death happened in a manner quite close to its biblical depiction. According to the story, David sent Joab a message, telling him to have Uriah placed in the front lines, in heavy fighting, and then have the troops around Uriah fall back to leave him standing alone, where he was sure to be killed. Joab didn't quite follow David's instructions to the letter, perhaps because he realized just how obvious such a ploy would be. Instead, he sent Uriah and a number of other officers to a particularly well-defended area of the besieged city, where many of them, including Uriah, were killed. David's response to the news puts into words the low value he placed on the lives of others, even his most loyal officers: "Do not be upset about the matter; the sword consumes all equally" (2 Sam. 11:25). In other words, David is happy to sacrifice a number of his best men to ensure that he will have a clear path to taking the woman of his choice. Everything about this seems realistic enough, with one exception. The Bible tells us that the message instructing Joab to have Uriah killed was delivered by Uriah himself: "David wrote a letter to Joab, which he sent with Uriah" (11:14). This claim is necessary because the authors have just had David bring Uriah to Jerusalem to sleep with his wife. If that story was invented, so too the notion that Uriah was the one to deliver his own death warrant. The elimination of this feature does little to soften the cruelty David exhibited in this matter. A man died for David's lust—in fact, many men died, thinking that they were fighting for their king. But they were merely dying for him.

The biblical story takes a surprising twist at the end of Nathan's oracle. Not only will David be punished for his sins by experiencing Absalom's revolt, as we saw in the previous chapter, but the child about to be born to him and Bathsheba will die. The story of the infant's death is famous and moving: David fasts and prays for the seven days that the child lives, but stops once the baby has died, much to his servants' confusion. His explanation is authentically touching: "While the child was still alive, I fasted and wept because I thought 'Who knows? Yahweh may have mercy on me, and the child may live.' But now that he is dead, why should I fast? Can I bring him back again? I shall go to him, but he will never come back to me" (2 Sam. 12:22–23). It is a recognizably parental scene, one that still resonates as realistic today. But we have grown accustomed by now to David's public displays of grief: over Saul and Jonathan, over Abner, over Absalom. And we have come to realize that an emotionally accurate scene is not necessarily historically accurate. The death of the firstborn son is followed immediately in the Bible by the birth of a second son to David and Bathsheba. This, it turns out, is Solomon.

The story of the death of David and Bathsheba's firstborn son is, to put it gently, bizarre. First, it is odd that the child has no name. It was the custom to name a newborn immediately after birth, as we see in virtually every birth narrative in the Bible. Names held great importance in the ancient world. They defined one's relationship to kin or to the deity, and they often reflected the manner of the child's birth (the naming of Jacob's sons in Gen. 29–30 offers a good example). A nameless child would be an anomaly.

Second, Nathan's prophetic announcement of the infant's imminent death entails a logical inconsistency. When David repents for taking Bathsheba and having Uriah killed, we are told, Nathan responds: "Yahweh has removed your punishment; you shall not die. However, since you have spurned Yahweh by this deed, the child about to be born to you shall die" (2 Sam. 12:13–14). Nathan implies that the punishment for David's sin will be inflicted upon the child. Yet nowhere in the preceding oracle predicting Absalom's rebellion is it ever said that David would die.

Third, and most important, the death of the firstborn child renders the lengthy preceding account of its conception moot. If the firstborn son was to die, then why go to all the bother of making it clear that it was David's child? All of the demonstrations that David must be the father—Bathsheba's purification and Uriah's refusal to sleep with his wife—end up being a false lead, a blind motif. What difference does it make, in the end, if the baby is Uriah's or David's? The child has no effect on the larger story. Once Solomon is the second son, born long after Uriah's death, and his paternity therefore established beyond a doubt, the first child's paternity is a nonissue. The biblical authors do not waste words. If they wanted to make clear that David and Bathsheba's firstborn son was really David's child, they must have had a reason to do so. When we read the narrative, we expect that this unborn child will be of great importance, just from the amount of space the Bible devotes to the story of its conception and the proof of its paternity. Stories like these are reserved for major figures—even David himself doesn't have a birth story like this. The sudden death of this child renders the efforts of the biblical authors for naught.

All of this has led many scholars, correctly, to the conclusion that the account of the death of David and Bathsheba's firstborn, beginning with the last words of Nathan's oracle, is a later insertion into the original story.[4] It may be a successful representation of parental grief, but it fails on almost every other level. If it is excised, then Solomon is the first—and only—child that Bathsheba bore in David's house. All of the arguments for David's paternity of the firstborn then make much more sense: now they are arguments for *Solomon* being David's son. It is clear enough why it would be important for the biblical authors to establish this fact. Solomon followed David on the throne. If he were not really David's son, then he would not be a rightful heir, with all the natural rights that come with standard royal succession. He would be a usurper and the legitimacy of his reign thus undermined.

But why would the biblical authors feel the need to make this case? None of David's other sons are provided with detailed proofs of paternity, and no one would ever question them. Someone must have thought that Solomon was in fact not David's son, and it is to this charge that the Bible responds.

Why would Solomon's descent from David be in question? The most significant issue is Solomon's name.[5] It was the custom in Israel for the mother to name her children. We see this, for example, in the naming of Jacob's twelve sons by their mothers, Leah and Rachel. Bathsheba therefore was the one to name her son Solomon.[6] The child was born, as the Bible admits, after Uriah's death in Ammon—to which we will return presently. It is thus telling that Bathsheba should name her newborn son Solomon, which means "his replacement." Bathsheba gives her son a name that memorializes her deceased husband. If David were the father, this would be problematic. In the first place, we would expect David's son to be named after him, if anyone. Beyond this, we may well wonder what David would make of his son being named in honor of Bathsheba's first husband. Such a name would practically announce to the world that Bathsheba's affection still belonged to Uriah. It may have been the mother's right to name her child, but it is hard to imagine David allowing Uriah's memory to live on in David's son.

It is the discomfort that such a situation produces that probably led to Solomon being given a second name in the Bible, Jedidiah. Perhaps lost in translation is the wordplay inherent in this name: Jedidiah, "Beloved of Yahweh," is etymologically linked to David, "Beloved." This second name for Solomon—which is never used again—is an attempt to erase the connection to Uriah and replace it with a connection to David.

There is another reason to suspect that Solomon was not really David's son. Bathsheba was not merely a random beautiful woman. She was the daughter of Eliam, one of David's warriors. And Eliam, in turn, was the son of Ahitophel—the same Ahitophel who defected from David during Absalom's rebellion. Solomon was Ahitophel's great-grandson. If Ahitophel thought that his great-grandson stood in line for the succession to the throne, he hardly would have supported Absalom, which would all but guarantee that Ahitophel's offspring would never attain the kingship. Ahitophel would defect to Absalom only if he had no reason to think that Solomon might someday be king—because Solomon was not one of David's offspring.[7]

The biblical authors tried their best to disguise Solomon's true father. They created a scenario in which Bathsheba is virtually obligated by biology to become pregnant by David. They created a story in which David acts on the assumption that he is Solomon's father and in which Uriah acts in a way that publicly ensures this to be the case. But the authors could not overcome two unchangeable facts: Solomon's name and Bathsheba's genealogy. Both of these testify to Solomon's being Uriah's son, not David's.

No matter what stories the authors invented, Solomon's name still identified him as Uriah's son—and it is safe to say, given the Bible's detailed rendering of an alternative scenario, that there were those in Israel in David's day who recognized this fact. The story of the death of the firstborn son was created and inserted to address this lingering problem. Not only does the story make it chronologically impossible for Solomon to be Uriah's son, but it provides, quite cleverly, a new explanation for Solomon's name. Now he could be seen as the "replacement" not for Uriah, but for his ill-fated older sibling. This sort of naming is known from the Bible and elsewhere in the Near East. In Genesis 4 Eve gives her third son the name Seth, meaning "God has provided me with another offspring in place of Abel" (4:25), who had died at the hands of Cain. The eighth-century BCE Assyrian king Sennacherib, famous for his attacks on Judah during the reign of King Hezekiah, bears a name meaning "Sin [a Mesopotamian deity] has replaced brothers for me."[8] The biblical authors provided an alternative referent for Solomon's name and thereby removed the last potential link between Solomon and Uriah. They did so, however, at the cost of narrative logic. And in compounding the Bible's insistence that Solomon, despite his name, could not be Uriah's son, these authors lead us only more firmly to the conclusion that he was.

The biblical authors present David and Bathsheba's affair as the story of their child(ren). The reality is that the affair was just like any other: it was about sex. The Bible's presentation of Bathsheba as unknown to David is probably false. Most likely, David had known her, and had his eye on her, for nearly her entire life. She was, after all, the wife of one of his chosen warriors, the daughter of one of his chosen warriors, and the granddaughter of his trusted advisor. David was always one to take what he wanted, regardless of the claims of others. This is especially true of women, as Ahinoam, Abigail, and Michal could attest. We may imagine that with the army, and Uriah, engaged in a lengthy siege abroad, David saw the opportunity to take for himself the beautiful Bathsheba, whom he had long coveted. It was undoubtedly a surprise to discover that she was already pregnant with Uriah's child. But this would have been little more than a passing disappointment—after all, he had little invested in the baby, who was not his own. Bathsheba would enter David's harem as one of his many wives and concubines. The child would become whatever he would become. It was—so David thought—none of his concern.

Solomon had no deceased older brother. He was the first child born to Bathsheba after David took her into his harem. But he was not David's son; he was Uriah's. The Bible's attempts to persuade us otherwise are part of the standard biblical genre of apology. But this is not an apology for David—it is an apology for Solomon. Solomon would become king after David, but he had no right to the throne. Just as pro-David authors created an apology for how David came to reign in place of Saul, so too pro-Solomon authors created an apology for how Solomon came to reign in place of David. How this actually happened we will see presently. The Bible very much wants us to think that it was a natural succession, the son following the father. But it was not.

Adonijah

THE STORY OF SOLOMON'S succession—the next time we hear of Solomon after his birth—comes naturally at the end of David's life. After all his battles, against Israel's enemies, against Israel itself, and against his own son, David was old and tired. His body, which had carried him to so many victories, had finally broken down: "they covered him with bedclothes, but he was not warmed" (1 Kings 1:1). Even the notion that David needed others to put blankets on him testifies to his physical decline. His courtiers tried to comfort him with the company of a beautiful young girl, named Abishag. There is some irony in this: the man who had used so many women for his own ends now required a woman merely to keep him warm. But to no avail—"the king did not sleep with her" (1:4). No depiction of David's decline can be more pointed than this: his virility has abandoned him. Although the Bible makes no mention of it, it is only natural to wonder not only about David's physical health, but about his mental health as well. The Bible's silence is probably meant to suggest that David was still mentally sound, but the course of events would suggest otherwise.

After Absalom's death, the next in line for the throne was David's fourth son, Adonijah. He had only to wait for David to die, and he would become king. Yet for Adonijah—as for Absalom before him—waiting was unacceptable. He declared his intention to make himself king, in both words and actions that will be familiar: "he provided himself with chariots and horses, and fifty men to run before him" (1 Kings 1:5). This is precisely what Absalom had done, and with the same intentions. To make the comparison even clearer, the biblical authors tell us that Adonijah "was very handsome; he was born after Absalom" (1:6). Knowing that Solomon will be the one to succeed David, we can recognize all of this as foreshadowing: Adonijah will be more like Absalom than he might prefer.

As with Absalom, David does not prevent any of this. But this time it is not because Adonijah lives elsewhere or is preparing a coup in secret. Everything was out in the open—and yet David did nothing. Perhaps David did not know—he was, after all, confined to his bed—or perhaps he was incapable of knowing, senility having crept upon him. But everyone else knew, and took sides. Adonijah had important supporters: Joab, David's general, and Abiathar, one of David's priests. These were not just two members of David's court; they were two of David's oldest and most reliable friends, men who had been with him since the wilderness. For them to abandon David, they must have recognized that the end was coming. If Adonijah was to be king one way or the other, they had a chance to ingratiate themselves with him, to ensure that their status would be maintained in the new administration. Others, however, seem to have found Adonijah's actions precipitous. The priest Zadok, the general Benaiah, and, crucially, David's private army refused to follow Adonijah.

Adonijah threw himself a feast to celebrate his coronation. Unlike

Absalom, who went to Hebron to have himself crowned, Adonijah had no need to be secretive. He held his feast just outside Jerusalem itself, right under David's nose. His disdain for David—or at least his belief that David was powerless to stop him—is evident. The guest list for the feast comprised the royal family, though obviously not David, including all of Adonijah's younger brothers and all of the king's courtiers. It is clear that Adonijah had every expectation of being crowned and that much of the royal establishment shared his expectation. Naturally, Zadok and Benaiah were not invited, as they did not support Adonijah's cause. We are also told that Solomon was not invited, which appears to be an insult. All the rest of the princes were there, why not him? According to the biblical narrative, Adonijah would have no reason not to invite Solomon, no reason to think that Solomon alone would be against him. Solomon was not even listed in the Bible's own record of Adonijah's opponents. But when we remember who Solomon really was—a relative nobody, not a son of David—the lack of an invitation is easily understood.[9]

Although the Bible makes out Adonijah to be committing a coup, his self-promotion was probably justifiable. David was in no shape to be in command anymore. If he was unable to get out of bed, he was certainly unable to lead the nation to war. If he was unable to respond to Adonijah's actions, then he was unfit to make decisions about the fate of Israel. The fact that so much of the royal house supported Adonijah suggests that it was common knowledge that David's rule, for all practical purposes, had come to an end.[10]

It is not necessarily the case that Adonijah planned to become king in David's place, however. It was not uncommon in the ancient Near East for two kings to rule together because one was unable to rule adequately alone. Often this happened when a child attained the kingship—as in the case of the famous fifteenth-century BCE Egyptian queen Hatshepsut, who ruled alongside her young son Tuthmosis III. But it also happened when a king became too old to rule effectively and his son became coregent to take up the reins of power—as in the case of Tuthmosis III, who ruled for more than fifty years, and his son Amenophis II, who joined him on the throne for the final two years of his father's reign.[11] The aim of the coregency was to ensure a smooth succession from one monarch to the next, for the sake of both the royal family and the nation. If this was Adonijah's plan—and since he did not expect to have long to wait for David's death, it seems reasonable—then he should not be considered a rebel. He was, in fact, acting in the best interests of Israel, and most of David's court thought so as well.

Bathsheba's Request

ADONIJAH'S CORONATION, whether well-intentioned or not, would never come to pass. According to the Bible, the prophet Nathan told Bathsheba of Adonijah's plan and advised her to intervene with David on Solomon's behalf, "so that you may save your life and the life of your son Solomon" (1 Kings 1:12). The biblical authors thus make Nathan out to be the driving force behind Solomon's rise, while Bathsheba is merely Nathan's messenger and Solomon knows nothing about any of it. The first puzzling feature here is Nathan's suggestion that Bathsheba's and Solomon's lives would be in danger if Adonijah became king. There is no reason to think that this would be the case. Even if Solomon were Adonijah's younger brother, at least three steps removed from the throne according to the list of David's sons in 2 Samuel 3, he would be no threat to Adonijah's rule. And since Solomon was in fact not part of the royal family, there is no reason that Adonijah should have cared about him in the slightest. Nathan's warning about an unexplained threat to Solomon's life seems to serve only as a basis for the competition between Solomon and Adonijah to come.

More important, perhaps, we may wonder: what stake does Nathan have in Solomon in the first place? Even if Solomon were a member of the royal family, why should Nathan prefer that Solomon become king rather than Adonijah? Nothing indicates that Adonijah was ill-equipped to rule; on the contrary, he seemed to have all the ambition and support necessary to take over. Solomon, on the other hand, had not shown in any way that he was prepared for the throne. As one of David's youngest children—considerably younger than Adonijah, at least—he probably would not have received extensive training to be king. When Adonijah first begins planning for the kingship, we are not told that Nathan and the others sided with Solomon, only that they sided against Adonijah, and thus presumably with David. Nathan's sudden support for Solomon comes out of nowhere and makes little historical sense—especially when we remember that Solomon was not, in fact, one of David's sons.

Throughout the David story, Nathan is something of a shadowy figure. He appears only three times. The first is in 2 Samuel 7, where he delivers to David God's refusal to allow David to build the temple, and with it the promise of a continuous royal dynasty in Israel, including the promise that David's son would be the one to build a house for God. The second is after the Bathsheba affair, in Nathan's parable and condemnation of David. The third is here, where Nathan promotes Solomon in place of Adonijah. We have already seen that Nathan's first two appearances are literary rather than historical, and we may thus be dubious about the third as well. Moreover, it should be noted that all three of Nathan's appearances are directly related to Solomon— one predicting his birth, one at his birth, and one at the moment he becomes king—as if Nathan is an exclusively pro-Solomonic prophet. Even more interestingly, Nathan does not appear when a prophet is called for outside of a Solomonic context—in those cases, David has an established personal seer, named Gad. Nathan comes from nowhere to lay the groundwork for and eventually establish Solomon's kingship. And after Solomon has attained the throne, Nathan disappears from the narrative. In short, Nathan's very historical existence seems doubtful. He is a literary construct, introduced by the biblical authors for the sole purpose of validating Solomon in the name of God.

If we remove Nathan from the picture, then it was Bathsheba who approached David on her own. Nathan may have been introduced here in part to hide that very fact: to make Solomon's kingship God's will, rather than Bathsheba's. But it makes far more sense for Solomon's mother to advocate on his behalf, regardless of his status. Her request begins with what can only be described as a lie: "My lord, you yourself swore to your maidservant by Yahweh your God: 'Your son Solomon shall succeed me as king, and he shall sit upon my throne'" (1 Kings 1:17). David never could have said this. Despite all of his machinations, despite his conspiracy with Absalom, David seems always to have realized that the eldest living son would be the one to succeed him—this is in fact the very reason that Amnon had to die, rather than simply be skipped in favor of Absalom. There is no evidence that David had any plans to remove Adonijah from the succession, much less Adonijah's other brothers. And again, as Solomon was not David's son in the first place, David hardly could have promised that Solomon would be king. Outsiders attain the throne only from the outside—no king willingly gives up the dynastic principle.

After Bathsheba tells David about Adonijah's plans to make himself king—David has remained ignorant of them until now, though the feast is happening practically outside his palace window—she suggests that all of Israel is waiting to hear who David will choose to succeed him. Again, this is a lie—no one outside of this room, where Bathsheba is speaking to David, has any notion that Solomon ought to be king or has any right to be king. But Bathsheba positions David's decision as having national importance, perhaps playing on his infirmity, giving the aged king one last chance to affect Israel's fate. She concludes by repeating the warning of Nathan: "when my lord the king lies down with his fathers, my son Solomon and I will be regarded as traitors" (1 Kings 1:21). As before, this fear is baseless. Bathsheba and Solomon are unimportant. They have done nothing to mark themselves as traitors—at least, not until this very moment, when Bathsheba asks David to make Solomon king.

From start to finish, Bathsheba's speech is designed to play upon David's fragile mental state. The only truth in it is the description of Adonijah's plans—the one thing she presents to David as new in-

formation. What she presents as something David already knew—
that he had promised Solomon the throne—is the lie. David is being
shrewdly manipulated here. The man who once made all of Israel
dance like a marionette beneath his fingers is now rendered help-
less. He acquiesces to Bathsheba's lies: "The oath I swore to you by
Yahweh, the God of Israel, that your son Solomon should succeed me
as king and that he should sit upon my throne in my stead, I will fulfill
this very day!" (1:30).

Some have doubted whether this exchange ever really happened.[12]
It is, after all, another private conversation to which the biblical authors could not have been privy, and is thus open to doubt. It also
serves a clear apologetic purpose: to have David be the one to officially declare Solomon his successor, thus denying the possibility that
Solomon took the throne without David's consent (or even knowledge). We may also wonder whether Bathsheba's lie about David
having long ago declared that Solomon would be king is designed to
fool David or to fool the reader. At the same time, it would not be unreasonable for Bathsheba to take advantage of David's state and have
him pronounce Solomon king, even if David was not of sound mind.
Until there was a new king, David's words still had some currency. It
couldn't hurt to be able to say that David had approved of Solomon's
kingship. Perhaps most likely, Bathsheba went to David to see for
herself just how debilitated the king was. Did he have the capacity to
stand in the way of Solomon's kingship? She got her answer.

Solomon's Anointing

DAVID IS DESCRIBED AS giving full instructions for Solomon's
anointing. He calls for Zadok and Benaiah, the priest and general
who opposed Adonijah, and tells them to take Solomon, with David's warriors, to the Gihon spring, Jerusalem's famous water source.
There he will be anointed, the horn sounded, and the shout raised:
"Long live King Solomon!" (1 Kings 1:34). Then Solomon will be

taken to the palace and seated on David's own throne. This speech is unexpectedly lucid. It seems to contain information that David would not have had access to—such as the support of his army for Solomon, which even according to the biblical account David had not been told of. And it suggests that Solomon will be not a coregent with David, but the sole king in David's place, sitting alone on David's throne. But a kingship was not something a man gave up while still alive. A man stopped being king only when he stopped breathing. It is hard to imagine David giving these instructions.

On the other hand, it is easy to see why it would be important from the standpoint of the authors to put this speech in David's mouth. Again, it confirms that Solomon's kingship, down to the fine details of his anointing and including his replacement of David rather than coregency with him, was David's willing choice. As always, the biblical emphasis on David's participation suggests that perhaps he was not so closely involved.

Either way, the anointing of Solomon proceeded according to plan. He was taken to the Gihon spring by Zadok, Abiathar, and David's army and anointed with oil, and the horn was sounded. Then the biblical authors do something familiar. They tell us that "all the people shouted, 'Long live King Solomon!,'" and "all the people then went up behind him, playing on flutes and rejoicing greatly, and the earth was split open by their voices" (1 Kings 1:39–40). Somehow, the private ceremony turned into a very public celebration, as if to imply that everyone in Jerusalem had both heard about the anointing of Solomon and immediately supported it. But there is no explanation for how this would have come to pass. Solomon's anointing was a hasty affair, designed to take place before Adonijah had a chance to declare himself king—remember that Bathsheba's conversation with David, David's instructions, and the fulfillment of those instructions all occurred between the beginning of Adonijah's feast and the coronation at its conclusion. There is no time for the inhabitants of Jerusalem either to have been told about Solomon's ceremony—nor is it ever said that they were—or to have gathered at the Gihon spring.

And there is no reason that they should have been overjoyed at Solomon becoming king. Probably, there would have been less dancing and more asking of the question, "Who is Solomon?" This is another example of the biblical authors using "all the people" to persuade the reader: if "all the people" supported Solomon, how could we not?

The Gihon spring is less than a kilometer from En-Rogel, where Adonijah's feast was taking place. It is reasonable, then, that the Bible accurately portrays those attending the coronation at En-Rogel as hearing the sounds of the horn and the shouting from Solomon's parallel ceremony. The news quickly made its way to Adonijah: Solomon had beat him to the kingship. The biblical account of the message, reflecting the continuous attempts of the authors to make Solomon's kingship out to be almost universally popular, includes the note that "the king's courtiers came to congratulate our lord King David" (1 Kings 1:47), which must have been confusing for Adonijah, since "all the king's courtiers" were with him at his coronation feast. But what undoubtedly put an end to Adonijah's ceremony, and broke up the party permanently, was the discovery that the Cherethites and the Pelethites were with Solomon. The support of all of Israel probably would not have been enough to put Adonijah on the throne—after all, it was not enough to keep Absalom there in the face of David's royal militia. Solomon's coronation would go unchallenged.

The feature of the biblical story that seems least probable is the suddenness of Solomon's anointing. Opposition to Adonijah, which is readily explained, is quickly transformed into support for Solomon— even though Solomon seems to have been seeking precisely the same thing as Adonijah. People who have no stake in Solomon—not only the probably invented Nathan, but also Zadok and Benaiah and the army—throw their authority behind him with no obvious justification. Support takes time to build up, but the biblical account leaves no room for it.

In reconstructing the more historically likely course of events, we can rectify some of these inconsistencies. David's feebleness was apparent to all. It was the motivation for Adonijah's actions, which were more an attempt to save the kingship than to usurp it. Nevertheless, Adonijah acted unilaterally—an indication that David was truly in no shape to rule. His decision was the logical one, and the one supported by most of David's own administration. He was the next in line, and the continuity of the dynasty was of great importance. And there is no reason to doubt Adonijah's ability to lead.

But unilateral decisions are almost never without controversy. As David weakened, there was room for others with an eye on the throne to step up. Ironically, David was now in the same position Saul had been in so many years earlier: the first king in a hoped-for dynasty, with an assumption—though not an assurance—of lineal succession. David had seen in Saul's kingship the possibility that an outsider could step in. Others must have thought the same about David's. We should not see the decision to elevate Solomon as a sudden one, but rather as one that grew as David declined, in parallel with Adonijah's moves to take power. This would best explain the recurring claim that somehow Bathsheba's and Solomon's lives would be endangered if Adonijah became king: the two sides had been in increasing competition all along.

With no clear end to David's reign in sight—and thus no clear beginning for his successor—it must have been something of a waiting game. If David died, Adonijah would be the de facto king, at which point any other candidate would have a far more difficult path to the throne. In some respects, then, Adonijah did Solomon a favor by making his move while David was still alive. And Solomon's supporters must have been ready for it when the moment came. As soon as Adonijah moved to crown himself, Solomon's people did the same for their man. But they had no need of a large feast and a public celebration. They needed only a few men, a jug of oil, and a horn—and David's royal bodyguards standing beside them.

There is no need to posit any participation on David's part through all of this. He was incapacitated, nothing more than a figurehead, and one whose death all involved eagerly awaited. The real power, it is clear from Solomon's success over Adonijah, rested in the hands of

Benaiah and the Cherethites and Pelethites. We have already had occasion to observe that in a power vacuum, it is often the military that takes command, in the ancient world as today. With David incapable of leading them, his militia had the power to dictate their preferences. And when they gave their support to Solomon, he had command of the most powerful institution in Israel.

Adonijah would have realized the precariousness of his situation immediately upon hearing that Solomon had been anointed. He knew what happened after a coup to those with a rightful claim to the throne. His father had provided a blueprint. Now Solomon was in charge, and Adonijah was like one of Saul's descendants—a constant threat that he would sway popular opinion (which he already had) and that he would attempt to regain the throne (which he undoubtedly would). Adonijah had two courses of action: flee the country, or throw himself on Solomon's mercy. He chose the latter. He ran to the altar beside the ark in Jerusalem and clutched the horns on its corners. Everyone would have understood this as the traditional gesture of one seeking sanctuary—this is in fact exactly where that meaning of "sanctuary" comes from—a tradition that is already assumed in the earliest legal text of the Bible (Exod. 21:14).[13] Solomon may have felt that he had not yet accumulated enough power to kill Adonijah, who had the support of so many. He therefore let him live—for now.

With Adonijah's flight to the sanctuary, the debate over David's succession came to an end. David's eldest son lived in fear for his life. Solomon—an outsider, the son of Uriah the Hittite—sat uncontested on the throne over Judah and Israel. It would appear that Solomon had accomplished something truly remarkable. But in fact, it seems that Solomon had little to do with it. His first words in the Bible are his ruling that Adonijah should be allowed to live. Throughout all the machinations to make him king, including his coronation ceremony, Solomon is silent. Others always act on his behalf: Benaiah, Zadok, the military, and, most important, Bathsheba.[14] Solomon appears to be something of a pawn. The driving force behind his kingship was the new queen mother; Solomon's coup was really Bathsheba's coup.

How could Bathsheba, ostensibly just another one of David's many wives and concubines, garner enough support to put Uriah's son on the throne? It is crucial to note where the support came from. Solomon gained the kingship because David's warriors were behind him. And they were behind him because Solomon was almost one of their own. Bathsheba's father, Eliam, was one of David's warriors—so, too, her husband and Solomon's father, Uriah. Solomon did not grow up in David's court, as Adonijah had. He grew up among David's army. This was a military coup—David had always ruled on the strength of his private militia, and now that militia was claiming official command of the nation that it had, in effect, controlled for years.

Bathsheba, as one of David's wives, perhaps had more authority, or access to power, than others who might have wished their military sons to rise to the top. But she also may have had extra motivation. Her grandfather, remember, was Ahitophel, David's former advisor who turned his allegiance to Absalom. Ahitophel, as may be expected, did not survive the rebellion. The Bible says that when his advice was rejected in favor of Hushai's, he went home and hanged himself (2 Sam. 17:23). If he did truly commit suicide, it would be more logical for him to have done so only after Absalom had been killed—after all, had Absalom somehow emerged victorious even despite Hushai's subversive actions, Ahitophel would have remained a high-ranking member of the royal court. But it is equally possible that he did not commit suicide at all but was killed by David as punishment for his defection, just as Amasa was killed for his. It also seems likely that if Ahitophel had defected, his son Eliam had as well; though it is not unheard of for fathers to fight against sons, it need not be the most obvious choice either. And then there is Uriah, Bathsheba's first husband, whom David had killed—and whom, based on Bathsheba's naming her son Solomon, she never stopped loving. It is thus possible that Bathsheba had lost three of her male relatives, including her father and husband, to the sword. Solomon's kingship may have been Bathsheba's revenge: an opportunity to make right all of the wrongs that had befallen her family because of the king.[15]

If this reconstruction has any validity, it means that the fallout from Absalom's revolt was more widespread than may have been imagined. Not only did Absalom permanently scar David's previously unblemished power, but ironically, in defeating Absalom, David may have laid the groundwork for the ultimate downfall of his kingship and the end of his incipient dynasty. With Solomon's accession—not succession—to the throne, David's power was finally and completely gone. He was no longer king. He was merely an old man confined to his bed.

David's Death

THE FINAL CHAPTER OF the biblical story of David's life consists almost entirely of David's deathbed instructions to Solomon. It begins with a short speech that, like the oracle in 2 Samuel 7, is a seventh- or sixth-century BCE addition to the narrative based on the book of Deuteronomy. David tells Solomon to be strong—exactly as Moses, in his deathbed speech, tells Joshua to be strong (Deut. 31:6). He tells Solomon to "keep the charge of Yahweh your God" (Deut. 11:1); to walk in God's ways and observe all of his laws, commandments, rules, and admonitions (Deut. 26:17). These, David says, are recorded "in the Torah of Moses"—that is, Deuteronomy, to which, it should be noted, David has never paid much attention before this. All of this is in order that Solomon should "succeed in whatever you undertake" (Deut. 29:8). Then, David says, God will fulfill the promise he made about David: the promise of 2 Samuel 7. As Deuteronomy was written at least three hundred years after David lived, it is safe to conclude that David never said any of this.

Now David turns to the specific instructions. First, he tells Solomon to kill Joab. This is, to say the least, shocking—no one in all Israel, at least according to the biblical narrative and probably in reality as well, was as loyal to David as Joab. David's rationale is baldly apologetic: Joab should die because he killed Abner and Amasa. Even in his last words David's reputation is upheld. Solomon needs no fictional reason to kill Joab, for Joab had taken Adonijah's side—correctly perceiving that to be the course truest to David's legacy. The opposing general was never allowed to live—as the cases of Abner and Amasa, mentioned by David himself, prove.

David also tells Solomon to deal with Shimei, the northerner who accused David of killing Saul's family. David had promised Shimei that he would not die—which at the time was a measure of David's decreased power after Absalom's revolt. Solomon can now do what David had been unable to. And it is as much in Solomon's interests to root out any potential troublemakers as it was in David's.

In neither of these cases did David need to tell Solomon what to do. Solomon—if he were only half as wise as the Bible makes him out to be—would be sure to do them on his own. And, like the speech lifted from Deuteronomy, it is certain that David did not tell Solomon what to do. Solomon had stolen the crown from David's head. There is no reason to think that he ever went to David for advice, or for anything else. David was not Solomon's father—he was nothing to Solomon anymore. These instructions exist to validate Solomon's actions as reprisals on David's behalf rather than as the understandable decisions of a new king wanting to consolidate his power.

With the final details out of the way, nothing was left for David but to die. In all likelihood, he died alone—no family was left to be at his bedside; perhaps only a servant or two were assigned by Solomon to keep watch and report the happy news. David had risen from the humblest of beginnings to become the mightiest king Israel had ever known. But he died without glory, his power, both physical and political, having long since slipped away.

Solomon Secures His Power

ONCE DAVID WAS GONE, Solomon had only to tie up the loose ends. He began, as expected, by dealing with Adonijah and his supporters. In the Bible, Adonijah dies mostly of stupidity. He is said to have gone to Bathsheba with a friendly request: might he perchance take David's last concubine, Abishag, as his wife? Solomon, when Bathsheba brings Adonijah's request to him, correctly interprets it: "Why request Abishag the Shunammite for Adonijah? Request the kingship for him!" (1 Kings 2:22). For this gross misconduct, Solomon has Benaiah, his general, kill Adonijah. It is impossible to imagine that Adonijah, who had been forced to seek sanctuary to save himself from Solomon, should now be so foolish as to try such a blatant attempt at a coup. Solomon had Adonijah killed for the obvious reason: he was the rightful heir to the throne that Solomon had stolen. The biblical story, however, absolves Solomon of any vindictiveness. He had given Adonijah a chance to live out his days in peace, the Bible tells us. It was Adonijah who brought about his own death.

From Adonijah, Solomon turned to the priest Abiathar. His life was spared, but he was confined to house arrest. His fellow Adonijah supporter Joab, however, was less fortunate. After seeing what had happened to Adonijah—or, equally likely, even before then—Joab tried to seek sanctuary at the altar, just as Adonijah had. Solomon had been lenient with Adonijah, at least at first. He would not be so with Joab; he sent Benaiah to seize him from the altar and kill him. Though this seems a violation of the principle of sanctuary, it was in fact in line with ancient Israelite custom: the altar provided no safety for those guilty of murder (Exod. 21:14). And, even if disingenuously, Solomon was perfectly capable of laying the deaths of Abner and Amasa at Joab's feet. Solomon could declare that he had rid Israel of its most dangerous man—without mentioning that Joab was probably most dangerous to Solomon himself.

Finally, Solomon dealt with Shimei. Shimei was confined to a house in Jerusalem—away from his home in Benjamin, where he might continue to stir up trouble—and given instructions that were nearly impossible to follow. He was not to leave his house—ever. Should he leave, he would die. Solomon only had to wait. And sure enough, eventually Shimei left, in pursuit of some runaway slaves. Like Adonijah and Joab, Shimei died by the sword of Benaiah.

One group remains that had supported Adonijah but never appears in the story again: Adonijah's younger brothers, the princes, the other sons of David who were invited to Adonijah's feast. The precise makeup of this group is unclear. The Bible mentions two sons born after Adonijah in Hebron, Shephatiah and Ithream, and ten others born in Jerusalem. Because none is ever mentioned by name again, it is hard to judge whether these lists are historically accurate. It seems safe to say, however, that David had other sons after Adonijah—they appear not only here, but also in the story of Absalom's murder of Amnon, where David is afraid that Absalom has killed not only his elder brother, but all the other princes as well. If David had other sons, what happened to them after Solomon became king? There is probably not an innocent explanation for their disappearance. After Adonijah's death, the rightful heir to David's throne would be the eldest of Adonijah's younger brothers, and so on down the line. David knew enough to eliminate all his predecessor's descendants to ensure the safety of his stolen crown. It is reasonable to assume that Solomon knew it just as well.

With these deaths, all the remaining ties to David's story were severed. Solomon could begin to rule without any entanglements inherited from his predecessor. Murder had been David's main path to power, and with these final murders, that path finally came to an end. With the last words of the chapter, the Bible formally transitions from the story of David to the story of Solomon: "The kingdom was secured in Solomon's hands" (1 Kings 2:46).

The Bible presents Solomon's kingship as David's choice. David declared that Solomon would succeed him; David gave the command for Solomon's coronation; David gave Solomon instructions for securing the kingdom. But Solomon's kingship was not David's choice. It happened without his consent, and even without his knowledge.

Solomon's kingship is presented as the divinely ordained continuation of David's dynasty. It had been predicted long before Solomon's birth; it was reaffirmed in David's own deathbed words. But Solomon's kingship was not a continuation of David's dynasty. Solomon was not David's son—he was the son of Uriah. Solomon had no right to the throne—he took it by force from Adonijah, the true heir, with the support of the army. Solomon was a usurper.

The biblical authors did all they could to hide this fact, though it must have been recognized by David and Solomon's contemporaries. But generations later, with king after king in Judah tracing his lineage back to David—the man who had created the kingdom of Judah in the first place—the biblical account won the day. And it has prevailed for the past three thousand years.

The realization that Solomon was not David's son has an effect beyond mere historical curiosity. The entire myth of the Davidic dynasty, built up over the centuries in ancient Israel, is based on a falsehood. There was no Davidic dynasty—the kingdom of Judah was ruled by a Solomonic dynasty. And the genealogies that trace the descent of Jesus back to David are equally problematic. Jesus's line may go back to Solomon—but David is out of the picture. And so too are David's sons, whom Solomon probably had killed as part of his Davidic housecleaning. David's line died with him.

The irony of Solomon's coup is that, in the end, David's legacy is the same as Saul's. Both were the first kings—Saul over Israel, David over Judah and over the united kingdom. Both must have had high hopes that their sons would succeed them and that a long-lasting dynasty would result. But neither would see his hopes realized. Saul and David were both outmaneuvered by an outsider, someone with no right to be king, who would come to wear the crown.

Solomon's Reign

THE ISRAELITES WHO LIVED through David's and Solomon's reigns witnessed a dramatic transformation of their land and culture. David had created two new kingdoms out of nothing: the kingdom of Judah, previously a region of independent communities, and the united kingdom of Judah and Israel. The inhabitants of Judah may not have felt that they needed a king—David imposed the kingship on them against their will—but once they had it, it was there to stay. David gave the Judahites a sense of nationhood and importance that they had never had previously. Long the minor area to the south of Israel's heartland, Judah could now see itself as equal to its northern cousins, even if it would take many generations for them to achieve that status fully. In the north, on the other hand, the Israelites were never pleased with having been subsumed into a larger polity. They had had their own king once, and with him the hopes for a lasting national identity. David had put that all to a quick end.

In some respects, the notion of the united kingdom, representing Israel's golden age, is a myth.[16] Israel and Judah were separate polities, with separate histories and traditions. In David, they had a common king, but not a common cause. The inhabitants of Israel and Judah did not consider themselves "Israelites" in the larger sense. They were members of their tribes, and clans, and families. The reluctance of the north to see itself as part of David's kingdom is evident from Shimei's curses, from Sheba's rallying cry, and from the renewed separation of Israel and Judah that was yet to come. The combination of the two kingdoms was an accomplishment of David's force and will—it was really the kingdom of David, not the kingdom of Israel.

Memories of independence have long lives. In our time, we have witnessed what appears to be the disintegration of well-established nations—the USSR and Czechoslovakia, for example—not to mention the regular cries of those peoples unable to reassert their independence. This is not really disintegration, however; it is a return to older territorial and ethnic boundaries. David may have brought the north and south together, but this was a unification neither side ever asked for. And within two generations, when the force of David's personality had faded, one would become two again.[17]

Nevertheless, it was this united monarchy that David bequeathed to Solomon. David had struggled all his life to create and maintain his kingdom. He had little time or energy to do much more with it—as noted earlier, David's kingship looked very much like Saul's.

Solomon, however, faced no challenges to his rule at any point, and fought no wars. He had the freedom to take what David had started and turn Israel into a real state, with centralized rule extending to all corners of the kingdom. David transformed Israel from a loose collection of tribes into a legitimate, if incipient, ancient Near Eastern nation. Solomon transformed the kingship from a glorified tribal chiefdom into a true Near Eastern monarchy.

On multiple levels Solomon built on foundations laid by David. David made some forays into international relations, including some minor conquests and some tentative diplomatic ties. But he spent most of his energy securing Israel's new borders. His efforts resulted in a state that, during Solomon's reign, became more of a player on the international stage. Solomon married an Egyptian princess—thereby becoming the first Israelite king to establish diplomatic connections with the superpower on the Nile. He developed commercial dealings across the Near East that brought new wealth into Israel, largely using the trade routes to the south that David had secured. And with that wealth Solomon followed the standard model of Near Eastern kings: he kept it for himself, using it to decorate his palace, build an elaborate ivory throne, and purchase horses for the royal stables. It is unclear whether the majority of Israel reaped any benefit from Solomon's riches. It is telling that even the Bible does not suggest that anyone but Solomon grew wealthy during his reign.

David had founded a new cult in Jerusalem, centered on the ancient icon of the ark of the covenant and the altar that accompanied it. Solomon, famously, built a new house for the ark, a magnificent temple. But Solomon's temple was not like other Israelite sanctuaries. He didn't want to have just another local cultic site. He wanted his temple to be grand on an internationally recognized scale. Archaeology has uncovered palaces from ancient Turkey to Syria that have architectural designs remarkably close to those of the temple described in the Bible.[18] This makes sense, as the Bible tells us that Solomon had the temple built by foreigners: the Phoenicians from Tyre. We saw that David probably envisioned the Jerusalem cult as a confirmation of God's approval of his kingship. Solomon would make the divine-royal link explicit by building not only the temple, but a new palace just beside it, in a single complex on the Temple Mount. Like David, Solomon offered sacrifices before his new cultic site, though Solomon's were a bit more grandiose: 22,000 oxen and 120,000 sheep, according to the Bible. Like David, Solomon acted as priest, confirming that this great temple was a royal temple, the cult a royal cult. Solomon built the temple to be the religious center of the nation—but, as king, he was inextricably linked to it. Church and state were anything but separate.

One of the most significant results of David's reign was the end of Israel's own old-fashioned ad hoc tribal armies, which had served Israel for generations. They may not have been the best fighting forces, but they kept the Israelites grounded in their long-established kinship groups and reinforced a communal model of mutual self-defense. The victory of David's royal militia during Absalom's revolt demonstrated the weakness of the old system and inaugurated a new era of the centralized royal military.[19] Solomon, again adopting the practices of Israel's more powerful neighbors, instituted a policy of military conscription, thereby taking advantage of the sheer manpower afforded by the populace and combining it with the rigor of a formal centralized army.[20] The Israelites could not have been very pleased with this development. Even as it enhanced national security, it came at a severe cost to the traditional way of life. This popular displeasure is reflected in the prophet Samuel's pessimistic prediction of what it would mean for Israel to have a king: "He will take your sons and appoint them as his charioteers and horsemen, and to run before his chariots" (1 Sam. 8:11).

Saul, as we saw, had only the most insignificant of royal courts, consisting of a few relatives who helped him command the army. David largely maintained this pattern, though he introduced a few more figures: a scribe, a recorder, priests. Solomon, however, exploded the traditional forms of government. He too had generals, a scribe, a recorder, and priests. But whereas Saul's and David's governments were essentially local, tied to the person of the king, Solomon created a true national administration. He divided Israel into twelve districts, each governed by a prefect. Crucially, these districts did not correspond to the twelve tribes of Israel. Solomon redrew the map of Israel, breaking up long-standing affiliations and creating new administrative regions that crossed traditional boundaries. The purpose of this redistricting was to dissolve the tribal system entirely. Tribes had their own leaders, their own cultures, their own priorities. In theory, a tribe could try to secede, to return to its original independent status. Solomon would have none of this.[21]

Moreover, these new administrative districts were created mainly for the purpose of taxation. Each district was responsible for providing Solomon's court—and Solomon's horses—with provisions for one month of the year, in rotation. Israel had no experience with national taxation; neither Saul nor David had taxed his subjects. This was a new imposition, and another predicted by Samuel: "He will take a tenth part of your grain and vintage and give it to his eunuchs and courtiers . . . he will take a tenth part of your flocks, and you shall become his servants" (1 Sam. 8:15, 17). Although military conscription was unwelcome, at least it served a clear national purpose. Solomon's royal taxation, however, served nothing other than Solomon.

Solomon's most significant administrative action was instituting a policy of forced labor—not on conquered peoples, as David had done with Ammon, but on Israel itself, and specifically on the northern kingdom. Solomon undertook major building projects—not only the temple and palace, but new fortifications of major cities throughout Israel. At three sites in particular, Hazor, Megiddo, and Gezer, archaeological excavation has revealed what some believe to be the remains of Solomon's construction.[22] The massive walls and gates that were built under Solomon are on a scale far beyond anything Israel had known before. These sites, and others, were built as royal outposts—as the Bible puts it, "garrison towns, chariot towns, and cavalry towns"—intended not to empower their local regions, but to assert Solomon's royal power throughout his territory.[23]

In the end, it was these administrative impositions of taxation and forced labor that would undo all of David's and Solomon's achievements. After Solomon's death, the leaders of the northern tribes came to his son, Rehoboam, and demanded that Solomon's policies be reversed: "Your father made our yoke heavy. Now lighten the harsh labor of your father and the heavy yoke that he laid on us, and we will serve you" (1 Kings 12:4). Rehoboam refused, and Israel seceded, returning to the independence it had known before David. Solomon's descendants would continue to rule Judah from David's capital in Jerusalem. But the two kingdoms would never be unified again.

DAVID CREATED SOMETHING NEW in Israel: a legitimate state, with secure borders and increasing international recognition. Solomon took David's emerging nation and tried to bring it up to the standards of the great powers of the region. From where Solomon sat—on the throne—this meant enhancing the status of the kingship so that it no longer resembled a tribal chiefdom. This meant having a magnificent temple and palace. This meant military conscription. This meant taxation. This meant royally sponsored building projects, even if they had to be built on the backs of the people. Israel was not ready for such changes. It had survived and, in its provincial way, thrived under its traditional tribal system. The Israelites saw the new style of monarchy as an imposition, forcing them into unfamiliar cultural patterns, for ends that seemed to not benefit them. David and especially Solomon were ahead of their time. The cost of their innovations was the disintegration of the nation David had worked so hard to create.[24]

CONCLUSION

THE PROCESS OF CONSTRUCTING DAVID's legacy began even before
his death, with the composition of the pro-David apology with which
we have primarily been concerned here. As we saw in the previous
chapter, the narrative of David's decline and death in the first chapters of 1 Kings is intrinsically connected with the story of Solomon's
rise to power. It presents a David who is confused and easily taken
advantage of, which hardly seems to serve an apologetic purpose with
regard to David. Instead, this story is needed to establish Solomon's
credential to rule. Rather than defend David against any charges, it
uses David to defend Solomon, to show that he gained the throne
with David's blessing and that Solomon's retributive actions against
his political opponents were undertaken on David's instructions. The
story of David's last days belongs not to David's apology, but to Solomon's.[1]

David's apology thus properly ends before his death, shortly after
he has resumed power in the wake of Absalom's rebellion. And this
is probably when we should date the composition of the apology as
well. It should be no surprise that the apology was written even while
David was still on the throne. Although the narrative does glorify
David, its main purpose is to exculpate him, to defend him against ac-
cusations leveled by his contemporaries: that he was a murderer and
most important a usurper. The apology defends David's right to sit
on the throne; after his death, the arguments on both sides would be

moot. It is also likely that it was Absalom's revolt that occasioned the composition of the apology. When David first became king, although he was a usurper, his power was undeniable. His military strength and political savvy forced Judah and Israel to accept him as their ruler. In such a circumstance an apology would hardly be warranted—even if David was an illegitimate king, the people had no means to do anything about it. After Absalom's rebellion, however, when David's power was at its weakest, even the Bible acknowledges that many people in both Judah and Israel were reluctant to return to David. It was during Absalom's revolt that the explicit accusation of murdering Saul and his family was hurled at David. This was the moment that required a full accounting of why David had the right to be king, that required a detailed denial of all the charges of illegitimacy and criminality that had been latent for years but had raced to the surface when David's power was finally challenged.[2]

This view of the story of David, the recognition that it is an apology, has ramifications for how we understand the Bible as a whole. We have been taught by generations of religious authorities that the history in the Bible is literally true. Even when we have agreed to discard the mythical (the creation, the flood, the splitting of the sea) or even the semimythical (the patriarchs, Moses), when we read the so-called historical books, especially the books of Samuel and Kings, we tend to read them as just that: historical. But no writing comes without an agenda, especially in the ancient world, before the idea of "objective" history entered human consciousness. And the biblical story of David preserved in the books of Samuel is no exception. It is, in fact, the very opposite of objective history. It is apologetic revision, its agenda evident at nearly every turn.

Even when the biblical authors take it upon themselves to depict events from the past, it is not what we call history today. It is, rather, ideology expressed in the historiographical genre. Not a word of the David story—and perhaps the entire Bible—is intended solely to describe things as they truly were. Much of the Bible was written so long after the events it describes that there was no possibility for its authors to access the objective past. The story of the Exodus may have some kernel of truth to it—we cannot state definitively that it is wholly fictional. But the biblical description of the Exodus uses the distant past to make a point about the present. The David story is different in that the past it describes was barely past at all. Its audience had lived through David's reign—indeed, his reign was not yet finished when the story was composed. There was no need merely to *tell* the Israelites of David's time their own story. What was necessary was to *reshape* their conceptions of their story.

The apology for David, a tenth-century BCE composition, was taken up and embedded in the more substantial seventh- or sixth-century BCE historical work that stretches from the beginning of the book of Joshua to the end of 2 Kings. Three hundred years after David lived and died, there was no further need to defend him. An uninterrupted succession of Judahite kings had traced their lineage back to David, the king who created the nation of Judah. He was their founder, both nationally and genealogically, and the success of their family in holding on to the crown—especially in contrast to the politically volatile northern kingdom—was evidence enough of David's greatness and God's favor toward him. It is from this later viewpoint that we get the explicit theologizing of David's dynasty: "Your house and your kingship shall be secure before me; your throne shall be established forever" (2 Sam. 7:16). These seventh- or sixth-century authors are responsible for David's final speech to Solomon, which was heavily influenced by the contemporary book of Deuteronomy: "Yahweh will fulfill the promise that he made concerning me: 'If your descendants are scrupulous in their conduct, walking before me faithfully, with all their heart and soul, there will never cease to be one of your descendants on the throne of Israel'" (2 Kings 2:4). It is these later writers who reconfigured David not only as blameless, but as actively righteous, as a model against whom all future kings were judged: "You have not been like my servant David, who kept my commandments and followed me with all his heart, doing only what was right in my sight" (1 Kings 14:8). Even the most ardently pro-David authors of the tenth-century BCE apology could not have said such a thing. But time heals all wounds.

In the fourth century BCE, after Israel had returned from the Babylonian exile and the temple was rebuilt, the need was felt for a new recounting of Israel's history. Long past was the need to legitimate David's kingship. The Israel that existed now was David's Israel, and he was to be emphatically glorified as the nation's founding hero. The new narrative of David's life would be based on the apology from the books of Samuel, but every story that might make David look anything less than perfect was excised. In the retelling of Chronicles, therefore, no mention is made of David's service under Saul, his flight to the wilderness, the death of Nabal, David's time with the Philistines, his affair with Bathsheba and Uriah's death, the death of Amnon, Absalom's revolt, or the conflict between Solomon and Adonijah. This whitewashed David is presented as the perfect king. Moreover, since in the fourth century the institution of kingship in Israel had ended and been replaced by a temple-centered leadership, extra attention was paid to David's role as the founder of the Jerusalem cult. Though the tradition that Solomon was the one who actually built the temple could not be overcome, the authors of Chronicles did everything possible to make David into its true founder. Thus, before his death David is depicted as not only bringing the ark to Jerusalem and setting up its altar, but also organizing the Levites and priests according to their cultic responsibilities, establishing the regular cycle of cultic music and worship, providing men to guard the temple and its treasuries, and even bringing in the raw materials to build the temple and giving Solomon an exact written blueprint of how it should be built. Though Solomon is credited with the temple's construction, he is portrayed as no more than a glorified foreman. David is the architect.

By the end of the Old Testament period, Israel was truly David's nation, both politically and religiously. Dreams of Israel's future glory were pinned to the renewal of David's kingship: at the eschaton, or the end of time, says the prophet Zechariah, "Yahweh will shield the inhabitants of Jerusalem; the feeblest of them shall be in that day like

David, and the House of David like a divine being, like a messenger of Yahweh, before them" (Zech. 12:8). It is no wonder, then, that when the early followers of Jesus tried to position him as the fulfillment of God's plan for Israel, they adopted David's legacy. David was so fundamental that Matthew begins his Gospel with the genealogy leading from David to Jesus. A talmudic rabbi laid down a clear dictum: "Whoever says that David sinned is simply mistaken."[3] David's transformation from a deeply flawed human to a perfected type was complete.

This book has tried to undo that transformation, to peel back the layers of literary interpretation and recover the human David. We are now in a position to think more broadly about his life—what he accomplished, and at what costs.

On a personal level, David achieved what most only dream of. He rose from the humblest of beginnings to become the most powerful man whom Israel had ever known. He proved himself to be a superior military strategist and a brilliant political tactician. Perhaps more important, David changed the face of Israel. He coalesced the scattered communities of Judah into a kingdom, one that would last for more than four hundred years, longer even than its historically dominant northern counterpart. He unified Israel and Judah under a single crown, a union that no one before had accomplished, or perhaps even considered possible. He incorporated into Israel territories that had long been independent enclaves, foremost among them Jerusalem. He turned Jerusalem into a royal capital and a major cultic center. He secured and expanded Israel's borders. For the first time in generations, the Philistines ceased to be a threat. The Ammonites went from a menacing neighbor to a vassal state. Major trade routes to the south were opened. Diplomatic relations to the north were initiated. David left an Israel more secure, more capable of defending itself, and more important internationally than it had ever been before.

David reshaped Israel, but there was significant loss along the way. Success rarely comes without a price. The sublimation of the once-independent northern tribes into David's unified kingdom occasioned great resentment against David and Judah. Before David, the two territories had coexisted peacefully, each recognizing the other as a non-threatening neighbor. Once they were combined, against Israel's will, the narrative changed: now Israel felt the need to separate itself from Judah, and thus Judah became viewed as a problem. By forcing Israel and Judah together, David polarized them. Once they were separate, Judah looked to bring Israel back into the fold, though as a vassal state rather than as equals; Israel, for its part, wanted to do the same to Judah. For much of the next two hundred years, Judah and Israel were in a near-constant state of war with each other. It is impossible to know whether these conflicts would have erupted had David not created the united kingdom. It is certain that the conflicts that did occur can be traced back to David.

David began the process of unraveling the fabric of traditional Israelite tribal society. He put an end to the long-standing tribal armies—perhaps a good for the security of the state, but a step toward the hated military conscription that would occur under Solomon. He undermined the established kinship-based system of land tenure, the inviolable rights of families, clans, and tribes to their property. He trampled on the ancient cultic traditions, seizing the venerated ark of the covenant and using it to his economic advantage. He disregarded his responsibility as an Israelite leader to ensure that justice was upheld, that the rights of the individual were maintained—a job that had once fallen to local elders but now rested on the king's shoulders. On the whole, David ignored or disdained the needs of his subjects. Their desire simply to live as they always had was subsumed by his desire to become something new.

Amid all the national upheaval David's kingship created, we cannot forget the human toll. As David gained power, many people died—or were murdered. Nabal, Saul, Jonathan, Abner, Ishbaal, Rechab, Baanah, Uriah, Amnon, Absalom, Amasa, Ahitophel, Sheba—and those are just the ones whose names we know. There were surely many, many others, including Saul's remaining sons and grandsons. David and his militia must have slain hundreds if not thousands of opponents over the years—often Israelites—from David's time in Philistia to Absalom's revolt. Communities were destroyed: the Jebusites, the longtime inhabitants of Jerusalem, saw their entire culture wiped away so that David could have a new capital. David left a wake of death and destruction behind him as he moved mercilessly toward the throne.

We have no first-person reports of David's life, no personal letters that might shed light on his character. We have only his actions. It is only by what he did that we can assess what kind of a man he was. He was not kind or generous. He was not loving. He was not faithful or fair. He was not honorable or trustworthy. He was not decent by almost any definition. What he was, was ambitious and willing to abandon all of these positive qualities to achieve that ambition. David was a successful monarch, but he was a vile human being.

Some may observe that David was no different from any aspiring monarch of his day, especially a usurper—that all of his actions can be seen as in line with the standards of the time, as no more than real-politik, and that to castigate him too strongly is to ignore his cultural context. The first part of this is true enough. David was not the only person in the ancient Near East to use murder as a stepping stone to power. But to absolve him for this reason carries a faint whiff of moral relativism. Just because some people murdered to gain power in the ancient world—just as today—does not mean it was culturally acceptable. Most people were not murdering others left and right in an attempt to become king. They sacrificed potential power in exchange for the social good. And, it should be remembered, the particular society in which David lived was very clear about its intolerance for murder: "He who fatally strikes a man shall be put to death" (Exod. 21:12); "Whoever sheds the blood of man, by man shall his blood be shed, for in his image did God make man" (Gen. 9:6). Indeed, the very lengths to which the biblical authors go to absolve David of these murders—and the curses against Joab that they put into David's mouth—demonstrate the cultural values of the ancient Israelites. David, even in his own day, was considered guilty of horrific crimes. We cannot judge him any differently.

No one wishes to claim as their founding figure a usurper, a traitor, a murderer. Yet this is the situation we face. There are various ways to deal with this reality. We could essentially ignore it: take a Machiavellian stance, that the end justifies the means. We could worry less about *how* David accomplished what he did and instead recognize *what* those accomplishments ended up meaning. By both creating a kingdom of Judah and bringing it together with the northern kingdom of Israel under a single crown, David gave Israel a sense of nationhood that it would not otherwise have had. We think of some peoples in the ancient Near East as nations—the Arameans, the Philistines, the Phoenicians—but they never actually had any unified national self-conception. No Philistine would have thought to describe himself as such; he would have been an Ekronite, an Ashkelonite, an Ashdodite. Before David, even in the time of Saul, the same was true in Israel: one was a Benjaminite, or an Ephraimite, or a Danite. Israel is Israel, a true national body, because of David. This national self-identification can be credited with being at the root of Israel's survival over the millennia, through war, exile, and diaspora.

The modern state of Israel is directly dependent on David's political accomplishments. The very notion of a political unity that stretches from the Negev to the Galilee, a notion we now take for granted, was David's previously unimagined dream. The name "Israel" itself, so natural to us now, was a conscious decision on the part of the modern state's founders, and one that they debated intensely. In deciding on "Israel," they chose the name of David's unified nation, linking the emergence of Israel in the twentieth century CE with the emergence of Israel in the tenth century BCE. The flag that waves throughout

Israel, and in synagogues and on other Jewish buildings all over the world, bears the Star of David. David bestowed Israel with a sense of its own independence that it had never had before, and that it would experience only rarely for the next three millennia—but that is at the very heart of the modern independent state of Israel. Geographically, politically, and ideologically, the Israel we know today is the embodiment of David's legacy.

By taking the ark to Jerusalem and founding a cultic site there, David laid the groundwork for Jerusalem to become the holiest city in the world. Without David, Jerusalem would have had no temple— the religious center of Israel for a thousand years, including during Jesus's lifetime, and the focus of Judaism's hopes for restoration ever since then. The eschatological idea of the heavenly Jerusalem, the new Jerusalem, found in both the New Testament and in Jewish texts, is built on the foundations David laid in the earthly Jerusalem. From the Crusades to our own time, disputes over who has the right to possess Jerusalem, to call it a capital, are all based on the city's recognized sanctity. It is the city of Isaiah, of Jesus, and even of Muhammad. But above all it is the City of David.

Often unrecognized is the effect that David had on the Bible itself, both by his unification of Judah and Israel and by his inauguration of the Jerusalem cult. Before David, Israel and Judah were never considered a single entity. Yet think of all the biblical passages that presume their essential unity: everywhere that Judah is included under the heading of "Israel"—most notably the narratives involving Jacob and his twelve sons. These stories, which we think of as fundamental and especially ancient parts of Israel's past, could not have been conceived of without David. They are reflections of the united monarchy, not prefigurations of it. Every passage that is written from a pro-Judah perspective—the whole of both books of Kings, for example— depends on David's creation and elevation of the kingdom of Judah. Every text that celebrates the Jerusalem temple and its cult owes its existence to David. This means all of Leviticus and Deuteronomy, Isaiah, Ezekiel, Lamentations, Ezra, Nehemiah, Chronicles, and, at least implicitly, almost all of the Psalms—these are books that could not have been written without David. These are only the most obvious examples. With only a few exceptions, some or all of every book in the Hebrew Bible is rooted in David's kingdom and David's cult. More than most people realize, the Bible is really David's book.

It is possible, then, to look at the results of David's actions—a nation, a holy city, and, in the Bible, the basis of the Judeo-Christian religions—and conclude that these ends are more valuable than the means by which they were achieved. This view is especially tempting since we continue to live under the influence of David's accomplishments. But this also makes it susceptible to charges of cultural egocentrism. In a thousand years, if the Judeo-Christian traditions have fallen victim to the same fate as almost every other religion in history and disappeared, will historians still consider David's actions justifiable? Even today, what might a person outside of the Judeo-Christian tradition think of David? We need not be proud of him merely because we are part of the culture he helped to create.

In fact, as we see more clearly what David did on the way to creating our culture, we recognize that his actions, far from being uniquely guided and approved by God, are at times virtually indistinguishable from those of his ancient Near Eastern contemporaries. This should have important ramifications for how we view ourselves. We can no longer maintain that Judaism, or its religious descendants, is exceptional by virtue of its divinely ordained origins. Had the Arameans, or the Assyrians, or the Hittites survived rather than the Israelites, they would be telling the same story we are. Our existence and self-importance are no more due to David than the nonexistence and lack of importance of the Hittites are due to Hattušili. Judaism emerged from a cultural landscape in which it, and its founding figure, were anything but unique. We may not blame earlier generations for attributing Israel's survival to divine salvation, but neither should we feel free to perpetuate the propaganda of the past to inflate our own sense of self-worth over other peoples. We come from entirely unexceptional origins. If we are to consider ourselves special in the world, it will have to be because of who we are and how we act today—not because of David, and certainly not because of how he acted.

THOUGH IT IS TEMPTING to throw David's sins into the dustbin of history, it is irresponsible to do so. The past matters. If David's historical existence is irrelevant, if all that matters is the biblical depiction, then the Bible becomes a mere storybook and David no better than a fictional character. Ironically, by recognizing the fundamentally literary nature of the biblical account, we can recognize the historical realities standing behind it. There *was* a David. He lived in a particular place and time, and his actions changed the world. We cannot accept the results he achieved without accepting the rest of him as well, the man in full. We cannot wish away our intimate association with the historical David and with the crimes he committed. We can, however, come to terms with it and with what it means for us.

The ambivalence we feel about David, when faced with the need to balance his lasting achievements against the reality of his behavior, parallels other modern feelings of moral uncertainty. The United States has long grappled with the guilt of driving millions of Native Americans off of their ancestral lands. Columbus Day has changed from a national day of celebration to one of soul-searching. And yet we are proud to be Americans, to call this land our home—just as we are proud to call Jerusalem our spiritual capital, despite the native Jebusites who were wiped off the map for it to become so. The Civil War ripped apart the fabric of American society, exposing the deep cultural differences between the northern and southern states and inflicting wounds that still have not entirely healed 150 years later. Yet we recognize the lasting value of holding the Union together by force—just as we recognize the lasting value of David's creating by brute force, against popular will, a unified Israel. Among the most significant debates at the time this book was being written was the issue of targeting and killing those considered to be enemies of the state.

Although we morally abhor the notion of state-sponsored murder, we are also aware that a case can be made that the continuing existence of the nation may be at stake—just as a case can be made that Judaism and Christianity as we know them may not have existed had David not murdered those who stood in his way. Moral ambivalence is a good thing, especially when it comes to the distant past. It tempers our pride in the present with the recognition that a price was paid to reach this point. It forces us to ask whether we would have made the same choices, knowing what we know now about how those choices turned out. And it permits us to accept what happened without wishing that it had to have been that way. Moral ambivalence is, in short, the sign of a maturing—if not yet fully mature—society.

The David of history was who he was and did what he did—and there is nothing we can do to change that. The David of legend, however, is a cultural construction. He is a product not of historical reality, but of our own self-definition, and that of those who have preceded us. Recognition of the disconnect between the historical David and the legendary David is crucially important. The very fact that we have reconstructed David is meaningful. When we understand his humanity—when we see David clearly as a product of and a participant in a world very different from our own—the choices we have made in our own systems of values and behavior are brought into sharp relief. Our national and religious founding figure did things of which we cannot approve, things that we cannot accept as part of our cultural fabric. This is to our credit. We should be proud of the fact that we find the historical David difficult, even repelling. Our morals and actions are not mere replicas of those of the ancient world, despite our deep attachment to the people and events of that world. They are, rather, our own. We are not constrained by the past—we re-create it in our own image. If we are fundamentally opposed to the model of the historical David, it is because we have grown as a culture. Our values take precedence, and, as the historical David clearly shows, this is demonstrably for the better.

In the end, perhaps the healthiest—and the truest—way to deal with the import of the historical David is to accept, maybe even gladly, that he was a fairly dislikable man. We know enough about the ancient world to know that many aspects of it stand in opposition to our own cultural standards: slavery, the treatment of women, bloody animal sacrifices, monarchy itself, to name only the most obvious. For all our reverence of it, none of us would want to live in the world of the Bible. David is part of that world, not ours. We have spent the past three thousand years evolving as a culture, developing and cultivating values that we hold dear, that we teach our children and inscribe in our cherished documents. The difference between the David we want to see—the David we have created—and the David who actually walked the earth three thousand years ago is the difference between the world that we have chosen to become and the world we have left behind. If the historical David didn't strike us as problematic, it would speak rather badly of our cultural growth in the intervening millennia. The more we can see that David is not like us, but is deeply different, the more we can recognize how far we have come. An appreciation of history allows us to see ourselves more clearly.

"DAVID, KING OF ISRAEL, lives and endures." This was the song I grew up singing, probably the first context in which I ever heard or uttered David's name. Almost thirty years would pass before I understood about whom I was really singing. There are two Davids—and the song is about both. The David of legend lives in our cultural imagination and endures in our liturgy, in our scriptures, and in our hopes. The David of history lives in our desire to understand the past, in our search for something like the truth among the millennia of accreted tradition. And he endures in our recognition that we are who we are both because of and in spite of him.

ACKNOWLEDGMENTS

THIS BOOK WOULD NOT HAVE been possible without the help and support of four distinct parties. First, my family: Gillian, Zara, and Iris, who sustain me daily both wittingly and unwittingly. Nothing I do is accomplished without their sacrifices and love, and I am always grateful.

There were three fine gentlemen who agreed, without coercion, to read the manuscript in full. Without their comments and gentle critiques—and sometimes not-so-gentle criticisms—the book would have suffered greatly. Thanks, therefore, are due to my father, Clifford Baden, my first and still best editor; my colleague and friend Professor Bruce Gordon; and Bill Goettler, who pushed me to write this sort of book even before I knew I wanted to do so.

Roger Freet and the entire team at HarperOne have demonstrated repeatedly the value of a publisher that cares about both the material and the author. They have been continually supportive and generous at every stage along the way, making this as pleasant an experience as one could hope for.

This book would, without exaggerating at all, simply not have existed without my dear friend and co-conspirator, Professor Candida Moss. She not only opened the door for this project at its inception, she pulled me through it and showed me the way. She is the finest scholar and best exemplar I know, and my debts to her neither begin nor end with this work.

NOTES

Introduction

1. See also Ezek. 37:24–25.
2. *Psalms of Solomon* 17:21; *b. Sanh.* 98a–b.
3. *Jewish Antiquities*, VI. 307.
4. See Louis Ginzberg, *Legends of the Jews*, vol. 2 (2d ed.; Philadelphia: Jewish Publication Society, 2003), 903 n. 72.
5. Matthew Henry, *Commentary on the Whole Bible*, vol. 2 (Old Tappen, NJ: Revell, 1925), 413.
6. On the early date of the majority of 2 Samuel, see the extensive treatment of Baruch Halpern, *David's Secret Demons: Messiah, Murderer, Traitor, King* (Grand Rapids, MI: Eerdmans, 2001), 57–72.
7. *b. Ber.* 3b–4a.
8. See Paul A. Riemann, "Dissonant Pieties: John Calvin and the Prayer Psalms of the Psalter," in *Inspired Speech* (ed. J. Kaltner and L. Stulman; *Journal for the Study of the Old Testament*, Supplement Series 378; London: T&T Clark, 2004), 354–400.

Chapter 1: David's Youth

1. There is some disagreement in the Bible as to whether Jesse had seven sons (1 Chron. 2:13–15) or eight (as here). For discussion, see

P. Kyle McCarter, *I Samuel* (Anchor Bible 8; New York: Doubleday, 1980), 276. For our purposes, it is less important which number is correct and more significant that the dispute exists at all, for it raises the question of the Bible's ultimate trustworthiness when it comes to historical facts. Indeed, the number seven has such regular symbolic value throughout the Bible, and elsewhere in the ancient Near East, that either figure may be considered historically dubious, especially as Samuel preserves the names only of the elder three. See Steven L. McKenzie, *King David: A Biography* (Oxford: Oxford Univ. Press, 2000), 52–54.

2. Although the Bible does not give David's age explicitly in these stories, he must be more than a mere child. He shepherds his father's flock (1 Sam. 16:11), a task not left to children (see Gen. 37:2, where Joseph does the same job at age seventeen); he is strong enough to carry Saul's heavy arms (1 Sam. 16:21); his father is already old by the time of the battle against the Philistines (17:12); and his three elder brothers are fighting (17:13), which means they must be older than twenty, the standard fighting age in ancient Israel (cf., e.g., Num. 26:2)—and on the reasonable assumption that Jesse's sons were born in sequential years, that puts David at approximately age fifteen (with his remaining four elder brothers filling the gap from ages sixteen to nineteen).

3. 4QMMT C10. Compare this with what we find in the New Testament, in Luke 24:44: "Everything written about me in the law of Moses, the prophets, and the Psalms must be fulfilled."

4. See, e.g., Mark 12:36 (citing Ps. 110:1), Acts 2:25–28 (Ps. 16:8–11), Acts 4:25–26 (Ps. 2:1–2), Rom. 4:6–8 (Ps. 32:1–2), Rom. 11:9–10 (Ps. 69:22–23), Heb. 4:7 (Ps. 95:7–8).

5. *b. B. Bat.* 14b.

6. John Calvin, *Commentary on the Psalms*, preface (1571).

7. Some named, and some unnamed; see, e.g., Gen. 38:1, 2; Exod. 2:1; Lev. 24:10; Judg. 13:2; 19:1; 1 Sam. 1:1; 21:7; 1 Kings 20:13, 35; 22:34; 2 Kings 4:1; Ruth 1:1.

8. On the editorial nature of this verse, see McCarter, *I Samuel*, 304.

9. That particular profession may also render unlikely David's claim that he is unable to wear armor, "for I am not used to them" (1 Sam. 17:39).

10. Almost all—but not all. For the Septuagint version preserves Saul's assessment of David as a mere boy, not a warrior, which remains in contradiction with the description of David in 1 Sam. 16:18.

11. McCarter, *I Samuel*, 306–9.

12. This is, in fact, how the rabbis of the Talmud understood the situation: "David wrote the Book of Psalms, including in it the works of ten elders, namely, Adam, Melchizedek, Abraham, Moses, Heman, Jeduthun, Asaph, and the three sons of Korah" (*b. B. Bat.* 14b–15a). Although there are no superscriptions mentioning Adam, the rabbis assigned him one verse, Ps. 139:16 ("Your eyes saw my unformed limbs / they were all recorded in your book; in due time they were formed / to the very last one of them"), and for Melchizedek, Ps. 110 (despite its Davidic superscription, because it states in v. 4, "You are a priest forever, after the manner of Melchizedek"). Abraham was equated with Ethan (Ps. 89). Notably, they make no mention of Solomon, despite the two psalms with his name in the title.

13. 1 Chron. 6:16–33; 15:16–22; 16:4–36, 41–42; etc.

14. See, e.g., the city-state of Ugarit, which flourished on the northern coast of the Levant in the Late Bronze Age, a few centuries before David, where the king was the primary cultic officiant. See Paolo Merlo and Paolo Xella, "The Rituals," in *Handbook of Ugaritic Studies* (ed. Wilfred G. E. Watson and Nicolas Wyatt; Handbuch der Orientalistik 39; Leiden: Brill, 1999), 287–304 (at 296–300).

15. Another psalm of lament, Ps. 54, receives a similar heading, though with reference to a different episode: "Of the leader, with instrumental music. A *maskil* [a type of song] about David, when the Ziphites came and told Saul, 'Know that David is hiding among us.'" Again, there is nothing specific to the narrative in the psalm—indeed, the headings for Pss. 3 and 54 could easily be interchanged. See further Rolf Rendtorff, "The Psalms of David: David in the Psalms," in *The Book of Psalms: Composition and Reception* (ed. P. W. Flint and P. D.

Miller; Supplements to Vetus Testamentum 99; Leiden: Brill, 2005), 53–64.

16. Note particularly those psalms in the Septuagint that have both the superscription mentioning David and an explicit date long after David's time: Ps. 71, which refers to "the first of those who were taken captive"; Ps. 96, which says "when the temple was built after the captivity"; and Ps. 137, which is said to be by Jeremiah. McKenzie, *King David*, 39.

17. Samuel Horsley, *The Book of Psalms*, vol. 1 (London: F. C. & J. Rivington, 1815), xiv. On the misattribution of the psalms to David, see McKenzie, *King David*, 39–43.

18. The earlier prophet's words are, broadly, found in Isa. 1–39, and the exilic prophet's in Isa. 40–55. According to many scholars, there is a third prophet to be identified in Isa. 56–66.

19. Tryggve N. D. Mettinger, *King and Messiah: The Civil and Sacral Legitimation of the Israelite Kings* (Lund: Gleerup, 1976), 175.

20. The main internal difficulty in the chapter is found in 17:50–51: in the first of these verses, we are told that David killed Goliath with his slingshot; in the second, that he killed Goliath by cutting off his head, the stone having merely knocked the giant down. This confusion stems, however, from the combining of the independent David and Goliath story with that found in the Septuagint; the Greek version does not have 17:50 in it.

21. This same Elhanan seems to be mentioned only in one other passage, 2 Sam. 23:24, which is merely a list of David's elite warriors.

22. We probably are able even to identify when the older stories were reassigned to David. In 1 Sam. 17:54, the Bible notes that David took the head of Goliath to Jerusalem, which is distinctly confusing insofar as Jerusalem was, at the time, a non-Israelite city and would not become Israelite until David, as king, captured it. It thus is likely that the adoption of the Goliath story occurred some time thereafter in order to bolster David's royal reputation.

Chapter 2: David in Saul's Service

1. See Th. P. J. van den Hout, "Apology of Hattušili III," in *The Context of Scripture*, vol. 1 (ed. William W. Hallo; Leiden: Brill, 1997), 199–204; Harry A. Hoffner Jr., "Propaganda and Political Justification in Hittite Historiography," in *Unity and Diversity: Essays in the History, Literature, and Religion of the Ancient Near East* (ed. H. Goedicke and J. J. M. Roberts; Baltimore: Johns Hopkins Univ. Press, 1975), 49–62. For other ancient Near Eastern royal apologies with similar features to the David story, see Michael B. Dick, "The 'History of David's Rise to Power' and the Neo-Babylonian Succession Apologies," in *David and Zion* (ed. B. F. Batto and K. L. Roberts; Winona Lake, IN: Eisenbrauns, 2004), 3–19.

2. See most prominently P. Kyle McCarter's seminal article "The Apology of David," *Journal of Biblical Literature* 99 (1980): 489–504. Early steps in this direction were taken by Niels Peter Lemche, "David's Rise," *Journal for the Study of the Old Testament* 10 (1978): 2–25.

3. For a full treatment of this inscription, known as the Tel Dan Stele, see George Athas, *The Tel Dan Inscription: A Reappraisal and a New Interpretation* (New York: T&T Clark, 2003).

4. See the assessment of the David story by Albrecht Alt, "The Formation of the Israelite State in Palestine," in Alt, *Essays on Old Testament History and Religion* (Garden City: Doubleday, 1967), 223–309: "It is the creation of a genuine historian, who conceals rather than reveals his historical purpose" (268).

5. See J. Maxwell Miller and John H. Hayes, *A History of Ancient Israel and Judah* (Louisville, KY: Westminster John Knox, 2006), 139–41.

6. On the nature of Israelite political organization before the monarchy, see the classic study of Alt, "Formation," 227–32.

7. On the influence of the Philistine threat on the emergence of kingship in Israel, see Alt, "Formation," 252–55. It is an oversimplification to tie the emergence of the Israelite kingship exclusively to external pressure, though the Philistine threat may have been the tipping point. For a more nuanced and complete view, see

Carol Meyers, "Kinship and Kingship: The Early Monarchy," in *The Oxford History of the Biblical World* (ed. Michael D. Coogan; Oxford: Oxford Univ. Press, 1998), 178–83; Israel Finkelstein, "The Emergence of the Monarchy in Israel: Environmental and Socio-Economic Aspects," *Journal for the Study of the Old Testament* 44 (1989): 43–74.

8. Many scholars have described Saul's position in anthropological terms as a "chiefdom" rather than as a real kingship. See James W. Flanagan, "Chiefs in Israel," *Journal for the Study of the Old Testament* 20 (1981): 47–73; Frank S. Frick, *The Formation of the State in Ancient Israel: A Survey of Models and Theories* (Social World of Biblical Antiquity Series 4; Sheffield: Journal for the Study of the Old Testament, 1985). For an assessment of these approaches, see Paula McNutt, *Reconstructing the Society of Ancient Israel* (Library of Ancient Israel; Louisville, KY: Westminster John Knox, 1999), 112–42. On the archaeological evidence for the nature of Israel during Saul's reign, see Baruch Rosen, "Subsistence Economy in Iron Age I," in *From Nomadism to Monarchy: Archaeological and Historical Aspects of Early Israel* (ed. I. Finkelstein and N. Na'aman; Jerusalem: Yad Itzhak Ben-Zvi, 1994), 339–51.

9. See Alt, "Formation," 255: "The king ruled the national army; his authority only really came into effect in camp and in battle and had hardly any function in peacetime. It was a kingship for the sole purpose of defence against the Philistines."

10. The similarity between the narratives of Saul's exploits as king and those of the Israelite leaders in the book of Judges has long been noted. See Alt, "Formation," 240–43.

11. On the kinship structure of Israelite society, see Norman K. Gottwald, *The Tribes of Yahweh: A Sociology of the Religion of Liberated Israel, 1250–1050 BCE* (Biblical Seminar 66; Sheffield: Sheffield Academic, 1999), 237–341.

12. The standard work on the Sea Peoples is Trude Dothan and Moshe Dothan, *People of the Sea: The Search for the Philistines* (New York: Macmillan, 1992).

13. Lawrence E. Stager, "Forging an Identity: The Emergence of Ancient Israel," in *The Oxford History of the Biblical World* (ed. Michael D. Coogan; Oxford: Oxford Univ. Press, 1998), 113–24.

14. Stager, "Forging," 90–91.

15. Stager, "Forging," 126.

16. See Alt, "Formation," 235–37. On occasion such raids would make the headlines, so to speak, especially in locations particularly prone to Philistine attack by virtue of their location or relative prosperity. Thus, e.g., a number of narratives recount the heroic actions of various Israelites against Philistine raiding parties at the town of Lehi. See N. L. Tidwell, "The Philistine Incursions into the Valley of Rephaim," in *Studies in the Historical Books of the Old Testament* (ed. J. A. Emerton; Supplements to Vetus Testamentum 30; Leiden: Brill, 1979), 190–212 (at 198–200).

17. A notable example, featuring a figure well known from the Bible, is the role of Nebuchadnezzar II as the head of the Babylonian army in 605 BCE, during the reign of his father Nabopolassar. See further Silvia Zamazalová, "The Education of Neo-Assyrian Princes," in *The Oxford Handbook of Cuneiform Culture* (ed. K. Radner and E. Robson; Oxford: Oxford Univ. Press, 2011), 313–30.

18. Some scholars have seen fit to view Jonathan's exploits as parallel to those of the judges, which would suggest that he was quite the military leader indeed. See P. Kyle McCarter, *I Samuel* (Anchor Bible 8; New York: Doubleday, 1980), 251.

19. On the *'elep* ("thousand") military unit, see Gottwald, *Tribes*, 270–76.

20. Lawrence E. Stager, in his seminal article "The Archaeology of the Family in Early Israel" (*Bulletin of the American Schools of Oriental Research* 260 [1985]: 1–35), suggests that in the wake of significant population increase in Israel around David's time, the land was unable to sustain the population as it had before, with the result that many were forced to look for nonagricultural work, such as entering the military (at 25–28). This observation dovetails nicely with the tradition that David was the youngest of his brothers (however many there were). The family's landholdings would devolve on the

eldest of Jesse's sons, with diminishing inheritance down the line. If the portrayal of David as the youngest is not merely a literary convention, then David would be more in need of another line of work than most. See also Steven L. McKenzie, *King David: A Biography* (Oxford: Oxford Univ. Press, 2000), 54, 59.

21. Baruch Halpern, *David's Secret Demons: Messiah, Murderer, Traitor, King* (Grand Rapids, MI: Eerdmans, 2001), 124–32 (quotation on 126).

22. This phenomenon will be recognizable to anyone familiar with the famous tie between Harvard and Yale's dominant football team in 1968, proclaimed in the headlines of the Harvard Crimson newspaper as "Harvard Beats Yale 29–29."

23. On the Philistine population estimate, see Israel Finkelstein, "The Philistine Countryside," *Israel Exploration Journal* 46: 225–42.

24. On this poetic phenomenon, see James L. Kugel, *The Idea of Biblical Poetry: Parallelism and Its History* (Baltimore: Johns Hopkins Univ. Press, 1981), 42–44.

25. In Mesopotamia, this may have occurred at the annual New Year's festival, when officials from around the kingdom converged to celebrate the holiday and when royal appointments were reaffirmed or renegotiated. See Karel van der Toorn, "The Babylonian New Year Festival," in *Congress Volume Leuven 1989* (ed. J. A. Emerton; Supplements to Vetus Testamentum 43; Leiden: Brill, 1991), 331–44 (esp. 334–35).

26. The Bible presents Michal as the second of Saul's daughters offered to David, the first being Merab, Saul's eldest, the offer of whom has to be withdrawn because she has already been engaged to someone else (1 Sam. 18:17–19). This rather useless detour from the narrative exists solely to fulfill Saul's promise from the Goliath story, as recorded in 1 Sam. 17:25: "The man who kills him will be rewarded by the king with great riches; he will also give him his daughter in marriage." The Goliath story being fictional, so too the episode of Saul offering Merab that depends on it. See McCarter, *I Samuel*, 306.

27. See Amélie Kuhrt, *The Ancient Near East: c. 3000–330 BC* (2 vols.; London: Routledge, 1995), 1:63.

28. See Martin Noth, *The History of Israel* (New York: Harper & Row, 1960), 184 n. 1.

29. For much of Israelite history, it was not uncommon for Israelites to keep idols, particularly of what are called household gods. The same word used here, *teraphim*, is found in the story of Jacob and Laban in Gen. 31, in which Rachel takes the idol from her father's house to bring on her journey to Canaan, as well as in the lesser-known story of the Danite priest in Judg. 18, in which the idol is assumed to be part of the standard priestly inventory. It would not be until the seventh century BCE, during the reign of Josiah, that such personal idols were deemed inappropriate (2 Kings 23:24)—and even then most Israelites didn't know about or ignored this condemnation of such idols. See Susan Ackerman, *Under Every Green Tree: Popular Religion in Sixth-Century Judah* (Harvard Semitic Monographs 46; Winona Lake, IN: Eisenbrauns, 2001).

30. Some viewed ecstatic prophecy in Israel and elsewhere through a distinctly negative lens. See Robert R. Wilson, *Prophecy and Society in Ancient Israel* (Philadelphia: Fortress, 1980), 103–6, 182–83. Note particularly his observation that ecstatic behavior in tenth- to seventh-century BCE Assyria was "seen as a form of insanity" (103). See also Robert R. Wilson, "Prophecy and Ecstasy: A Reexamination," *Journal of Biblical Literature* 98 (1979): 321–37.

31. See, almost unimaginably recently, George Stein, "The Case of King Saul: Did He Have Recurrent Unipolar Depression or Bipolar Affective Disorder?—Psychiatry in the Old Testament," *British Journal of Psychiatry* 201 (2011): 212.

32. Hans Wilhelm Hertzberg, *I & II Samuel* (Old Testament Library; Philadelphia: Westminster, 1964), 141.

33. The aforementioned Tel Dan Stele and the Black Obelisk of Shalmaneser, respectively. For the latter, see K. Lawson Younger Jr., "Black Obelisk," in *The Context of Scripture*, vol. 2 (ed. William H. Hallo; Leiden: Brill, 2000), 269–70.

34. See Julian Morgenstern, "David and Jonathan," *Journal of Biblical Literature* 78 (1959): 322–25 (at 322).

35. See the scholarship cited in Saul M. Olyan, "'Surpassing the Love of Women': Another Look at 2 Samuel 1:26 and the Relationship of David and Jonathan," in *Authorizing Marriage? Canon, Tradition, and Critique in the Blessing of Same-Sex Unions* (ed. M. D. Jordan; Princeton, NJ: Princeton Univ. Press, 2006), 7–16 (esp. n. 1).

36. On the meaning of "love" as "covenant loyalty," see the classic study of W. L. Moran, "The Ancient Near Eastern Background of the Love of God in Deuteronomy," *Catholic Biblical Quarterly* 25 (1963): 77–86. On this meaning as it relates to Jonathan's love for David, see J. A. Thompson, "The Significance of the Verb *Love* in the David-Jonathan Narratives in 1 Samuel," *Vetus Testamentum* 24 (1974): 334–38.

37. This is not the typical rendering of this verse, which is usually translated "More wonderful to me was your love than the love of women." While both translations are syntactically possible, I prefer the one that, as elsewhere in the story, explicitly portrays Jonathan as the lover and David as the beloved, without any real sense of reciprocity on David's part. The translation suggested here may have some support from the Septuagint, which renders this verse as "Your love fell upon me like the love of women."

38. See Steven Seidman, *The Social Construction of Sexuality* (New York: W. W. Norton, 2003).

39. On sexuality in the ancient world, see Eva Cantarella, *Bisexuality in the Ancient World* (2d ed.; New Haven, CT: Yale Univ. Press, 2002).

40. Olyan, "'Surpassing.'"

41. This may be another case in which "love" has political overtones: the people's love of David suggests that they were already announcing their loyalty to his anticipated kingship. See Moran, "Ancient Near Eastern Background," 81.

42. Jo Ann Hackett, "'There Was No King in Israel': The Era of the Judges," in *The Oxford History of the Biblical World* (ed. Michael D. Coogan; Oxford: Oxford Univ. Press, 1998), 132–64 (at 151).

43. See Morgenstern, "David and Jonathan."

44. Hackett, "There Was No King," 151.

45. McKenzie, *King David*, 106.

46. Jon D. Levenson, "1 Samuel 25 as Literature and as History," *Catholic Biblical Quarterly* 40 (1978): 11–28.

47. This custom seems to have been known outside of Israel as well. See Matitiahu Tsevat, "Marriage and Monarchical Legitimacy in Ugarit and Israel," *Journal of Semitic Studies* 3 (1958): 237–43.

48. That David probably attempted a coup was recognized by McKenzie, *King David*, 87–88, though without linking it to Ahinoam.

Chapter 3: David in the Wilderness

1. On the geography of ancient Israel, see Yohanan Aharoni, *The Land of the Bible: A Historical Geography* (Philadelphia: Westminster, 1979), 21–42; Amihai Mazar, *Archaeology of the Land of the Bible*, vol. 1 (Anchor Bible Reference Library; New York: Doubleday, 1992), 1–9.

2. The story also serves a historiographical purpose that has little to do with David. It is part of a drawn-out explanation of how the family of Zadok came to be the priests in Jerusalem. The literary connections go back to 1 Sam. 2, in which the priest Eli was told that his priestly family would come to an end. One descendant will be spared, Eli was told, but eventually he too will be replaced by "a faithful priest" who will "go before my anointed one forever" (2:35). The sole descendant of Eli is Abiathar; the faithful priest is his rival Zadok, who replaces Abiathar during the reign of Solomon; the "anointed one" is David, or the royal descendants of David's line. Eli's priestly line, with the exception of Abiathar, is destroyed, as promised, by Doeg the Edomite in Nob. And when Solomon eventually dismisses Abiathar from his priestly duties, it says in 1 Kings 2:27, it "fulfilled the word of Yahweh regarding the House of Eli." See P. Kyle McCarter, *I Samuel* (Anchor Bible 8; New York: Doubleday, 1980), 366; Steven L. McKenzie, *King David: A Biography* (Oxford: Oxford Univ. Press, 2000), 92.

3. Most Bibles read "cave" for "stronghold" here, but it has long been recognized that this is a text-critical error. Note that in the continuation of this brief episode, in 22:4, David's hideout is referred to as a "stronghold." It was therefore most likely a fortified settlement (see McCarter, *I Samuel*, 357). This unfortunately renders the modern tourist attraction of the "cave of Adullam" rather more symbolic than historical.

4. On kinship culture in ancient Israel, see Philip J. King and Lawrence E. Stager, *Life in Biblical Israel* (Library of Ancient Israel; Louisville, KY: Westminster John Knox, 2001), 36–61.

5. It may be noted that the term used here, "saved," is the same one used regularly to describe the actions of the judges in the book of Judges, thereby suggesting that David—rather than Saul, as one might expect—was taking on the role of the tribal leader. See Hans Wilhelm Hertzberg, *I & II Samuel* (Old Testament Library; Philadelphia: Westminster, 1964), 190.

6. See 1 Kings 22:10: "The King of Israel and King Jehoshaphat of Judah were seated on their thrones, dressed in robes, on the threshing floor at the entrance of the gate of Samaria."

7. See N. L. Tidwell, "The Philistine Incursions into the Valley of Rephaim," in *Studies in the Historical Books of the Old Testament* (ed. J. A. Emerton; Supplements to Vetus Testamentum 30; Leiden: Brill, 1979), 190–212: "Behind the stories which . . . ostensibly refer to decisive encounters between David and the Philistines there lie accounts of what were originally nothing more than the successful routing of Philistine raiding parties engaged in foraging for supplies for local garrisons or intent on destroying the harvested crops of the Israelites as they lay exposed on the threshing floors" (202).

8. For a different, though equally unflattering, view of David's time in Keilah, see Nadav Na'aman, "David's Sojourn in Keilah in Light of the Amarna Letters," *Vetus Testamentum* 60 (2010): 87–97.

9. McKenzie, *King David*, 107.

10. See Baruch Halpern, *David's Secret Demons: Messiah, Murderer, Traitor, King* (Grand Rapids, MI: Eerdmans, 2001), 272–73.

11. It is certain that, whatever may be historically authentic in this story, the name of David's victim, Nabal, is not. This name is descriptive of his character and is part of the literary agenda of the biblical authors. We have no way of ascertaining what his real name may have been. On Nabal's name, see Jon D. Levenson, "1 Samuel 25 as Literature and as History," *Catholic Biblical Quarterly* 40 (1978): 11–28.

12. On the institution of levirate marriage, see Eryl W. Davies, "Inheritance Rights and the Hebrew Levirate Marriage," *Vetus Testamentum* 31 (1981): 138–44, 257–68.

13. See Deut. 10:18; 14:29; 16:11, etc.

14. See the brilliant essay of Levenson, "1 Samuel 25."

15. See John Bright, *A History of Israel* (Louisville, KY: Westminster John Knox, 2000), 193–94.

16. The location of Gath was long a matter of dispute, but recent excavations have firmly identified it as Tell es-Safi. See Aren M. Maier, ed., *Tell Es-Safi/Gath I: The 1996–2005 Seasons* (Ägypten und Altes Testament 69; Wiesbaden: Harrassowitz, 2012).

17. On the *habiru*, see Moshe Greenberg, *The hab/piru* (New Haven, CT: American Oriental Society, 1955).

18. This parallel to David's story was noted by Niels Peter Lemche, "David's Rise," *Journal for the Study of the Old Testament* 10 (1978): 2–25 (at 12). On Idrimi's inscription, see Sidney Smith, *The Statue of Idrimi* (London: British Institute of Archaeology in Ankara, 1949).

19. See Greenberg, *Hab/piru*, 64–65.

20. On the Amarna letters, see William L. Moran, *The Amarna Letters* (Baltimore: Johns Hopkins Univ. Press, 1992).

21. Some of these were noted by Lemche, "David's Rise," 11–14. See also George E. Mendenhall, *The Tenth Generation: The Origins of the Biblical Tradition* (Baltimore: Johns Hopkins Univ. Press, 1973), 135–36.

22. On the connection of *habiru* and Hebrews, see Nadav Na'aman, "Habiru and Hebrews: The Transfer of a Social Term to the Literary Sphere," *Journal of Near Eastern Studies* 45 (1986): 271–86.

23. It is possible that even the description of Saul's death is meant to denigrate him. Suicide, often seen as a noble death in the Greco-

Roman world, was not viewed quite so positively in the ancient Near East. See W. Boyd Barrick, "Saul's Demise, David's Lament, and Custer's Last Stand," *Journal for the Study of the Old Testament* 73 (1997): 25–41.

24. This mechanism for calling the tribes to war was probably understood as an implicit curse—that the recipients should suffer the fate of the dismembered body should they not join their compatriots in battle. See McCarter, *I Samuel*, 203.

25. The motivation for the inhabitants of Jabesh-Gilead in particular to undertake this mission is found in the earlier narrative of how Saul became king: by defending the town against the attacks of the Ammonites.

26. See Meir Malul, "Was David Involved in the Death of Saul on the Gilboa Mountain?," *Revue Biblique* 103 (1996): 517–45 (at 532–36).

27. See Keith W. Whitelam, *The Just King: Monarchic Judicial Authority in Ancient Israel* (Journal for the Study of the Old Testament, Supplement Series 12; Sheffield: Journal of the Study of the Old Testament, 1979), 104–5.

28. See P. Kyle McCarter, *II Samuel* (Anchor Bible 9; New York: Doubleday, 1984), 63. The best indication for this interpretation is the identification of the informant as an Amalekite, the archetypical evildoer in the Bible. Once he was identified as such, the Israelite audience might well have assumed that everything the Amalekite said would be a lie and that he should be suspected of looting, a classic Amalekite behavior.

29. For details, see D. M. Gunn, "Narrative Patterns and Oral Tradition in Judges and Samuel," *Vetus Testamentum* 24 (1974): 286–317 (esp. 286–97).

30. Pushing this idea further, Malul, "Was David Involved," suggests that David had established a fifth column within Saul's ranks and that Saul fell at the hands of his own men, who had betrayed him. This reconstruction is tempting, but it relies on taking much of the narrative of David's time at Saul's court as accurate historical representation, which, as we have seen, is problematic.

Chapter 4: David Becomes King

1. On the history of Hebron, see Avi Ofer, "Hebron," in *The New Encyclopedia of Archaeological Excavations in the Holy Land* (4 vols.; ed. Ephraim Stern; New York: Simon & Schuster, 1993), 2:606–9.

2. See Steven L. McKenzie, *King David: A Biography* (Oxford: Oxford Univ. Press, 2000), 114–15.

3. See Tryggve N. D. Mettinger, *King and Messiah: The Civil and Sacral Legitimation of the Israelite Kings* (Lund: Gleerup, 1976), 118: "David's earlier distribution of spoils between 'the elders of Judah' (1 S 30,26–31) was made with the conscious aim to prepare the way for his recognition by these."

4. This was the standard practice in Egypt, e.g.: "The allegiance of these vassals was initially secured by the imposition upon them of a binding oath, renewed from time to time and always at the accession of a new pharaoh" (Margaret S. Drower, "Syria *c.* 1550–1400 B.C.," in *The Cambridge Ancient History*, vol. 2.1 [ed. I. E. S. Edwards et al.; Cambridge: Cambridge Univ. Press, 1973], 469).

5. See Martin Noth, *The History of Israel* (New York: Harper & Row, 1960), 183; John Bright, *A History of Israel* (Louisville, KY: Westminster John Knox, 2000), 196; Baruch Halpern, *David's Secret Demons: Messiah, Murderer, Traitor, King* (Grand Rapids, MI: Eerdmans, 2001), 302–6.

6. This was recognized as early as the nineteenth century; see Adolf Kampenhausen, "Philister und Hebräer zur Zeit Davids," *Zeitschrift für die alttestamentliche Wissenschaft* 6 (1886): 43–97.

7. This may well be due to David's relationship with Ammon, the long-time aggressor toward Gilead. See Halpern, *David's Secret Demons*, 301.

8. There seems to be a five-year gap between Saul's rule and Ishbaal's, since David is said to rule in Hebron for seven years, but Ishbaal rules in the north for only two (2 Sam. 2:10–11). This has occasioned much scholarly speculation: perhaps David actually took control in Judah while Saul was still on the throne in

Israel (McKenzie, *King David*, 115–16; Halpern, *David's Secret Demons*, 230), or, more likely, it took five years for Abner and Ishbaal to consolidate power and drive the Philistines out of the north, thereby returning it to Israelite control (J. Alberto Soggin, "The Reign of 'Ešba'al, Son of Saul," in Soggin, *Old Testament and Oriental Studies* [Biblica et Orientalia 29; Rome: Pontifical Biblical Institute, 1975], 31–49 [esp. 34–40]). It is also quite possible that in driving out the Philistines, Abner and Ishbaal were also responsible for the destruction and incorporation into Israel of the major independent city-states in the north, most notably Megiddo (Halpern, *David's Secret Demons*, 154–56). Such a situation might explain the oddity that Ishbaal and Abner are depicted as governing from Mahanaim, across the Jordan, rather than from anywhere in Israel itself. Mahanaim seems to have been the provisional capital of the north while the Philistines still occupied much of Israel's former territory (McCarter, *II Samuel*, 87). It might also explain the power dynamic between Abner and Ishbaal. Abner, as the head of the army, would have been responsible for the defeat of the Philistines and thereby had the power to rule had he wanted it. But to return Israel to its former glory meant restoring the dynasty that had been interrupted by the Philistine presence. If the dynastic succession had truly been uninterrupted, then Abner would not have had to make Ishbaal king—everyone in Israel would have known that Ishbaal was the rightful monarch. But if the succession had been interrupted, and in the interim Abner had made himself the most important man in the north, then Israel may well have looked to him, wondering whether Saul's line would be reestablished on the throne.

9. On Ishbaal's name, see McCarter, *II Samuel*, 85–87.

10. See Jakob H. Grønbaek, *Die Geschichte vom Aufstieg Davids (1. Sam 15–2 Sam 5): Tradition und Komposition* (Copenhagen: Prostant Apud Muksgaard, 1971), 229–30. This is not to say that single combat was unknown as a means of deciding battles. If it were completely invented, then this story, and even more so the Goliath story, would

be unintelligible to the ancient audience. There is a relief from the Mesopotamian site of Tell Halaf from roughly David's time that depicts a moment almost identical to this one: two warriors, each grabbing the head of the other, each stabbing the other simultaneously in the side (see Y. Yadin, "Let the Young Men, I Pray Thee, Arise and Play Before Us," *Journal of the Palestine Oriental Society* 21 [1938]: 110–16). Yet a realistic scenario does not mean a historical one (again, see the Goliath story).

11. See McKenzie, *King David*, 118.

12. See A. K. Grayson, "Assyrian Rule of Conquered Territory in Ancient Western Asia," in *Civilizations of the Ancient Near East* (ed. Jack M. Sasson; Peabody, MA: Hendrickson, 1995), 959–68 (esp. 964–65). Of particular interest is the observation that vassal treaties were often concluded as "'gunboat diplomacy,' where only after moving the army into position, or even launching some attacks, was an agreement acceptable to the Assyrians reached" (964). This is precisely what we see in the conflict between David and Israel.

13. The era of Saul, David, and Solomon coincides with just such a decline, in both Egypt and Mesopotamia. See Donald B. Redford, *Egypt, Canaan, and Israel in Ancient Times* (Princeton, NJ: Princeton Univ. Press, 1992), 283–92; Steven W. Hollaway, "Assyria and Babylonia in the Tenth Century BCE," in *The Age of Solomon: Scholarship at the Turn of the Millennium* (Studies in the History and Culture of the Ancient Near East 11; ed. L. K. Handy; Leiden: Brill, 1997), 202–16.

14. Working on the assumption that it was not fictional, Zafrira Ben-Barak offers legal arguments for why Ishbaal would be obligated to return Michal to David in "The Legal Background to the Restoration of Michal to David," in *Studies in the Historical Books of the Old Testament* (ed. J. A. Emerton; Supplements to Vetus Testamentum 30; Leiden: Brill, 1979), 15–29.

15. The rabbis of the Mishnah saw exactly what was going on here: in discussing the fact that David walked behind the bier of Abner, they commented, "That was but to pacify the people" (*m. Sanh.* 2:3).

16. On David's participation in Abner's death, see James C. VanderKam,

"Davidic Complicity in the Deaths of Abner and Eshbaal: A Historical and Redactional Study," *Journal of Biblical Literature* 99 (1980): 521–39.

17. On the import in the Bible of mutilating enemies, see Tracy M. Lemos, "Shame and Mutilation of Enemies in the Hebrew Bible," *Journal of Biblical Literature* 125 (2006): 225–41.

18. See, emphatically, Halpern, *David's Secret Demons*, 310.

19. See Noth, *History*, 186: "It is in fact unlikely that David tried to accelerate the almost inevitable course of events by instigating a murder instead of calmly and shrewdly awaiting the end of Eshbaal's reign as king."

20. See Albrecht Alt, "The Formation of the Israelite State in Palestine," in Alt, *Essays on Old Testament History and Religion* (Garden City: Doubleday, 1967), 223–309 (at 286).

21. See Noth, *History*, 187–88; Siegfried Herrmann, *A History of Israel in Old Testament Times* (Philadelphia: Fortress, 1975), 153–54.

22. It seems likely that after the Philistines found themselves unable to deal with David militarily, they decided to deal with him diplomatically. Though the Bible does not relate any such agreements, it is telling that after these initial attacks, the Philistines do not appear again in the David story—nor, for that matter, in the account of Solomon's career on the throne. Given the constant Philistine aggression toward Israel in the generations before David, this lengthy peace is almost certainly the result of a treaty.

23. Niccolò Machiavelli, *The Prince* (Chicago: Univ. of Chicago Press, 1998), 9.

24. On famine in ancient Israel and the Bible, see William H. Shea, "Famine," in *The Anchor Bible Dictionary* (6 vols.; ed. D. N. Freedman; New York: Doubleday, 1992), 2:769–73.

25. On the relationship of kings and fertility, see A. S. Kapelrud, "King David and the Sons of Saul," in *The Sacral Kingship* (Studies in the History of Religions 4; Leiden: Brill, 1959), 294–301 (esp. 299–301); A. S. Kapelrud, "King and Fertility: A Discussion of II Sam

21:1–14," in *Interpretationes ad Vetus Testamentum* (Osla: Land og Kirke, 1955), 113–22.

26. On Gibeon, see Joseph Blenkinsopp, *Gibeon and Israel: The Role of Gibeon and the Gibeonites in the Political and Religious History of Early Israel* (Society for Old Testament Studies Monographs 2; Cambridge: Cambridge Univ. Press, 1972).

27. The rabbis of the Talmud asked the same question—"Where do we learn that Saul put to death the Gibeonites?"—and determine that, in fact, he never had (*b. Yebam.* 78b).

28. Some scholars do assume that there is a historical basis for Saul's attempt to wipe out the Gibeonites. See McCarter, *II Samuel*, 441; Halpern, *David's Secret Demons*, 306–12.

29. Most scholars agree that the account in 2 Sam. 21 is chronologically displaced and belongs before 2 Sam. 9. See McCarter, *II Samuel*, 262–65. This is perhaps the only reasonable explanation for David's question at the beginning of 2 Sam. 9: "Is there anyone still left of the House of Saul with whom I can keep faith for the sake of Jonathan?" (9:1).

30. On Meribbaal's name, see the brilliant analysis of McCarter, *II Samuel*, 124–25.

31. See Jacob Klein, "Enki and Ninmah," in *The Context of Scripture*, vol. 1 (ed. William W. Hallo; Leiden: Brill, 1997), 516–18.

32. On Meribbaal's disability, see the pioneering work of Jeremy Schipper, *Disability Studies and the Hebrew Bible: Figuring Mephibosheth in the David Story* (Library of Hebrew Bible/Old Testament Studies 441; New York: T&T Clark, 2006).

33. See, e.g., the regular introductory feature in letters from Canaanite vassals to their Egyptian overlords: "I fall at the feet of my lord seven times and seven times" (William L. Moran, *The Amarna Letters* [Baltimore: Johns Hopkins Univ. Press, 1992], passim).

34. The Septuagint preserves the contrary notion, that David will provide the food for Meribbaal, and some have taken this version as the more authentic. See McCarter, *II Samuel*, 262.

35. See, e.g., J. N. Postgate, *Neo-Assyrian Royal Grants and Decrees* (Rome: Pontifical Biblical Institute, 1969).

36. For a biblical example of how deeply ingrained the custom of permanent possession of hereditary lands was, see the story of Naboth's vineyard in 1 Kings 21.

37. See McKenzie, *King David*, 145.

38. On the cult of the deceased in ancient Israel, see the classic work of Elizabeth Bloch-Smith, *Judahite Burial Practices and Beliefs About the Dead* (Journal for the Study of the Old Testament: Supplement Series 123; Sheffield: Sheffield Academic Press, 1992).

Chapter 5: David's Kingdom

1. It is notable that the three most significant sites in southern Canaan in the two centuries before David are the three that are most prominent in the David story: Hebron, Jerusalem, and Gath. See Avi Ofer, "The Monarchic Period in the Judaean Highland: A Spatial Overview," in *Studies in the Archaeology of the Iron Age in Israel and Jordan* (ed. A. Mazar; Journal for the Study of the Old Testament: Supplement Series 331; Sheffield: Sheffield Academic, 2001), 14–37 (at 26–27).

2. On the archaeology of Jerusalem, particularly from David's time, see Jane M. Cahill, "Jerusalem at the Time of the United Monarchy: The Archaeological Evidence," in *Jerusalem in Bible and Archaeology: The First Temple Period* (Society of Biblical Literature Symposium Series 18; ed. A. G. Vaughn and A. E. Killebrew; Leiden: Brill, 2003), 13–80.

3. See P. Kyle McCarter, *II Samuel* (Anchor Bible 9; New York: Doubleday, 1984), 141; Albrecht Alt, "The Formation of the Israelite State in Palestine," in Alt, *Essays on Old Testament History and Religion* (Garden City: Doubleday, 1967), 223–309 (at 282–83).

4. See John Bright, *A History of Israel* (Louisville, KY: Westminster John Knox, 2000), 195.

5. See most prominently Nadav Na'aman, "The Contribution of the Amarna Letters to the Debate on Jerusalem's Political Position in the Tenth Century BCE," *Bulletin of the American Schools of Oriental Research* 304 (1996): 17–27.

6. On the Egyptian administration of Canaan in the second millennium BCE, see Donald B. Redford, *Egypt, Canaan, and Israel in Ancient Times* (Princeton, NJ: Princeton Univ. Press, 1992), 192–213.

7. Steven L. McKenzie (*King David: A Biography* [Oxford: Oxford Univ. Press, 2000], 55) has suggested that Zeruiah was not David's sister, and was in fact not even a woman, but was rather the father of Joab and his brothers and had no relation to David whatsoever. This is possible, but as McKenzie admits, speculative.

8. See M. Delcor, "Les Kéréthim et les Cretois," *Vetus Testamentum* 28 (1978): 409–22.

9. Many scholars have argued that the report of the construction of David's palace in 2 Sam. 5:11–12 is chronologically displaced and belongs in fact much later in David's reign (see McCarter, *II Samuel*, 145–46). The same argument has been made, in fact, about David's bringing the ark to Jerusalem. These arguments may well be correct but have little effect on the discussion here.

10. See Eilat Mazar, "Did I Find King David's Palace?" *Biblical Archaeology Review* 32 (2006): 16–27, 70.

11. On the wide diversity of cultic sites in Israel, see Ziony Zevit, *The Religions of Ancient Israel: A Synthesis of Parallactic Approaches* (London: Continuum, 2001), 123–266.

12. See the variants on this theme in Gen. 28:10–22; 35:1–15; Hosea 12:5.

13. See Susan Ackerman, "Who Is Sacrificing at Shiloh? The Priesthoods of Israel's Regional Sanctuaries," in *Levites and Priests in Biblical History and Tradition* (ed. M. Leuchter and J. M. Hutton; Society of Biblical Literature—Ancient Israel and Its Literature 9; Atlanta: Society of Biblical Literature, 2011), 25–43; Israel Finkelstein, "The History and Archaeology of Shiloh from the Middle Bronze Age II to Iron Age II," in *Shiloh: The Archaeology of a Biblical Site* (ed. I. Fin-

kelstein; Tel Aviv: Monograph Series of Tel Aviv University, 1993), 371–89.

14. On the connection of Kiryath-jearim and the ark, see Joseph Blenkinsopp, "Kiriath-jearim and the Ark," *Journal of Biblical Literature* 88 (1969): 143–56.

15. See Martin Noth, *The History of Israel* (New York: Harper & Row, 1960), 191.

16. See H. B. Huffmon, "Shalem," in *Dictionary of Deities and Demons in the Bible* (2d ed.; ed. K. Van der Toorn et al.; Leiden: Brill, 1999), 755–57.

17. There are numerous ancient Near Eastern parallels, both thematic and specific, to David's bringing the ark into his new capital. Most notable are Assyrian texts from the ninth to eighth centuries BCE that describe the founding of a new capital, upon which the king "invites" the deities—that is, brings their idols—into the city, accompanied by sacrifices, music, and feasting. See P. Kyle McCarter, "The Ritual Dedication of the City of David in 2 Samuel 6," in *The Word of the Lord Shall Go Forth* (ed. C. L. Meyers and M. O'Connor; Winona Lake, IN: Eisenbrauns, 1983).

18. Shiloh may have been out of the question, as it appears to have been destroyed by the Philistines in Saul's time. See Jer. 7:12–14, and for the archaeological evidence in support of this, see I. Finkelstein, "Shiloh," in *The New Encyclopedia of Archaeological Excavations in the Holy Land* (4 vols.; ed. E. Stern; New York: Simon & Schuster, 1993), 4:1366–70.

19. Some have suggested that in fact this is the account of how Kiryath-jearim, once a Gibeonite city, became Israelite: that David conquered it and took the ark as booty. See R. A. Carlson, *David, the Chosen King: A Traditio-Historical Approach to the Second Book of Samuel* (Uppsala: Almqvist & Wiksells, 1964), 58–60.

20. Although the text says simply that David offered these sacrifices "after six steps," this does not mean after only the first six. See McCarter, *II Samuel*, 171.

21. See P. Kyle McCarter, *I Samuel* (Anchor Bible 8; New York: Double-

day, 1980): "Israelite kingship had an important sacerdotal aspect (cf. Ps 110:4; etc.) that seems to have been refuted only in postmonarchical times" (186). See also Roland de Vaux, *Ancient Israel: Its Life and Institutions* (Biblical Resource Series; Grand Rapids, MI: Eerdmans, 1997), 113–14; Aelred Cody, *A History of Old Testament Priesthood* (Analecta biblica 35; Rome: Pontifical Biblical Institute, 1969), 98–107.

22. On the burnt and well-being offerings, see Jacob Milgrom, *Leviticus 1–16* (Anchor Bible 3; New York: Doubleday, 1991), 172–76, 217–25.

23. On the invention of the guilt and purification offerings, see Milgrom, *Leviticus*, 1–16, 176–77.

24. The existence of temple markets for sacrificial animals is attested famously in Matt. 21:12–13.

25. See E. Lipínski, ed., *State and Temple Economy in the Ancient Near East* (2 vols.; Leuven: Departement Oriëntalistiek, 1979).

26. On the economy of the medieval pilgrimage sites, see Esther Cohen, "Roads and Pilgrimages: A Study in Economic Interaction," *Studi Medievali* 21 (1980): 321–41.

27. On the Christian cult of the saints and relics, see Peter Brown, *The Cult of the Saints: Its Rise and Function in Late Christianity* (Chicago: Univ. of Chicago Press, 1981); Candida Moss, *The Myth of Persecution: How Ancient Christians Invented a Story of Martyrdom* (San Francisco: HarperOne, 2013).

28. See George E. Mendenhall, "The Census Lists of Numbers 1 and 26," *Journal of Biblical Literature* 77 (1958): 52–66.

29. See Philip J. King and Lawrence E. Stager, *Life in Biblical Israel* (Library of Ancient Israel; Louisville, KY: Westminster John Knox, 2001), 89: "The threshing of the cereal took place on open, level surfaces, often elevated to catch the breeze needed for winnowing."

30. Benjamin Mazar, "Jerusalem: The Early Periods and the First Temple Period," in *The New Encyclopedia of Archaeological Excavations in the Holy Land*, 2:698–701 (at 699).

31. See the classic work of Henri Frankfort, *Kingship and the Gods: A Study of Ancient Near Eastern Religion as the Integration of Society and*

Nature (Chicago: Univ. of Chicago Press, 1948); Ivan Engnell, *Studies in Divine Kingship in the Ancient Near East* (2d ed.; Oxford: Basil Blackwell, 1967).

32. Amélie Kuhrt, *The Ancient Near East: c. 3000–330 BC* (2 vols.; London: Routledge, 1995), 1:66–70.

33. Kuhrt, *Ancient Near East*, 1:277.

34. See Barry J. Kemp, "Old Kingdom, Middle Kingdom, and Second Intermediate Period *c.* 2686–1552 BC," in B. G. Trigger et al., *Ancient Egypt: A Social History* (Cambridge: Cambridge Univ. Press, 1983), 71–182 (at 71–76).

35. Even in Israel, however, there may have been a closer link between king and deity than one might expect: it has been argued that the king was seen as God's son. See Tryggve N. D. Mettinger, *King and Messiah: The Civil and Sacral Legitimation of the Israelite Kings* (Lund: Gleerup, 1976), 254–93.

36. Kuhrt, *Ancient Near East*, 2:580.

37. Kuhrt, *Ancient Near East*, 2:659.

38. On the diverse scholarly opinions regarding the composition and dating of 2 Sam. 7, see McCarter, *II Samuel*, 210–31.

39. A famous example is the appointment by Sargon the Great in the twenty-third century BCE of his daughter, Enheduanna, as the chief priestess, which inaugurated a tradition of Mesopotamian kings placing their daughters in this role that lasted for the next six centuries (Kuhrt, *Ancient Near East*, 1:50). On David's sons as priests, see Cody, *History of Old Testament Priesthood*, 103–5.

40. For the majority of the reconstruction offered here, and for further details, see the exceptional work of Baruch Halpern, *David's Secret Demons: Messiah, Murderer, Traitor, King* (Grand Rapids, MI: Eerdmans, 2001), 144–98.

41. See Øystein S. LaBianca and Randall W. Younker, "The Kingdoms of Ammon, Moab, and Edom: The Archaeology of Society in Late Bronze/Iron Age Transjordan (*ca.* 1400–500 BCE)," in *The Archaeology of Society in the Holy Land* (ed. Thomas E. Levy; London: Leicester Univ. Press, 1995), 399–415.

42. What is described, rather, is the treatment of the defeated captives, two-thirds of whom David had put to death. The punishment of individuals is the result of an isolated battle, not a territorial conquest. (Were this notice to be understood as recording the conquest of Moab as a whole, it would mean that David had two-thirds of the entire Moabite population killed, which seems excessive even by David's standards.)

43. Two ready examples come from the Bible itself: the Israelite king Hoshea revolted against Assyrian domination upon the death of Tiglath-Pileser III and the coronation of his son Shalmaneser V, with the result that the northern kingdom was attacked and destroyed forever; and the Judahite king Hezekiah revolted against the Assyrians when the kingship of Sargon II passed on to his son Sennacherib, again with disastrous results.

44. See K. A. D. Smelik, "The Inscription of King Mesha," in *The Context of Scripture*, vol. 2 (ed. William H. Hallo; Leiden: Brill, 2000), 137–38.

45. The clue to this reconstruction, as recognized by Halpern, lies in the framework of the narrative in 2 Sam. 8:3–13. The report begins with the notice that David defeated Hadadezer "when he was on his way to set up his monument at the river" (8:3), a notice that, read in isolation, could refer to the Euphrates, to the north of Aram. Yet the report ends with the notice that "David erected a monument when he returned from defeated Aram in the Valley of Salt" (8:13). The "Valley of Salt" is the area of the Dead Sea—known in antiquity, quite reasonably, as the "Sea of Salt"—and the monuments referred to at the beginning and end of the narrative are surely one and the same: a victory stela commemorating the defeat of Ammon, of the sort found all over the ancient Near East. Thus "the river" mentioned in 8:3 must be not the Euphrates, but rather the Jordan.

46. There are two lists of David's officials (2 Sam. 8:16–18; 1 Chron. 18:15–17), and Adoram is mentioned only in the second. Most scholars believe the lists to be two variants of a single original (see McCarter, *II Samuel*, 257), yet it seems more than mere coincidence

that the list mentioning Adoram comes after the account of the Ammonite war, when his services would have been most naturally put to use. See Carol Meyers, "Kinship and Kingship: The Early Monarchy," in *The Oxford History of the Biblical World* (ed. Michael D. Coogan; Oxford: Oxford Univ. Press, 1998), 194–95. It is also worth noting that Adoram is said to have served under Solomon, and even briefly under his son Rehoboam, which suggests that he attained his position late in David's reign (McKenzie, *King David*, 149).

47. Archaeological surveys confirm the location of Edom in the Negev during the eleventh to tenth centuries BCE, rather than in its later heartland across the Jordan to the east, which was settled only in the eighth century BCE. See Nadav Na'aman, "Israel, Edom, and Egypt in the Tenth Century BCE," *Tel Aviv* 19 (1992): 71–93; Burton MacDonald, "Early Edom: The Relation Between the Literary and Archaeological Evidence," in *Scripture and Other Artifacts* (ed. M. D. Coogan et al.; Louisville, KY: Westminster John Knox, 1994), 230–46.

48. See John S. Holladay, "The Kingdoms of Israel and Judah: Political and Economic Centralization in the Iron IIA–B (ca. 1000–750 BCE)," in *The Archaeology of Society in the Holy Land* (ed. Thomas E. Levy; London: Leicester Univ. Press, 1998), 383.

49. See Halpern, *David's Secret Demons*, 244.

50. Halpern, *David's Secret Demons*, 133–41.

Chapter 6: David Under Attack

1. On the two names for David and Abigail's son, and a possible original "Daluiah" from which both are derived, see P. Kyle McCarter, *II Samuel* (Anchor Bible 9; New York: Doubleday, 1984), 101.

2. It has been suggested that Chileab's disappearance from the story, and from the line of succession, should be attributed to an early death. See Steven L. McKenzie, *King David: A Biography* (Oxford: Oxford Univ. Press, 2000), 161.

3. There were evidently two areas known as Geshur: this one, in Trans-jordan to the northeast, and another near Philistine territory to the southwest. It is, logically, the latter that the Bible tells us David raided during his time with Achish; it is mentioned also in Josh. 13:2–3.

4. See Baruch Halpern, *David's Secret Demons: Messiah, Murderer, Traitor, King* (Grand Rapids, MI: Eerdmans, 2001), 233–34.

5. The same is undoubtedly true of David's overtures to Jabesh-Gilead just after taking the throne in Hebron. Both Geshur and Gilead are regions over which Ishbaal is said to have been king in 2 Sam. 2:9 (where we should read "Geshurites" for the usual "Ashurites"; see McCarter, *II Samuel*, 82–83).

6. That is, the same reason it is historically unlikely that Saul would have offered Michal to David in marriage accounts for why David, after marrying Michal, did not have any children by her.

7. A comparable law exists in the Hittite law codes as well. See Harry A. Hoffner Jr., "Hittite Laws," in *The Context of Scripture*, vol. 2 (ed. W. W. Hallo; Leiden: Brill, 2000), 106–119 (at 118).

8. See Jon D. Levenson and Baruch Halpern, "The Political Import of David's Marriages," *Journal of Biblical Literature* 99 (1980): 507–18.

9. It has been speculated that Tamar was in fact Absalom's daughter, rather than his sister, in an early version of the story. See Jack M. Sasson, "Absalom's Daughter: An Essay in Vestige Historiography," in *The Land That I Will Show You* (ed. J. A. Dearman and M. P. Graham; Journal of the Study of the Old Testament, Supplement Series 343; Sheffield: Sheffield Academic, 2001), 179–96.

10. The connection of Ruth to David is made in the last five verses of the book of Ruth, recognized by all scholars as a later addition to the story. See Edward F. Campbell Jr., *Ruth* (Anchor Bible 7; New York: Doubleday, 1975), 172–73.

11. Intriguingly, the phrase used for Tamar's garment in 2 Sam. 13, *ketonet passim*, appears only one other place in the Bible: it is the same phrase that describes Joseph's famous tunic, the ill-translated "multicolored coat" (it was more likely a long-sleeved tunic, according

to 2 Sam. 13:18, the customary clothing of unmarried princesses). Here, then, is yet another connection between the stories of Tamar and Joseph: both of these unusual garments are torn as the result of an act of fraternal aggression.

12. On a more detailed level, both stories use a relatively rare Hebrew word for "violate"—it appears at the beginning of the Dinah story, where Shechem "saw her and took her and violated her" (Gen. 34:2), and at the end of the Tamar story, where "Absalom hated Amnon because he had violated his sister Tamar" (2 Sam. 13:22). There is yet another, more striking verbal parallel between the two narratives, evident in both the English and, even more so, the Hebrew. As Tamar pleads with Amnon not to rape her, she says to him, "Such things are not done in Israel—don't do such an outrageous thing" (2 Sam. 13:12). When Dinah's brothers hear of her rape, they are distressed because Shechem "had committed an outrage in Israel by lying with Jacob's daughter—a thing not to be done" (Gen. 34:7). Both texts describe rape as an outrage (Hebrew *nebalah*), both qualify this with "in Israel," and both add to this description the statement that such things should not be done. The similarity of this latter clause is even closer in Hebrew than it is in English: in the Tamar story it says *lo ye'aseh ken*, and in the Dinah story it says *ken lo ye'aseh*.

13. Other elements of the narrative add to this impression; e.g., there are only four characters in the tale: Amnon, Absalom, Tamar, and Jonadab. After this episode, only Amnon and Absalom continue in the story—Tamar and Jonadab disappear from the biblical narrative. It also should be noted that neither is mentioned before this story, even though one is David's daughter and the other is his nephew. We may also wonder at the report of Absalom's encounter with Tamar after the rape: somehow, simply by seeing her in a state of despair, Absalom concludes, with remarkable accuracy, that Amnon had raped her.

14. See Halpern, *David's Secret Demons*, 89.

15. Note that David apparently had little use for chariots, as is apparent from the account of his defeat of Hadadezer: "David hamstrung all the chariot horses" (2 Sam. 8:4). If David had chariots, he would

have taken the horses rather than destroyed them. See André Lemaire, "The United Monarchy," in *Ancient Israel* (2d ed.; ed. Hershel Shanks; Washington, DC: Biblical Archaeology Society, 1999), 91–120 (at 104).

16. See Philip J. King and Lawrence E. Stager, *Life in Biblical Israel* (Library of Ancient Israel; Louisville, KY: Westminster John Knox, 2001), 60–61.

17. This is the basis of the prophet Amos's castigation of Israel's leaders: "You enemies of the righteous, you takers of bribes, you who subvert in the gate the cause of the needy!" (Amos 5:12).

18. See Martha Roth, "The Laws of Hammurabi," in *The Context of Scripture*, vol. 2 (ed. William H. Hallo; Leiden: Brill, 2000), 335–53. See more broadly Keith W. Whitelam, *The Just King: Monarchic Judicial Authority in Ancient Israel* (Journal for the Study of the Old Testament, Supplement Series 12; Sheffield: Journal of the Study of the Old Testament, 1979), 17–37.

19. See further Whitelam, *Just King*, 137–42.

20. See McKenzie, *King David*, 167: "It was an illustration of how out of touch with his people David had become."

21. The pattern established in the premonarchic period, of tribes coming together to fight only in times of crisis, that is, for defensive purposes alone, was dramatically disrupted by David's expansionist leanings and, equally important, his private militia, which required no tribal assistance or ratification before engaging in battle. See Rainer Albertz, *A History of Israelite Religion in the Old Testament Period* (2 vols.; Old Testament Library; Louisville, KY: Westminster John Knox, 1994), 1:115–16.

22. See Hayim Tadmor, "Traditional Institutions and the Monarchy: Social and Political Tensions in the Time of David and Solomon," in *Studies in the Period of David and Solomon and Other Essays* (ed. T. Ishida; Winona Lake, IN: Eisenbrauns, 1982), 239–57.

23. Halpern, *David's Secret Demons*, 365–71, goes much further and suggests the possibility that Absalom promised the north a restoration of its previous independence.

24. The number of the concubines, ten, is intriguing. It may simply be taken as a typical "biblical" number, more symbolic than accurate. At the same time, it lines up neatly with another semimysterious group of ten in David's life: the ten sons, aside from Solomon, who are said to have been born to David in Jerusalem (2 Sam. 5:13–15). The ten concubines are unnamed, as are the mothers of the ten Jerusalemite sons, which is unusual given the genealogical information provided about the sons born in Hebron in 2 Sam. 3:2–5. It would seem likely that one of these enumerations has influenced the other: either the ten concubines were part of the original story, and David was said to have had ten sons on that account, or, more likely, the list of the ten sons is original and the mention of ten concubines meant to provide each of those sons with a mother from David's harem.

25. On royal advisors in Assyria, see Amélie Kuhrt, *The Ancient Near East: c. 3000–330 BC* (2 vols.; London: Routledge, 1995), 2:523–25. For Egypt, see Barry J. Kemp, "Old Kingdom, Middle Kingdom, and Second Intermediate Period *c*. 2686–1552 BC," in B. G. Trigger et al., *Ancient Egypt: A Social History* (Cambridge: Cambridge Univ. Press, 1983), 71–182 (at 84).

26. As suggested by McCarter, *II Samuel*, 395.

27. This is the technical meaning of "All of Israel had fled, each man to his tent" in 2 Sam. 19:9. See McCarter, *II Samuel*, 419.

28. See Stanley A. Cook, "Notes on the Composition of 2 Samuel," *American Journal of Semitic Languages and Literature* 16 (1900): 145–77 (at 159–60).

29. Halpern, *David's Secret Demons*, 90 n. 29.

30. Halpern, *David's Secret Demons*, 364–81, boldly suggests that David had never really been king of Israel before Absalom's defeat and that the revolt was in fact an opportunity for David to attain power on a new and far broader scale. The temptations offered by his argument are great, especially for a work like the present one, but Halpern's counterreading of the biblical presentation is too much even for this author to accept.

31. This statement of Meribbaal is often taken as rhetorical, the focus being placed on Meribbaal's proclamation of loyalty to David. But the division of Saul's land between Meribbaal and Ziba seems unlikely given everything we know about David's character, and so perhaps more weight than usual should be placed on the first part of Meribbaal's statement.

32. McCarter, *II Samuel*, 419.

33. See Halpern, *David's Secret Demons*, 91.

Chapter 7: David in Decline

1. In the Talmud, David is held up as the model of repentance (*b. 'Abod. Zar.* 4b–5a).

2. On menstrual impurity and purification rituals in the ancient Near East, see Jacob Milgrom, *Leviticus 1–16* (Anchor Bible 3; New York: Doubleday, 1991), 950–53.

3. This conclusion is supported by the reference to a story from Judg. 9:50–55 placed in David's mouth in 2 Sam. 11:21.

4. See fundamentally Timo Veijola, "Solomon: Bathsheba's Firstborn," in *Reconsidering Israel and Judah: Recent Studies on the Deuteronomistic History* (ed. Gary N. Knoppers and J. Gordon McConville; Winona Lake, IN: Eisenbrauns, 2000), 340–57, and intimated already as early as Stanley A. Cook, "Notes on the Composition of 2 Samuel," *American Journal of Semitic Languages and Literature* 16 (1900): 145–77 (at 156–57).

5. For the following, see Baruch Halpern, *David's Secret Demons: Messiah, Murderer, Traitor, King* (Grand Rapids, MI: Eerdmans, 2001), 401–2. For the classic statement of the argument that Solomon was Uriah's son, see Veijola, "Solomon."

6. Although the biblical text that we have says "he named him Solomon," referring ostensibly to David, it has been recognized since as long ago as the eleventh century CE that the text requires cor-

rection to "she named him Solomon." See further Veijola, "Solomon," 344.

7. See Halpern, *David's Secret Demons*, 402. It also has been conjectured that Ahitophel defected to Absalom precisely because of David's murder of Uriah, his grandson-in-law (Steven L. McKenzie, *King David: A Biography* [Oxford: Oxford Univ. Press, 2000], 168).

8. On the basis of such parallel names, some scholars have accepted the biblical notion that Solomon was named in memory of the deceased firstborn son. See P. Kyle McCarter, *II Samuel* (Anchor Bible 9; New York: Doubleday, 1984), 303. Yet these analogies do not resolve the internal logical problems of the biblical narrative.

9. See Halpern, *David's Secret Demons*, 402.

10. See James W. Flanagan, "Court History or Succession Document? A Study of 2 Samuel 9–20 and 1 Kings 1–2," *Journal of Biblical Literature* 91 (1972): 172–81 (at 174–75).

11. See Donald B. Redford, "The Coregency of Tuthmosis III and Amenophis II," *Journal of Egyptian Archaeology* 51 (1965): 107–22.

12. See McKenzie, *King David*, 178.

13. On the concept of sanctuary in the Bible, see William H. C. Propp, *Exodus 19–40* (Anchor Bible 2A; New York: Doubleday, 2006), 208–10.

14. In many ways Solomon's lack of action is reminiscent of the presentation of David in Saul's court: neither does anything that could be construed as ambitious, yet both end up sitting on the throne nonetheless. See Gary N. Knoppers, *Two Nations Under God: The Deuteronomistic History of Solomon and the Dual Monarchies* (Harvard Semitic Monographs 52; Atlanta: Scholars, 1993), 67–68.

15. See Halpern, *David's Secret Demons*, 406.

16. See Margaret M. Gelinas, "United Monarchy–Divided Monarchy: Fact or Fiction?" in *The Pitcher Is Broken* (ed. S. W. Holloway and L. K. Handy; Journal of the Study of the Old Testament, Supplement Series 190; Sheffield: Sheffield Academic, 1995), 227–37.

17. On Israel's inherent dualism, see Albrecht Alt, "The Formation

of the Israelite State in Palestine," in Alt, *Essays on Old Testament History and Religion* (Garden City: Doubleday, 1967), 223–309 (at 274–85); Tryggve N. D. Mettinger, *King and Messiah: The Civil and Sacral Legitimation of the Israelite Kings* (Lund: Gleerup, 1976), 298–300.

18. For an overview of these long-recognized parallels, see John M. Monson, "The Temple of Solomon: Heart of Jerusalem," in *Zion: City of Our God* (ed. R. S. Hess and G. J. Wenham; Grand Rapids, MI: Eerdmans, 1999), 1–22.

19. See Alt, "Formation," 271–74; Baruch Halpern, *The Constitution of the Monarchy in Israel* (Harvard Semitic Monographs 25; Chico, CA: Scholars, 1981), 242–44.

20. On the change from David's military to Solomon's, see Chris Hauer Jr., "The Economics of National Security in Solomonic Israel," *Journal for the Study of the Old Testament* 18 (1980): 63–73.

21. See G. Ernest Wright, "The Provinces of Solomon (1 Kings 4:7–19)," *Eretz-Israel* 8 (1967): 58*–68*. The discovery of a set of ninth-century BCE administrative inscriptions from the northern capital of Samaria, however, makes clear that the tribal system was not completely obliterated by Solomon's redistricting. See Lawrence E. Stager, "The Archaeology of the Family in Early Israel," *Bulletin of the American Schools of Oriental Research* 260 (1985): 1–35 (at 24).

22. The attribution to Solomon of the construction at these sites is hotly contested in archaeological circles. For an overview of this debate, see Israel Finkelstein, "The Archaeology of the United Monarchy: An Alternative View," *Levant* 28 (1996): 177–87, and Amihai Mazar, "Iron Age Chronology: A Response to Israel Finkelstein," *Levant* 29 (1997): 157–67.

23. See Halpern, *David's Secret Demons*, 423–24.

24. See Alt, "Formation," 308: "The empire created by David and Solomon with such amazing speed [was] a swing of the political pendulum, which went too far, beyond the prevailing inclinations and capabilities of the people of Palestine at the time."

Conclusion

1. On the distinction of 1 Kings 1–2 from the rest of the David story, see P. Kyle McCarter, *II Samuel* (Anchor Bible 9; New York: Doubleday, 1984), 12–13; Henry Wansbrough, "The Finale of the Davidic Succession Narrative?," in *Biblical and Near Eastern Essays* (ed. C. McCarthy and J. F. Healey; Journal for the Study of the Old Testament, Supplement Series 375; London: T&T Clark, 2004), 37–56.

2. See James W. Flanagan, "Social Transformation and Ritual in 2 Samuel 6," in *The Word of the Lord Shall Go Forth* (ed. C. L. Meyers and M. O'Connor; Winona Lake, IN: Eisenbrauns, 1983), 361–72: "Legitimacy [is] the primary, indispensable stabilizer for new authority structures and . . . the need to legitimate is especially pressing when the new structures do not rest easily upon traditional values" (364).

3. *b. Šabb.* 56a. This is admittedly a minority opinion.

SCRIPTURE INDEX

SUBJECT INDEX